THE GOLD HUNTERS

By J. D. BORTHWICK

THE GOLD HUNTERS

By J. D. BORTHWICK

A First-Hand Picture of Life in California
Mining Camps in the Early Fifties

EDITED BY
HORACE KEPHART

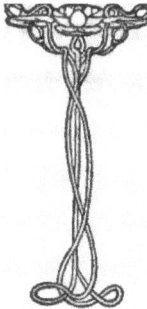

INTERNATIONAL FICTION LIBRARY
CLEVELAND   NEW YORK
Made in U.S.A.

PRESS OF

THE COMMERCIAL BOOKBINDING CO.CLEVELAND

ISBN: 978-1-6673-0477-9 paperback
ISBN: 978-1-6673-0478-6 hardcover

INTRODUCTION

CALIFORNIA under Spanish and Mexican rule was a lotus-land of lazy, good-natured, hospitable friars, of tame and submissive Indian neophytes, of vast savannas swarming with half-wild herds, of orchards and gardens, vineyards and olive groves. There was no mining, no lumbering, no machinery, no commerce other than a contraband exchange of hides and tallow for clothing, merchandise and manufactures. There was no art, no science, no literature, no news, save at rare intervals, from the outer world. One day was like another from generation to generation. Everyone was content with his mode of life or ignorant of any other. War never harassed the Franciscans' drowsy realm, nor ever threatened, beyond a few opéra bouffe affairs that began and ended in loud talk and bloodless gesticulation.

Under the old Spanish law, foreign commerce was prohibited and foreign travelers were excluded from California. But Boston traders managed to evade it by collusion with local officials; and strangers did enter the land ; sailors and merchants of divers nationalities came across seas and settled along the coast, while hunters and trappers crossed overland from the States. Generally they were welcomed and encouraged to establish themselves in California, though in defiance of the Mexican government. The foreigners, being for the most part men of enterprise and energy, were respected and became influential.

Many of them married into native California families, were naturalized, and acquired large estates. Among the Americans was John A. Sutter, formerly a Swiss military officer, who, in 1839, was permitted to build a fortified post on the present site of Sacramento. He received a large grant of land around it, and became a Mexican official.

As a result of the Mexican war, California was ceded to the United States on the 2d of February, 1848. Nine days earlier an event occurred that was destined to fix upon this splendid province the fascinated gaze of all the world. On the 24th of January, at Colonel Sutter's mill, near the present Coloma, a workman named James W. Marshall discovered gold.

Within a few months amazingly rich placers were found in river bars, creeks and gulches, of this and the surrounding region. During the first year or two of discovery it was not unusual for a miner to wash or dig up a hundred ounces of gold in a day. Some lucky strikes were made of five to ten times this amount, and nuggets were picked up of from $1,000 to $20,000 value. Within a few hundred yards of a populous town, a man stubbed his toe against a protruding rock ; glaring in wrath at the stumbling-block, he was thunderstruck at the sight of more gold than quartz. A market gardener, abusing his sterile soil for producing cabbages that were all stalk, was quickly placated by finding gold adhering to their roots; the cabbage-patch was successfully worked for years, and pieces of gold of many pounds weight were taken from it. Stories went abroad of places where the precious metal was blasted out in chunks, of ledges so rich that it could be picked out of the fissures with a bowie-knife, of men digging up gold as they would potatoes, and of a competence being amassed by a few hours' work with a tin spoon.

For two or three months the tales that came from the diggings were received with incredulity ; but when larger and larger shipments of the yellow metal kept coming to the coast there was a wild stampede for the gold-fields.

"Settlements were completely deserted; homes, farms and stores abandoned. Ships deserted by their sailors crowded the bay at San Francisco (there were five hundred of them in July, 1850); soldiers deserted wholesale, churches were emptied, town councils ceased to sit; merchants, clerks, lawyers and judges and criminals, everybody, flocked to the foothills. Soon, from Hawaii, Oregon and Sonora, from the Eastern States, the South Seas, Australia, South America and China came an extraordinary flow of the hopeful and adventurous. In the winter of '48 the rush began from the States to Panama, and in the spring across the plains. It is estimated that 80,000 men reached the coast in 1849, about half of them coming overland; three-fourths were Americans." By 1851 the number of actual miners had risen to about 140,000. From across the Atlantic there came Britons, Germans, Frenchmen, Italians, others speaking strange tongues, until the mines of California were likened to so many towers of Babel, and pantomime often took the part of speech.

Never before had there been brought together, in a far quarter of the earth, a body of men of so varied trades and professions all massed in a twinkling to one common pursuit. Social distinctions vanished at a touch. Soft-handed lawyers and clergymen wielded pick and shovel side-by-side with born navvies, cooked their own meals and washed their own clothes. No honest labor lowered the dignity of a gentleman, since that gentleman needs must wait upon himself and provide for himself with the work of his own hands. Out of this common necessity grew, as it were overnight, a natural democracy in which all men met each other on an equal footing. No deference was paid save to conspicuous ability of such sort as was useful in the work at hand.

The popular notion of a miner is that of a rude and reckless fellow who "works one day with a tin pan and gets drunk the next." There were, indeed, many of this ilk in the gold-diggings; but in the main, the miners of '49 were a picked and superior class of men. It was not as if a bonanza had been struck within easy reach of the riffraff of the nations. California, by the shortest route, was two thousand miles from any well populated part of America, five thousand from a European port. The journey thither was expensive, and most of the men who undertook it were such as had accumulated, by their own industry, a good "stake" at home. They were adventurers, to be sure; but what is an adventurer? One who hazards a chance, especially a chance of danger. That is the spirit which starts almost any enterprise that demands courage, determination and self-reliance. Beyond this, the argonauts were notably capable and intelligent men, as their works soon proved. An unbiased observer said of them: "Perhaps in no other community so limited could one find so many well-informed and clever men – men of all nations who bave added the advantages of traveling to natural abilities and a liberal education." Most of them were charged with spontaneous and persistent energy. Immediately, as by an electric shock, the California of dreaming friars and lazy vaqueros was tossed aside and an amazing industry whirred into action.

When San Francisco was laid in ashes, not a day was wasted in lamentation. Before the debris had fairly cooled the work of rebuilding was started with a rush. Soon the sand-hills were leveled, and rocks were blasted out to make room for a greater city. Brick buildings rose where there had been nothing but shanties or canvas tents. Foundries were built and shops were fitted with machinery brought half around the world. To provide rapid transit to the mines, large river steamers, of the same model as those used on the Hudson, were bought in New York, and, incredible as it may seem, these toplofty and fragile craft were navigated around South America, by way of the Straits of Magellan, and most of them came safe into the Golden Gate. (The author of this book declares his belief that a premium of 99 per cent, would not have insured them at Lloyd's for a trip from Dover to Calais.) The mines themselves were as so many ant-hills swarming with hurrying workers. Where water was scarce, canals were dug, or flumes were run for miles along mountain sides and carried over gorges or valleys by viaducts; even a large river was borne half a mile by an aqueduct high above its native bed. So rapid was the development of the country that, as our author says, California became a full-grown State while one-half the world still doubted its existence.

Gold mining, of course, was a gamble; while some "struck it rich" many others worked hard for nothing. So gambling was in the very air. And so long as common labor commanded at least five dollars a day, so long as ships by the hundred lay idle at their docks because sailors would rather take their chances in the mines than a steady wage of two or three hundred dollars a month, there was bound to be reckless extravagance and wild dissipation. Most of the miners were young men, too active, ebullient, vivacious, for quiet amusements in their hours of leisure. There was no home life nor anything to suggest it. In 1850 only two per cent, of the population of the mining counties were women, and probably most of these were of loose character. There was no standard of respectability to be lived up to. So long as a man did not interfere with the rights of others, he was perfectly free, if he chose, to go to the devil in his own way. Against the toil and hardships of the mining-field, against the gloom of disappointment or the wild elation of success, human nature demanded a counterpoise of some sort – and the only places in all the wide land where the miner could find comfort, luxury, gaiety, were the saloons and gambling-houses.

There being no sheriffs or policemen worthy the name, every man went armed, prepared at an instant's notice to redress his own real or fancied grievances. Shootings and stabbings were frequent, though in much less number actually than such conditions might be expected to provoke – most men think twice before stirring up trouble in a company where everybody carries a loaded gun and knows how to use it. Formal law was powerless, through corrupt or inefficient officers, to keep in check the many scoundrels and desperadoes that infested the cities and the diggings; so the miners themselves administered summary justice by means of extemporized courts, and for high crimes were prompt to inflict the highest punishment after the verdict of Judge Lynch. It is undeniable that, in a pioneer society, such rough-and-ready justice was a necessity and that its effects were salutary.

Yet when the first fever of excitement had passed away, when the richest placers were exhausted, when men settled down from prospecting and "rushes" to the steady work of mining on a business basis, it is wonderful how quickly the social order changed for the better. Miners returning to San Francisco after a year's absence scarcely recognized the place. Substantial buildings of brick and stone were replacing the tinder-boxes that had been swept away by one "great fire" after another – dressed granite for some of them was even imported from China! Streets that had been rubbish-heaps and quagmires were orderly and clean. A large number of respectable women had arrived in California, and their influence was immediately noticeable in the refinement of dress and decorum of the men. Places of rational amusement had sprung up – clubs, reading-rooms, theaters – which replaced in great measure the gambling-houses. In very many instances a quiet domestic life had supplanted the old-time roistering in saloons. Few, if any, cities ever showed such rapid progress in manners and morals as well as in material things.

Many narratives have been published by men who participated in the stirring events of early California. From among them I have chosen, after long research, one written by a British artist, Mr. J. D. Borthwick, and issued in Edinburgh in 1857. The original book is now rare and sought for by collectors of western Americana. It is here reprinted in full, with certain errors corrected. I do not know of another story by an actual miner that is so well written and so true to that wonderful life in the Days of Gold.

Horace Kephart.
October, 1916.

CONTENTS

The Gold Hunters

CHAPTER I

ON TO THE GOLD FIELDS

ABOUT the beginning of the year 1851, the rage for emigration to California from the United States was at its height. All sorts and conditions of men, old, young, and middle-aged, allured by the hope of acquiring sudden wealth, and fascinated with the adventure and excitement of a life in California, were relinquishing their existing pursuits and associations to commence a totally new existence in the land of gold.

The rush of eager gold-hunters was so great that the Panama Steamship Company's office in New York used to be perfectly mobbed for a day and a night previous to the day appointed for selling tickets for their steamers. Sailing vessels were despatched for Chagres almost daily, carrying crowds of passengers, while numbers went by the different routes through Mexico, and others chose the easier, but more tedious, passage round Cape Horn.

The emigration from the Western States, was naturally very large, the in-habitants being a class of men whose lives are spent in clearing the wild forests of the West, and gradually driving the Indian from his hunting-ground.

Of these western-frontier men it is often said, that they are never satisfied if there is any white man between them and sundown. They are constantly moving westward; for as the wild Indian is forced to retire before them, so they, in their turn, shrinking from the signs of civilization which their own labors cause to appear around them, have to plunge deeper into the forest, in search of that wild border-life which has such charms for all who have ever experienced it.

To men of this sort, the accounts of such a country as California, thousands of miles to the westward of them, were peculiarly attractive; and so great was the emigration, that many parts of the Western States were nearly depopulated. The route followed by these people was overland, across the plains, which was the most congenial to their tastes, and the most convenient for them, as, besides being already so far to the westward, they were also provided with the necessary wagons and oxen for the journey. For the sake of mutual protection against the Indians, they traveled in trains of a dozen or more wagons, carrying the women and children and provisions, accompanied by a proportionate number of men, some on horses or mules, and others on foot.

In May, 1851, I happened to be residing in New York, and was seized with the California fever. My preparations were very soon made, and a day or two afterwards I found myself on board a small barque about to sail for Chagres with a load of California emigrants. Our vessel was little more than two hundred tons, and was entirely devoted to the accommodation of passengers. The ballast was covered with a temporary deck, and the whole interior of the ship formed a saloon, round which were built three tiers of berths: a very rough extempore table and benches completed the furniture. There was no invidious distinction of cabin and steerage passengers – in fact, excepting the captain's room, there was nothing which could be called a cabin in the ship. But all were in good spirits, and so much engrossed with thoughts of California that there was little disposition to grumble at the rough-and-ready style of our accommodation. For my own part, I knew I should have to rough it in California, and felt that I might just as well begin at once as wait till I got there.

We numbered about sixty passengers, and a nice assortment we were. The majority, of course, were Americans, and were from all parts of the Union; the rest were English, French, and German. We had representatives of nearly every trade, besides farmers, engineers, lawyers, doctors, merchants, and nondescript "young men."

The first day out we had fine weather, with just sea enough to afford the uninitiated an opportunity of discovering the difference between the lee and the weather side of the ship. The second day we had a fresh breeze, which towards night blew a gale, and for a couple of days we were compelled to lay to.

The greater part of the passengers, being from the Interior of the country, had never seen the ocean before, and a gale of wind was a thing they did not understand at all. Those who were not too sick to be able to form an opinion on the subject, were frightened out of their senses, and imagined that all manner of dreadful things were going to happen to the ship. The first night of the gale, I was awakened by an old fool shouting frantically to the company in general to get up and save the ship, because he heard the water rushing into her, and we should sink in a few minutes. He was very emphatically cursed for his trouble by those whose slumbers he had disturbed, and told to hold his tongue, and let those sleep who could, if he were unable to do so himself.

It was certainly, however, not very easy to sleep that night. The ship was very crank, and but few of the party had taken the precaution to make fast their luggage ; the consequence was, that boxes and chests of all sizes, besides casks of provisions, and other ship's stores, which had got adrift, were cruising about promiscuously, threatening to smash up the flimsy framework on which our berths were built, and endangering the limbs of any one who should venture to turn out.

In the morning we found that the cook's galley had fetched way, and the stove was rendered useless; the steward and waiters – landlubbers who were only working their passage to Chagres – were as sick as the sickest, and so the prospect for breakfast was by no means encouraging. However, there were not more than half-a-dozen of us who could eat anything, or could even stand on deck; so we roughed it out on cold beef, hard bread, and brandy-and-water.

The sea was not very high, and the ship lay to comfortably and dry; but, in the evening, some of the poor wretches below had worked themselves up to desperation, being sure, every time the ship laid over, that she was never coming up again. At last, one man, who could stand it no longer, jumped out of his berth, and, going down on his knees, commenced clapping his hands, and uttering the most dismal howls and groans, interspersed with disjointed fragments of prayers. He called on all hands to join him; but it was not a form of worship to which many seemed to be accustomed, for only two men responded to his call. He very kindly consigned all the rest of the company to a place which I trust none of us may reach, and prayed that for the sake of the three righteous men – himself and the other two – the ship might be saved. They continued for about an hour, clapping their hands as if applauding, and crying and groaning most piteously – so bereft of sense, by fear, that they seemed not to know the meaning of their incoherent exclamations. The captain, however, at last succeeded in persuading them that there was no danger, and they gradually cooled down, to the great relief of the rest of the passengers.

The next day we had better weather, but the sick-list was as large as ever, and we had to mess again on whatever raw materials we could lay our hands on – red-herrings, onions, ham, and biscuit.

We deposed the steward as a useless vagabond, and appointed three passengers to fill his place, after which we fared a little better – in fact, as well as the provisions at our command would allow. No one grumbled, excepting a few of the lowest class of men in the party, who had very likely never been used to such good living ashore.

When we got into the trade-winds we had delightful weather, very hot, but with a strong breeze at night, rendering it sufficiently cool to sleep in comfort. The all-engrossing subject of conversation, and of meditation, was of course California, and the heaps of gold we were all to find there. As we had secured our passage only as far as Chagres, our progress from that point to San Francisco was also a matter of constant discussion. We all knew that every steamer to leave Panama, for months to come, was already full, and that hundreds of men were waiting there to take advantage of any opportunity that might occur of reaching San Francisco; but among our passengers there were very few who were traveling in company; they were mostly all isolated individuals, each "on his own hook," and every one was perfectly confident that he at least would have no trouble in getting along, whatever might be the fate of the rest of the crowd.

We added to the delicacies of our bill of fare occasionally by killing dolphins. They are very good eating, and afford capital sport. They come in small shoals of a dozen or so, and amuse themselves by playing about before the bows of the vessel, when, getting down into the martingale under the bowsprit, one takes the opportunity to let drive at them with the "grains," a small five-pronged harpoon.

The dolphin, by the way, is most outrageously and systematically libeled. Instead of being the horrid, big-headed, crooked-backed monster which it is generally represented, it is the most elegant and highly-finished fish that swims.

For three or four days before reaching Chagres, all hands were busy packing up, and firing off and reloading pistols; for a revolver and a bowie-knife were considered the first items in a California outfit. We soon assumed a warlike appearance, and though many of the party had probably never handled a pistol in their lives before, they tried to wear their weapons in a negligé style, as if they never had been used to go without them.

There were now also great consultations as to what sort of hats, coats, and boots, should be worn in crossing the Isthmus. Wondrous accounts constantly appeared in the New York papers of the dangers and difficulties of these few miles of land-and-river travel, and most of the passengers, before leaving New York, had been humbugged into buying all manner of absurd and useless articles, many of them made of india-rubber, which they had been assured, and consequently believed, were absolutely necessary. But how to carry them all, or even how to use them, was the main difficulty, and would indeed have puzzled much cleverer men.

Some were equipped with pots, pans, kettles, drinking-cups, knives and forks, spoons, pocket-filters (for they had been told that the water on the Isthmus was very dirty), india-rubber contrivances, which an ingenious man, with a powerful imagination and strong lungs, could blow up and convert into a bed, a boat, or a tent – bottles of "cholera preventive," boxes of pills for curing every disease to which human nature is liable ; and some men, in addition to all this, determined to be prepared to combat danger in every shape, bade defiance to the waters of the Chagres river by buckling on india-rubber life-preservers.

Others of the party, who were older travelers, and who held all such accoutrements in utter contempt, had merely a small valise with a few necessary articles of clothing, an oil-skin coat, and, very probably, a pistol stowed away on some part of their person, which would be pretty sure to go off when occasion required, but not before.

At last, after twenty days' passage from New York, we made Chagres, and got up to the anchorage towards evening. The scenery was very beautiful. We lay about three-quarters of a mile from shore, in a small bay enclosed by high bluffs, completely covered with dense foliage of every shade of green.

We had but little time, however, to enjoy the scenery that evening, as we had scarcely anchored when the rain began to come down in true tropical style; every drop was a bucketful. The thunder and lightning were terrific, and in good keeping with the rain, which is one of the things for which Chagres is celebrated. Its character as a sickly wretched place was so well known that none of us went ashore that night; we all preferred sleeping aboard ship.

It was very amusing to watch the change which had been coming over some of the men on board. They seemed to shrink within themselves, and to wish to avoid being included in any of the small parties which were being formed to make the passage up the river. They were those who had provided themselves with innumerable contrivances for the protection of their precious persons against sun, wind, and rain, also with extraordinary assortments of very untempting-looking provisions, and who were completely equipped with pistols, knives, and other warlike implements. They were like so many Robinson Crusoes, ready to be put ashore on a desert island; and they seemed to imagine themselves to be in just such a predicament, fearful, at the same time, that companionship with any one not provided with the same amount of rubbish as themselves, might involve their losing the exclusive benefit of what they supposed so absolutely necessary. I actually heard one of them refuse another man a chew of tobacco, saying he guessed he had no more than what he could use himself.

The men of this sort, of whom I am happy to say there were not many, offered a striking contrast to the rest in another respect. On arriving at Chagres they became quite dejected and sulky, and seemed to be oppressed with anxiety, while the others were in a wild state of delight at having finished a tedious passage, and in anticipation of the novelty and excitement of crossing the Isthmus.

In the morning several shore-boats, all pulled by Americans, came off to take us ashore. The landing here is rather dangerous. There is generally a very heavy swell, causing vessels to roll so much that getting into a small boat alongside is a matter of considerable difficulty; and at the mouth of the river is a bar, on which are immense rollers, requiring good management to get over them in safety.

We went ashore in torrents of rain, and when landed with our baggage on the muddy bank of the Chagres river, all as wet as if we had swum ashore, we were immediately beset by crowds of boatmen, Americans, natives, and Jamaica niggers, all endeavoring to make a bargain with us for the passage up the river to Cruces.

The town of Chagres is built on each side of the river, and consists of a few miserable cane-and-mud huts, with one or two equally wretched-looking wooden houses, which were hotels kept by Americans. On the top of the bluff, on the south side of the river, are the ruins of an old Spanish castle, which look very picturesque, almost concealed by the luxurious growth of trees and creepers around them.

The natives seemed to be a miserable set of people, and the few Americans in the town were most sickly, washed-out-looking objects, with the appearance of having been steeped for a length of time in water.

After breakfasting on ham and beans at one of the hotels, we selected a boat to convey us up the river; and as the owner had no crew engaged, we got him to take two sailors who had run away from our vessel, and were bound for California like the rest of us.

There was a great variety of boats employed on the river – whale-boats, ships' boats, skiffs, and canoes of all sizes, some of them capable of carrying fifteen or twenty people. It was still raining heavily when we started, but shortly afterwards the weather cleared up, and we felt in better humor to enjoy the magnificent scenery. The river was from seventy-five to a hundred yards wide, and the banks were completely hidden by the dense mass of vegetation overhanging the water. There was a vast variety of beautiful foliage, and many of the trees were draped in creepers, covered with large flowers of most brilliant colors. One of our party, who was a Scotch gardener, was in ecstasies at such a splendid natural flower-show, and gave us long Latin names for all the different specimens. The rest of my fellow-passengers were a big fat man from Buffalo, two young Southerners from South Carolina, three New Yorkers, and a Swede. The boat was rather heavily laden, but for some hours we got along very well, as there was but little current. Towards the afternoon, however, our two sailors, who had been pulling all the time, began to flag, and at last said they could go no further without a rest. We were still many miles from the place where we were to pass the night, and as the banks of the river presented such a formidable barricade of jungle as to prevent a landing, we had the prospect of passing the night in the boat, unless we made the most of our time; so the gardener and I volunteered to take a spell at the oars. But as we ascended the river the current became much stronger, and darkness overtook us some distance from our intended stopping-place.

It became so very dark that we could not see six feet ahead of us, and were constantly bumping against other boats coming up the river. There were also many boats coming down with the current at such a rate, that if one had happened to run into us, we should have had but a poor chance, and we were obliged to keep shouting all the time to let our whereabouts be known.

We were several times nearly capsized on snags, and, as we really could not see whether we were making any way or not, we came to the determination of making fast to a tree till the moon should rise. It was now raining again as heavily as ever, and having fully expected to make the station that evening, we had taken no provisions with us. We were all very wet, very hungry, and more or less inclined to be in a bad humor. Consequently, the question of stopping or going ahead was not determined without a great deal of wrangling and discussion. However, our two sailors declared they would not pull another stroke

– the gardener and myself were in favor of stopping – and as none of the rest of our number were at all inclined to exert themselves, the question was thus settled for them, although they continued to discuss it for their own satisfaction for some time afterwards.

It was about eight o'clock, when, catching hold of a bough of a tree twelve or fifteen feet from the shore, we made fast. We could not attempt to land, as the shore was so guarded by bushes and sunken branches as to render the nearer approach of the boat impossible.

So here we were, thirteen of us, with a proportionate pile of baggage, cramped up in a small boat, in which we had spent the day, and were now doomed to pass the night, our miseries aggravated by torrents of rain, nothing to eat, and, worse than that, nothing to drink, but, worse than all, without even a dry match wherewith to light a pipe. If ever it is excusable to chew tobacco, it surely is on such an occasion as this. I had worked a good deal at the oar, and from the frequent alterations we had experienced of scorching heat and drench-ing rain, I felt as if I could enjoy a nap, notwithstanding the disagreeableness of our position; but, fearing the consequences of sleeping under such circum-stances in that climate, I kept myself awake the best way I could.

We managed to get through the night somehow, and about three o'clock in the morning, as the moon began to give sufficient light to let us see where we were, we got under way again, and after a couple of hours' hard pulling, we arrived at the place we had expected to reach the evening before.

It was a very beautiful little spot – a small natural clearing on the top of a high bank, on which were one or two native huts, and a canvas establishment which had been set up by a Yankee, and was called a "Hotel." We went to this hotel, and found some twenty or thirty fellow-travelers, who had there enjoyed a night's rest, and were now just sitting down to breakfast at a long rough table which occupied the greater part of the house. The kitchen consisted of a cooking-stove in one corner, and opposite to it was the bar, which was supplied with a few bottles of bad brandy, while a number of canvas shelves, ranged all round, constituted the dormitory.

We made up for the loss of our supper by eating a hearty breakfast of ham, beans, and eggs, and started again in company with our more fortunate fellow-travelers. The weather was once more bright and clear, and confined as we were between the densely wooded and steaming banks of the river, we found the heat most oppressive.

We saw numbers of parrots of brilliant plumage, and a great many monkeys and alligators, at which there was a constant discharge of pistols and rifles, our passage being further enlivened by an occasional race with some of the other boats.

The river still continued to become more rapid, and our progress was consequently very slow. The two sailors were quite unable to work all day at the oars; the owner of the boat was a useless encumbrance; he could not even steer; so the gardener and myself were again obliged occasionally to exert ourselves. The fact is, the boat was overloaded; two men were not a sufficient crew; and if we had not worked ourselves, we should never have got to Cruces. I wanted the other passengers to do their share of work for the common good, but some protested they did not know how to pull, others pleaded bad health, and the rest very coolly said, that having paid their money to be taken to Cruces, they expected to be taken there, and would not pull a stroke; they did not care how long they might be on the river.

It was evident that we had made a bad bargain, and if these other fellows would not lend a hand, it was only the more necessary that some one else should. It was rather provoking to see them sitting doggedly under their umbrellas, but we could not well pitch them overboard, or put them ashore, and I comforted myself with the idea that their turn would certainly come, notwithstanding their obstinacy.

After a tedious day, during which we had, as before, deluges of rain, with intervals of scorching sunshine, we arrived about six o'clock at a native settlement, where we were to spend the night.

It was a small clearing, with merely two or three huts, inhabited by eight or ten miserable-looking natives, mostly women. Their lazy listless way of doing things did not suit the humor we were in at all. The invariable reply to all demands for something to eat and drink was *poco tiempo*, (by-and-by), said in that sort of tone one would use to a troublesome child. They knew very well we were at their mercy – we could not go anywhere else for our supper – and they took it easy accordingly. We succeeded at last in getting supper in instalments – now a mouthful of ham, now an egg or a few beans, and then a cup of coffee, just as they would make up their minds to the violent exertion of getting these articles ready for us.

About half-a-dozen other boat-loads of passengers were also stopping here, some fifty or sixty of us altogether, and three small shanties were the only shelter to be had. The native population crowded into one of them, and, in consideration of sundry dollars, allowed us the exclusive enjoyment of the other two. They were mere sheds about fifteen feet square, open all round; but as the rain was again pouring down, we thought of the night before, and were thankful for small mercies.

I secured a location with three or four others in the upper story of one of these places – a sort of loft made of bamboos about eight feet from the ground, to which we climbed by means of a pole with notches cut in it.

The next day we found the river more rapid than ever. Oars were now useless – we had to pole the boat up the stream; and at last the patience of the rest of the party was exhausted, and they reluctantly took their turn at the work. We hardly made twelve miles, and halted in the evening at a place called Dos Hermanos where were two native houses.

Here we found already about fifty fellow-travelers, and several parties arrived after us. On the native landlord we were all dependent for supper; but we, at least, were a little too late, as there was nothing to be had but boiled rice and coffee – not even beans. There were a few live chickens about, which we would soon have disposed of, but cooking was out of the question. It was raining furiously, and there were sixty or seventy of us, all huddled into two small places of fifteen feet square, together with a number of natives and Jamaica negroes, the crews of some of the boats. Several of the passengers were in different stages of drunkenness, generally developing itself in a desire to fight, and more particularly to pitch into the natives and niggers. There seemed a prospect of a general set-to between black and white, which would have been a bloody one, as all the passengers had either a revolver or a bowie-knife – most of them had both – and the natives were provided with their *machetes* – half knife, half cutlass – which they always carry, and know how to use. Many of the Americans, however, were of the better class, and used their influence to quiet the more unruly of their countrymen. One man made a most touching appeal to their honor not to "kick up a muss," as there was a lady "of their own color" in the next room, who was in a state of great agitation. The two rooms opened into each other, and were so full of men that one could hardly turn round, and the lady of our own color was of course a myth. However, the more violent of the crowd quieted down a little, and affairs looked more pacific.

We passed a most miserable night. We lay down as best we could, and were packed like sardines in a box. All wanted to sleep; but if one man moved, he woke half-a-dozen others, who again in waking roused all the rest; so sleep was, like our supper, only to be enjoyed in imagination, and all we could do was to wait intently for daylight. As soon as we could see, we all left the wretched place, none of us much improved in temper, or in general condition. It was still raining, and we had the pleasure of knowing that we should not get any breakfast for two or three hours.

We had another severe day on the river – hot sun, heavy rains, and hard work; and in the afternoon we arrived at Gorgona, a small village, where a great many passengers leave the river and take the road to Panama.

Cruces is about seven miles farther up the river, and from there the road to Panama is said to be much better, especially in wet weather, when the Gorgona road is almost impassable.

The village of Gorgona consisted of a number of native shanties, built, in the usual style, of thin canes, between any two of which you might put your finger, and fastened together, in basket fashion, with the long woody tendrils with which the woods abound. The roof is of palm leaves, slanting up to a great height, so as to shed the heavy rains. Some of these houses have only three sides, others have only two, while some have none at all, being open all round; and in all of them might be seen one or more natives swinging in a hammock, calmly and patiently waiting for time to roll on, or, it may be, deriving intense enjoyment from the mere consciousness of existence.

There was a large canvas house, on which was painted "Gorgona Hotel." It was kept by an American, the most unwholesome-looking individual I had yet seen; he was the very personification of fever. We had here a very luxurious dinner, having plantains and eggs in addition to the usual fare of ham and beans. The upper story of the hotel was a large loft, so low in the roof that one could not stand straight up in it. In this there were sixty or seventy beds, so close together that there was just room to pass between them; and as those at one end became tenanted, the passages leading to them were filled up with more beds, in such a manner that, when all were put up, not an inch of the floor could be seen.

After our fatigues on the river, and the miserable way in which we had passed the night before, such sleeping accommodation as this appeared very inviting; and immediately after dinner I appropriated one of the beds, and slept even on till daylight. We met here several men who were returning from Panama, on their way home again. They had been waiting there for some months for a steamer, by which they had tickets for San Francisco, and which was coming round the Horn. She was long overdue, however, and having lost patience, they were going home, in the vain hope of getting damages out of the owner of the steamer. If they had been very anxious to go to California, they might have sold their tickets, and taken the opportunity of a sailing-vessel from Panama; but from the way in which they spoke of their grievances, it was evident that they were home-sick, and glad of any excuse to turn tail and go back again.

We had frequently, on our way up the river, seen different parties of our fellow-passengers. At Gorgona we mustered strong; and we found that, notwithstanding the disadvantage we had been under of having an overloaded boat, we had made as good time as any of them.

A great many here took the road for Panama, but we determined to go on by the river to Cruces, for the sake of the better road from that place. All our difficulties hitherto were nothing to what we encountered in these last few miles. It was one continual rapid all the way, and in many places some of us were obliged to get out and tow the boat, while the rest used the poles.

We were all heartily disgusted with the river, and were satisfied, when we arrived at Cruces, that we had got over the worst of the Isthmus; for however bad the road might be, it could not be harder traveling than we had already experienced.

Cruces was just such a village as Gorgona, with a similar canvas hotel, kept by equally cadaverous-looking Americans.

In establishing their hotels at different points on the Chagres river, the Americans encountered great opposition from the natives, who wished to reap all the benefit of the travel themselves; but they were too many centuries behind the age to have any chance in fair competition; and so they resorted to personal threats and violence, till the persuasive eloquence of Colt's revolvers, and the overwhelming numbers of American travelers, convinced them that they were wrong, and that they had better submit to their fate.

One branch of business which the natives had all to themselves was mule-driving, and carrying baggage over the road from Cruces to Panama, and at this they had no competition to fear from any one. The luggage was either packed on mules, or carried on men's backs, being lashed into a sort of wicker-work contrivance, somewhat similar to those used by French porters, and so adjusted with straps that the weight bore directly down on the shoulders. It was astonishing to see what loads these men could carry over such a road ; and it® really seemed inconsistent with their indolent character, that they should perform, so actively, such prodigious feats of labor. Two hundred and fifty pounds weight was an average load for a man to walk off with, doing the twenty-five miles to Panama in a day and a half, and some men carried as much as three hundred pounds. They were well made, and muscular though not large men, and were apparently more of the Negro than the Indian.

The journey to Panama was generally performed on mules, but frequently on foot; and as the rest of our party intended to walk, I determined also to forego the luxury of a mule; so, having engaged men to carry our baggage, we set out about two o'clock in the afternoon.

The weather was fine, and for a short distance out of Cruces the road was easy enough, and we were beginning to think we should have a pleasant journey; but we were very soon undeceived, for it commenced to rain in the usual style, and the road became most dreadful. It was a continual climb over the rocky beds of precipitous gullies, the gully itself perhaps ten or twelve feet deep, and the dense wood on each side meeting overhead, so that no fresh air relieved one in toiling along. We could generally see rocks sticking up out of the water, on which to put our feet, but we were occasionally, for a considerable distance, up to the knees in water and mud.

The steep banks on each side of us were so close together, that in many places two packed mules could not pass each other; sometimes, indeed, even a single mule got jammed by the trunk projecting on either side of him. It was a most fatiguing walk. When it did not rain, the heat was suffocating; and when it rained, it poured.

There was a place called the "Half-way House," to which we looked forward anxiously as the end of our day's journey; and as it was kept by an American, we expected to find it a comparatively comfortable place. But our disappointment was great, when about dark, we arrived at this half-way house, and found it to be a miserable little tent, not much more than twelve feet square.

On entering we found some eight or ten travelers in the same plight as ourselves, tired, hungry, wet through, and with aching limbs. The only furniture in the tent consisted of a rough table three feet long, and three cots. The ground was all wet and sloppy, and the rain kept dropping through the canvas

overhead. There were only two plates, and two knives and forks in the establishment, so we had to pitch into the salt pork and beans two at a time, while
the rest of the crowd stood round and looked at us; for the cots were the only
seats in the place, and they were so rickety that not more than two men could
sit on them at a time.

More travelers continued to arrive; and as the prospect of a night in such
a place was so exceedingly dismal, I persuaded our party to return about half
a mile to a native hut which we had passed on the road, to take our chance of
what accommodation we could get there. We soon arranged with the woman,
who seemed to be the only inhabitant of the house, to allow us to sleep in it; and
as we were all thoroughly soaked, every sort of waterproof coat having proved
equally useless after the few days' severe trial we had given them, we looked
out anxiously for any of the natives coming along with our trunks.

In the meantime I borrowed a towel from the old woman of the shanty;
and as it was now fair, I went into the bush, and got one of our two sailors, who
had stuck by us, to rub me down as hard as he could. This entirely removed
all pain and stiffness; and though I had to put on my wet clothes again, I felt
completely refreshed.

Not long afterwards a native made his appearance, carrying the trunk of
one of the party, who very generously supplied us all from it with dry clothes,
when we betook ourselves to our couches. They were not luxurious, being a
number of dried hides laid on the floor, as hard as so many sheets of iron, and
full of bumps and hollows ; but they were dry, which was all we cared about,
for we thought of the poor devils sleeping in the mud in the half-way house.

The next morning, as we proceeded on our journey, the road gradually improved as the country became more open. We were much refreshed by a light
breeze off the sea, which we found a very agreeable change from the damp and
suffocating heat of the forest; and about mid-day, after a pleasant forenoon's
walk, we strolled into the city of Panama.

CHAPTER II

ACROSS THE ISTHMUS

ON our arrival we found the population busily employed in celebrating one of their innumerable *dias de fiesta.* The streets presented a very gay appearance. The natives, all in their gala-dresses, were going the rounds of the numerous gaudily-ornamented altars which had been erected throughout the town ; and mingled with the crowd were numbers of Americans in every variety of California emigrant costume. The scene was further enlivened by the music, or rather the noise, of fifes, drums, and fiddles, with singing and chanting inside the churches, together with squibs and crackers, the firing of cannon, and the continual ringing of bells.

The town is built on a small promontory, and is protected, on the two sides facing the sea, by batteries, and, on the land side, by a high wall and a moat. A large portion of the town, however, lies on the outside of this.

Most of the houses are built of wood, two stories high, painted with bright colors, and with a corridor and veranda on the upper story; but the best houses are of stone, or sun-dried bricks plastered over and painted.

The churches are all of the same style of architecture which prevails throughout Spanish America. They appeared to be in a very neglected state, bushes, and even trees, growing out of the crevices of the stones. The towers and pinnacles are ornamented with a profusion of pearl-oyster shells, which, shining brightly in the sun, produce a very curious effect.

On the altars is a great display of gold and silver ornaments and images; but the interiors, in other respects, are quite in keeping with the dilapidated uncared-for appearance of the outside of the buildings.

The natives are white, black, and every intermediate shade of color, being a mixture of Spanish, Negro, and Indian blood. Many of the women are very handsome, and on Sundays and holidays they dress very showily, mostly in white dresses, with bright-colored ribbons, red or yellow slippers without stockings, flowers in their hair, and round their necks, gold chains, frequently composed of coins of various sizes linked together. They have a fashion of making their hair useful as well as ornamental, and it is not unusual to see the ends of three or four half-smoked cigars sticking out from the folds of their hair at the back of the head; for though they smoke a great deal, they never seem to finish a cigar at one smoking. It is amusing to watch the old women going to church. They come up smoking vigorously, with a cigar in full blast, but, when they get near the door, they reverse it, putting the lighted end into their mouth, and in this way they take half-a-dozen stiff pulls at it, which seems to have the effect of putting it out. They then stow away the stump in some of the recesses of their "back hair," to be smoked out on a future occasion.

The native population of Panama is about eight thousand, but at this time there was also a floating population of Americans, varying from two to three thousand, all on their way to California; some being detained for two or three months waiting for a steamer to come round the Horn, some waiting for sailing vessels, while others, more fortunate, found the steamer, for which they had tickets, ready for them on their arrival. Passengers returning from San Francisco did not remain any time in Panama, but went right on across the Isthmus to Chagres.

The Americans, though so greatly inferior in numbers to the natives, displayed so much more life and activity, even in doing nothing, that they formed by far the more prominent portion of the population. The main street of the town was densely crowded, day and night, with Americans in bright red flannel shirts, with the universal revolver and bowie-knife conspicuously displayed at their backs.

Most of the principal houses in the town had been converted into hotels, which were kept by Americans, and bore, upon large signs, the favorite hotel names of the United States. There were also numbers of large American stores or shops, of various descriptions, equally obtruding upon the attention of the public by the extent of their English signs, while, by a few lines of bad Spanish scrawled on a piece of paper at the side of the door, the poor natives were informed, as mere matter of courtesy, that they also might enter in and buy, if they had the wherewithal to pay. Here and there, indeed, some native, with more enterprise than his neighbors, intimated to the public – that is to say, to the Americans – in a very modest sign, and in very bad English, that he had something or other to sell; but his energy was all theoretical, for on going into his store you would find him half asleep in his hammock, out of which he would not rouse himself if he could possibly avoid it. You were welcome to buy as much as you pleased ; but he seemed to think it very hard that you could not do so without giving him at the same time the trouble of selling.

Although all foreigners were spoken of as *los Americanos* by the natives, there were among them men from every country in Europe. The Frenchmen were the most numerous, some of whom kept stores and very good restaurants. There were also several large gambling saloons, which were always crowded, especially on Sundays, with natives and Americans gambling at the Spanish game of monte; and, of course, specimens were not wanting of that great American institution, the drinking saloon, at the bars of which a brisk business was done in brandy-smashes, whisky-skins, and all the other refreshing compounds for which the Americans are so justly celebrated.

Living in Panama was pretty hard. The hotels were all crammed full ; the accommodation they afforded was somewhat in the same style as at Gorgona, and they were consequently not very inviting places. Those who did not live in hotels had sleeping-quarters in private houses, and resorted to the restaurants for their meals, which was a much more comfortable mode of life.

Ham, beans, chicken, eggs, and rice, were the principal articles of food. The beef was dreadfully tough, stringy, and tasteless, and was hardly ever eaten by the Americans, as it was generally found to be very unwholesome.

There was here at this time a great deal of sickness, and absolute misery, among the Americans. Diarrhœa and fever were the prevalent diseases. The deaths were very numerous, but were frequently either the result of the imprudence of the patient himself, or of the total indifference as to his fate on the part of his neighbors, and the consequent want of any care or attendance whatever. The heartless selfishness one saw and heard of was truly disgusting. The principle of "every man for himself" was most strictly followed out, and a sick man seemed to be looked upon as a thing to be avoided, as a hindrance to one's own individual progress.

There was a hospital attended by American physicians, and supported to a great extent by Californian generosity; but it was quite incapable of accommodating all the sick; and many a poor fellow, having exhausted his funds during his long detention here, found, when he fell sick, that in parting with his money he had lost the only friend he had, and was allowed to die, as little cared for as if he had been a dog.

An American characteristic is a weakness for quack medicines and spe-
cifics, and numbers of men here fell victims to the national mania, chiefly
Yankees and Western men. Persons coming from a northern climate to such a
place as Panama, are naturally apt at first to experience some slight derange-
ment of their general health, which, with proper treatment, is easily rectified;
but these fellows were all provided with cholera preventive, fever preventive,
and boxes of pills for the prevention and the cure of every known disease.
The moment they imagined that there was anything wrong with them, they
became alarmed, and dosed themselves with all the medicines they could
get hold of, so that when they really were taken ill, they were already half
poisoned with the stuff they had been swallowing. Many killed themselves
by excessive drinking of the wretched liquor which was sold under the name
of brandy, and others, by eating ravenously of fruit, green or ripe, at all hours
of the day, or by living, for the sake of economy, on gingerbread and spruce-
beer, which are also American weaknesses, and of which there were several
enterprising Yankee manufacturers.

The sickness was no doubt much increased by the outrageously filthy state
of the town. There seemed to be absolutely no arrangement for cleanliness
whatever, and the heavy rains which fell, and washed down the streets, were
all that saved the town from being swallowed up in the accumulation of its own
corruption.

Among the Americans en route for California were men of all classes –
professional men, merchants, laborers, sailors, farmers, mechanics, and numbers of long gaunt Western men, with rifles as long as themselves. The hotels
were too crowded to allow of any distinction of persons, and they were accordingly conducted on ultra-democratic principles. Some faint idea of the style
of thing might be formed from a notice which was posted up in the bar-room
of the most fashionable hotel. It ran as follows: "Gentlemen are requested to
wear their coats at table, if they have them handy." This intimation, of course,
in effect amounted to nothing at all, but at the same time there was a great
deal in it. It showed that the landlord, being above vulgar prejudices himself,
saw the necessity, in order to please all his guests, of overcoming the mutual
prejudices existing between broadcloth and fine linen, and red flannel with no
linen, – sanctioning the wearing of coats at table on the part of the former, by
making a public request that they would do so, while, of the shirt-sleeve gen-

tlemen, those who *had* coats, and refused to wear them, could still glory in the knowledge that they were defying all interference with their individual rights; and in behalf of the really coatless, those who could not call a coat their own, the idea was kindly suggested that that garment was only absent, because it was not "handy."

As may be supposed, such a large and motley population of foreigners, confined in such a place as Panama, without any occupation, were not remarkably quiet or orderly. Gambling, drinking, and cock-fighting were the principal amusements; and drunken rows and fights, in which pistols and knives were freely used, were of frequent occurrence.

The 4th of July was celebrated by the Americans in great style. The proceedings were conducted as is customary on such occasions in the United States. A procession was formed, which, headed by a number of fiddles, drums, bugles, and other instruments, all playing "Yankee Doodle" in a very free and independent manner, marched to the place of celebration, a circular canvas structure, where a circus company had been giving performances. When all were assembled, the Declaration of Independence was read, and the orator of the day made a flaming speech on the subject of George III. and the Universal Yankee nation. A gentleman then got up, and, speaking in Spanish, explained to the native portion of the assembly what all the row was about; after which the meeting dispersed, and the further celebration of the day was continued at the bars of the different hotels.

I met with an accident here which laid me up for several weeks. I suffered a good deal, and passed a most weary time. All the books I could get hold of did not last me more than a few days, and I had then no other pastime than to watch the humming-birds buzzing about the flowers which grew around my window.

As soon as I was able to walk, I took passage in a barque about to sail for San Francisco. She carried about forty passengers; and as she had ample cabin accommodation, we were so far comfortable enough. The company was, as might be expected, very miscellaneous. Some were respectable men, and others were precious vagabonds. When we had been out but a few days, a fever broke out on board, which was not, however, of a very serious character. I got a touch of it, and could have cured myself very easily, but there was a man on board who passed for a doctor, having shipped as such: he had been physicking the others, and I reluctantly consented to allow him to doctor me also. He began by giving me some horrible emetic, which, however, had no effect; so he continued to repeat it, dose after dose, each dose half a tumblerful, with still no effect, till, at last, he had given me so much of it, that he began to be alarmed for the consequences. I was a little alarmed myself, and putting my finger down my throat, I very soon relieved myself of all his villainous compounds. I think I fainted after it. I know I felt as if I were going to faint, and shortly afterwards was sensible of a lapse of time which I could not account for; but on inquiring of some of my fellow-passengers, I could find no one who had so far interested himself on my account as to be able to give me any information on the subject.

I took my own case in hand after that, and very soon got rid of the fever, although the emetic treatment had so used me up that for a fortnight I was hardly able to stand. We afterwards discovered that this man was only now making his *début* as a physician. He had graduated, however, as a shoemaker, a farmer, and I don't know what else besides; latterly he had practised as a horse-dealer, and I have no doubt it was some horse-medicine which he administered to me so freely.

We had only two deaths on board, and in justice to the doctor, I must say he was not considered to have been the cause of either of them. One case was that of a young man, who, while the doctor was treating him for fever, was at the same time privately treating himself to large doses, taken frequently, of bad brandy, of which he had an ample stock stowed away under his bed. About a day and a half settled him. The other was a much more melancholy case. He was a young Swede – such a delicate, effeminate fellow that he seemed quite out of place among the rough and noisy characters who formed the rest of the party. A few days before we left Panama, a steamer had arrived from San Francisco with a great many cases of cholera on board. Numerous deaths had occurred in Panama, and considerable alarm prevailed there in consequence. The Swede was attacked with fever like the rest of us, but he had no force in him, either mental or bodily, to bear up against sickness under such circumstances ; and the fear of cholera had taken such possession of him, that he insisted upon it that he had cholera, and that he would die of it that night. His lamentations were most piteous, but all attempts to reassure him were in vain. He very soon became delirious, and died raving before morning. None of us were doctors enough to know exactly what he died of, but the general belief was that he frightened himself to death. The church-service was read over him by the supercargo, many of the passengers merely leaving their cards to be present at the ceremony, and as soon as he was launched over the side, resuming their game where they had been interrupted ; and this, moreover, was on a Sunday morning. In future the captain prohibited all card-playing on Sundays, but throughout the voyage nearly one-half of the passengers spent the whole day, and half the night, in playing the favorite game of poker, which is something like brag, and at which they cheated each other in the most barefaced manner, so causing perpetual quarrels, which, however, never ended in a fight – for the reason, as it seemed to me, that as every one wore his bowie-knife, the prospect of getting his opponent's knife between his ribs deterred each man from drawing his own, or offering any violence whatever.

The poor Swede had no friends on board ; nobody knew who he was, where he came from, or anything at all about him; and so his effects were, a few days after his death, sold at auction by order of the captain, one of the passengers, who had been an auctioneer in the States, officiating on the occasion.

Great rascalities were frequently practised at this time by those engaged in conveying passengers, in sailing vessels, from Panama to San Francisco. There were such numbers of men waiting anxiously in Panama to take the first opportunity that offered of reaching California, that there was no difficulty in filling any old tub of a ship with passengers; and, when once men arrived in San Francisco, they were generally too much occupied in making dollars, to give any trouble on account of the treatment they had received on the voyage.

Many vessels were consequently despatched with a load of passengers, most shamefully ill supplied with provisions, even what they had being of the most inferior quality; and it often happened that they had to touch in distress at the intermediate ports for the ordinary necessaries of life.

We very soon found that our ship was no exception. For the first few days we fared pretty well, but, by degrees, one article after another became used up; and by the time we had been out a fortnight, we had absolutely nothing to eat and drink, but salt pork, musty flour, and bad coffee – no mustard, vinegar, sugar, pepper, or anything of the sort, to render such food at all palatable. It may be imagined how delightful it was, in recovering from fever, when one naturally has a craving for something good to eat, to have no greater delicacy in the way of nourishment than gruel made of musty flour, *au naturel.*

There was great indignation among the passengers. A lot of California emigrants are not a crowd to be trifled with, and the idea of pitching the supercargo overboard was quite seriously entertained; but, fortunately for himself, he was a very plausible man, and succeeded in talking them into the belief that he was not to blame.

We would have gone into some port for supplies but, of such grub as we had, there was no scarcity on board, and we preferred making the most of it to incurring delay by going in on the coast, where calms and light winds are so prevalent.

We killed a porpoise occasionally, and ate him. The liver is the best part, and the only part generally eaten, being something like pig's liver, and by no means bad. I had frequently tasted the meat at sea before; it is exceedingly hard, tough, and stringy, like the very worst beefsteak that can possibly be imagined ; and I used to think it barely eatable, when thoroughly disguised in sauce and spices, but now, after being so long under a severe salt-pork treatment, I thought porpoise steak a very delicious dish, even without any condiment to heighten its intrinsic excellence.

We had been out about six weeks, when we sighted a ship, many miles off, going the same way as ourselves, and the captain determined to board her, and endeavor to get some of the articles of which we were so much in need. There was great excitement among the passengers; all wanted to accompany the captain in his boat, but, to avoid making invidious distinctions, he refused to take any one unless he would pull an oar. I was one of four who volunteered to do so, and we left the ship amid clamorous injunctions not to forget sugar, beef, molasses, vinegar, and so on – whatever each man most longed for. We had four or five Frenchmen on board, who earnestly entreated me to get them even one bottle of oil.

We had a long pull, as the stranger was in no hurry to heave-to for us; and on coming up to her, we found her to be a Scotch barque, bound also for San Francisco, without passengers, but very nearly as badly off as ourselves. She could not spare us anything at all, but the captain gave us an invitation to dinner, which we accepted with the greatest pleasure. It was Sunday, and so the dinner was of course the best they could get up. It only consisted of fresh pork (the remains of their last pig), and duff; but with mustard to the pork, and sugar to the duff, it seemed to us a most sumptuous banquet; and, not having the immediate prospect of such another for some time to come, we made the most of the present opportunity. In fact, we cleared the table. I don't know what the Scotch skipper thought of us, but if he really could have spared us anything, the ravenous way in which we demolished his dinner would surely have softened his heart.

On arriving again alongside our own ship, with the boat empty as when we left her, we were greeted by a row of very long faces looking down on us over the side; not a word was said, because they had watched us with the glass leaving the other vessel, and had seen that nothing was handed into the boat; and when we described the splendid dinner we had just eaten, the faces lengthened so much, and assumed such a very wistful expression, that it seemed a wanton piece of cruelty to have mentioned the circumstance at all.

But, after all, our hard fare did not cause us much distress: we got used to it, and besides, a passage to California was not like a passage to any other place. Every one was so confident of acquiring an immense fortune there in an incredibly short time, that he was already making his plans for the future enjoyment of it, and present difficulties and hardships were not sufficiently appreciated.

The time passed pleasantly enough; all were disposed to be cheerful, and amongst so many men there are always some who afford amusement for the rest. Many found constant occupation in trading off their coats, hats, boots, trunks, or anything they possessed. I think scarcely any one went ashore in San Francisco with a single article of clothing which he possessed in Panama; and there was hardly an article of any man's wardrobe, which, by the time our voyage was over, had not at one time been the property of every other man on board the ship.

We had one cantankerous old Englishman on board, who used to roll out, most volubly, good round English oaths, greatly to the amusement of some of the American passengers, for the English style of cursing and swearing is very different from that which prevails in the States. This old fellow was made a butt for all manner of practical jokes. He had a way of going to sleep during the day in all sorts of places; and when the dinner-bell rang, he would find himself tied hand and foot. They sewed up the sleeves of his coat, and then bet him long odds he could not put it on, and take it off again, within a minute. They made up cigars for him with some powder in the inside; and in fact the jokes played off upon him were endless, the great fun being, apparently, to hear him swear, which he did most heartily. He always fancied himself ill, and said that quinine was the only thing that would save him ; but the quinine, like everything else on board, was all used up. However, one man put up some papers of flour and salt, and gave them to him as quinine, saying he had just found them in looking over his trunk. Constant inquiries were then made after the old man's health, when he declared the quinine was doing him a world of good, and that his appetite was much improved.

He was so much teased at last that he used to go about with a naked bowie-knife in his hand, with which he threatened to do awful things to whoever interfered with him. But even this did not secure him much peace, and he was such a dreadfully crabbed old rascal that I thought the stirring-up he got was quite necessary to keep him sweet.

After a wretchedly long passage, during which we experienced nothing but calms, light winds, and heavy contrary gales, we entered the Golden Gate of San Francisco harbor with the first and only fair wind we were favored with, and came to anchor before the city about eight o'clock in the evening.

CHAPTER III

A CITY IN THE MAKING

THE entrance to San Francisco harbor is between precipitous rocky headlands about a mile apart, which have received the name of the Golden Gate. The harbor itself is a large sheet of water, twelve miles across at its widest point, and in length forty or fifty miles, getting gradually narrower till at last it becomes a mere creek.

On the north side of the harbor falls in the Sacramento, a large river, to which all the other rivers of California are tributary, and which is navigable for large vessels as far as Sacramento city, a distance of nearly two hundred miles.

The city of San Francisco lies on the south shore, nearly opposite the mouth of the Sacramento, and four or five miles from the ocean. It is built on a semicircular inlet, about two miles across, at the foot of a succession of bleak sandy hills, covered here and there with scrubby brushwood. Before the discovery of gold in the country, it consisted merely of a few small houses occupied by native Californians, and one or two foreign merchants engaged in the export of hides and horns. The harbor was also a favorite watering-place for whalers and men-of-war cruising in that part of the world.

At the time of our arrival in 1851, hardly a vestige remained of the original village. Everything bore evidence of newness, and the greater part of the city presented a makeshift and temporary appearance, being composed of the most motley collection of edifices, in the way of houses, which can well be conceived. Some were mere tents, with perhaps a wooden front sufficiently strong to support the sign of the occupant; some were composed of sheets of zinc on a wooden framework; there were numerous corrugated iron houses, the most unsightly things possible, and generally painted brown ; there were many imported American houses, all, of course, painted white, with green shutters; also dingy-looking Chinese houses, and occasionally some substantial brick buildings; but the great majority were nondescript, shapeless, patchwork concerns, in the fabrication of which sheet-iron, wood, zinc, and canvas seemed to have been employed indiscriminately; while here and there, in the middle of a row of such houses, appeared the hulk of a ship, which had been hauled up, and now served as a warehouse, the cabins being fitted up as offices, or sometimes converted into a boarding-house.

The hills rose so abruptly from the shore that there was not room for the rapid extension of the city, and as sites were more valuable as they were nearer the shipping, the first growth of the city was out into the bay. Already houses had been built out on piles for nearly half-a-mile beyond the original high-water mark; and it was thus that ships, having been hauled up and built in, came to occupy a position so completely out of their element. The hills are of a very loose sandy soil, and were consequently easily graded sufficiently to admit of being built upon; and what was removed from the hills was used to fill up the space gained from the bay. This has been done to such an extent, that at the present day the whole of the business part of the city of San Francisco stands on solid ground, where a few years ago large ships lay at anchor; and what was then high-water mark is now more than a mile inland.

The principal street of the town was about three-quarters of a mile long, and on it were most of the bankers' offices, the principal stores, some of the best restaurants, and numerous drinking and gambling saloons.

In the Plaza, a large open square, was the only remaining house of the San Francisco of other days – a small cottage built of sun-dried bricks. Two sides of the Plaza were composed of the most imposing-looking houses in the city, some of which were of brick several stories high; others, though of wood, were large buildings with handsome fronts in imitation of stone, and nearly every one of them was a gambling-house.

Scattered over the hills overhanging the town, apparently at random, but all on specified lots, on streets which as yet were only defined by rude fences, were habitations of various descriptions, handsome wooden houses of three or four stories, neat little cottages, iron houses, and tents innumerable.

Rents were exorbitantly high, and servants were hardly to be had for money; housekeeping was consequently only undertaken by those who did not fear the expense, and who were so fortunate as to have their families with them. The population, however, consisted chiefly of single men, and the usual style of living was to have some sort of room to sleep in, and to board at a restaurant. But even a room to oneself was an expensive luxury, and it was more usual for men to sleep in their stores or offices. As for a bed, no one was particular about that;

a shake-down on a table, or on the floor, was as common as anything else, and sheets were a luxury but little thought of. Every man was his own servant, and his own porter besides. It was nothing unusual to see a respectable old gentleman, perhaps some old paterfamilias, who at home would have been horrified at the idea of doing such a thing, open his store in the morning himself, take a broom and sweep it out, and then proceed to blacken his boots.

The boot-blacking trade, however, was one which sprang up and flourished rapidly. It was monopolized by Frenchmen, and was principally conducted in the Plaza, on the long row of steps in front of the gambling saloons. At first the accommodation afforded was not very great. One had to stand upon one foot and place the other on a little box, while a Frenchman, standing a few steps below, operated upon it. Presently arm-chairs were introduced, and, the bootblacks working in partnership, time was economized by both boots being polished simultaneously. It was a curious sight to see thirty or forty men sitting in a row in the most public part of the city having their boots blacked, while as many more stood waiting for their turn. The next improvement was being accommodated with the morning papers while undergoing the operation ; and finally, the bootblacking fraternity, keeping pace with the progressive spirit of the age, opened saloons furnished with rows of easy-chairs on a raised platform, in which the patients sat and read the news, or admired themselves in the mirror on the opposite wall. The regular charge for having one's boots polished was twenty-five cents, an English shilling – the smallest sum worth mentioning in California.

In 1851, however, things had not attained such a pitch of refinement as to render the appearance of a man's boots a matter of the slightest consequence.

As far as mere eating and drinking went, living was good enough. The market was well supplied with every description of game – venison, elk, antelope, grizzly bear, and an infinite variety of wildfowl. The harbor abounded with fish, and the Sacramento river was full of splendid salmon, equal in flavor to those of the Scottish rivers, though in appearance not quite such a highly-finished fish, being rather clumsy about the tail.

Vegetables were not so plentiful. Potatoes and onions, as fine as any in the world, were the great stand-by. Other vegetables, though scarce, were produced in equal perfection, and upon a gigantic scale. A beetroot weighing a hundred pounds, and that looked like the trunk of a tree, was not thought a *very* remarkable specimen.

The wild geese and ducks were extremely numerous all round the shores of the bay, and many men, chiefly English and French, who would have scorned the idea of selling their game at home, here turned their sporting abilities to good account, and made their guns a source of handsome profit. A Frenchman with whom I was acquainted killed fifteen hundred dollars' worth of game in two weeks.

There were two or three French restaurants nearly equal to some of the best in Paris, where the cheapest dinner one could get cost three dollars; but there were also numbers of excellent French and American houses, at which one could live much more reasonably. Good hotels were not wanting, but they were ridiculously extravagant places ; and though flimsy concerns, built of wood, and not presenting very ostentatious exteriors, they were fitted up with all the lavish display which characterizes the fashionable hotels of New York. In fact, all places of public resort were furnished and decorated in a style of most barbaric splendor, being filled with the costliest French furniture, and a profusion of immense mirrors, gorgeous gilding, magnificent chandeliers, and gold and china ornaments, conveying an idea of luxurious refinement which contrasted strangely with the appearance and occupations of the people by whom they were frequented.

San Francisco exhibited an immense amount of vitality compressed into a small compass, and a degree of earnestness was observable in every action of a man's daily life. People lived more there in a week than they would in a year in most other places.

In the course of a month, or a year, in San Francisco, there was more hard work done, more speculative schemes were conceived and executed, more money was made and lost, there was more buying and selling, more sudden changes of fortune, more eating and drinking, more smoking, swearing, gambling, and tobacco-chewing, more crime and profligacy, and, at the same time, more solid advancement made by the people, as a body, in wealth, prosperity, and the refinements of civilization, than could be shown in an equal space of time by any community of the same size on the face of the earth.

The every-day jog-trot of ordinary human existence was not a fast enough pace for Californians in their impetuous pursuit of wealth. The longest period of time ever thought of was a month. Money was loaned, and houses were rented, by the month; interest and rent being invariably payable monthly and in advance. All engagements were made by the month, during which period the changes and contingencies were so great that no one was willing to commit himself for a longer term. In the space of a month the whole city might be swept off by fire, and a totally new one might be flourishing in its place. So great was the constant fluctuation in the prices of goods, and so rash and speculative was the usual style of business, that no great idea of stability could be attached to anything, and the ever-varying aspect of the streets, as the houses were being constantly pulled down, and rebuilt, was emblematic of the equally varying fortunes of the inhabitants.

The streets presented a scene of intense bustle and excitement. The sidewalks were blocked up with piles of goods, in front of the already crowded stores; men hurried along with the air of having the weight of all the business of California on their shoulders ; others stood in groups at the comers of the streets; here and there was a drunken man lying groveling in the mud, enjoying himself as uninterruptedly as if he were merely a hog; old miners, probably on their way home, were loafing about, staring at everything, in all the glory of mining costume, jealous of every inch of their long hair and flowing beards, and of every bit of California mud which adhered to their ragged old shirts and patchwork pantaloons, as evidences that they, at least, had "seen the elephant."

Troops of newly arrived Frenchmen marched along, en route for the mines, staggering under their equipment of knapsacks, shovels, picks, tin wash-bowls, pistols, knives, swords, and double-barrel guns – their blankets slung over their shoulders, and their persons hung around with tin cups, frying-pans, coffee-pots, and other culinary utensils, with perhaps a hatchet and a spare pair of boots. Crowds of Chinamen were also to be seen, bound for the diggings, under gigantic basket-hats, each man with a bamboo laid across his shoulder, from each end of which was suspended a higgledy-piggledy collection of mining tools, Chinese baskets and boxes, immense boots and a variety of Chinese "fixins," which no one but a Chinaman could tell the use of, – all speaking at once, gabbling and chattering their horrid jargon, and producing a noise like that of a flock of geese. There were continuous streams of drays drawn by splendid horses, and loaded with merchandise from all parts of the world, and horsemen galloped about, equally regardless of their own and of other men's lives.

Two or three auctioneers might be heard at once, "crying" their goods with characteristic California vehemence, while some of their neighbors in the same line of business were ringing bells to collect an audience – and at the same time one's ears were dinned with the discord of half-a-dozen brass bands, braying out different popular airs from as many different gambling saloons. In the midst of it all, the runners, or tooters, for the opposition river-steamboats, would be cracking up the superiority of their respective boats at the top of their lungs, somewhat in this style: "One dollar to-night for Sacramento, by the splendid steamer Senator, the fastest boat that ever turned a wheel from Long wharf – with feather pillows and curled-hair mattresses, mahogany doors and silver hinges. She has got eight young-lady passengers to-night, that speak all the dead languages, and not a colored man from stem to stem of her." Here an opposition runner would let out upon him, and the two would slang each other in the choicest California Billingsgate for the amusement of the admiring crowd.

Standing at the door of a gambling saloon, with one foot raised on the steps, would be a well-dressed young man, playing thimblerig on his leg with a golden pea, for the edification of a crowd of gaping greenhorns, some one of whom would be sure to bite. Not far off would be found a precocious little blackguard of fourteen or fifteen, standing behind a cask, and playing on the head of it a sort of thimblerig game with three cards, called "French monte." He first shows their faces, and names one – say the ace of spades – as the winning card, and after thimblerigging them on the head of the cask, he lays them in a row with their faces down, and goes on proclaiming to the public in a loud voice that the ace of spades is the winning card, and that he'll "bet any man one or two hundred dollars he can't pick up the ace of spades." Occasionally some man, after watching the trick for a little, thinks it is the easiest thing possible to tell which is the ace of spades, and loses his hundred dollars accordingly, when the youngster pockets the money and his cards, and moves off to another location, not being so soft as to repeat the joke too often, or to take a smaller bet than a hundred dollars.

There were also newsboys with their shrill voices, crying their various papers with the latest intelligence from all parts of the world, and boys with boxes of cigars, offering "the best Havana cigars for a bit a-piece, as good as you can get in the stores for a quarter." A "bit" is twelve and a half cents, or an English sixpence, and for all one could buy with it, was but little less useless than an English farthing.

Presently one would hear "Hullo! there's a muss!" (*Anglicé,* a row), and men would be seen rushing to the spot from all quarters. Auction-rooms, gambling-rooms, stores, and drinking-shops would be emptied, and a mob collected in the street in a moment. The "muss" would probably be only a *difficulty* between two gentlemen, who had referred it to the arbitration of knives or pistols; but if no one was killed, the mob would disperse, to resume their various occupations, just as quickly as they had collected.

Some of the principal streets were planked, as was also, of course, that part of the city which was built on piles; but where there was no planking, the mud was ankle-deep, and in many places there were mudholes, rendering the street almost impassable. The streets were the general receptacle for every description of rubbish. They were chiefly covered with bits of broken boxes and casks, fragments of hampers, iron hoops, old tin cases, and empty bottles. In the vicinity of the numerous Jew slop-shops, they were thickly strewed with old boots, hats, coats, and pantaloons; for the majority of the population carried their wardrobe on their backs, and when they bought a new article of dress, the old one which it was to replace was pitched into the street.

I often wondered that none of the enterprising "old clo" fraternity ever opened a business in California. They might have got shiploads of old clothes for the trouble of picking them up. Some of them doubtless were not worth the trouble, but there were always tons of cast-off garments kicking about the streets, which I think an "old clo" of any ingenuity could have rendered available. California was often said to be famous for three things – rats, fleas, and empty bottles; but old clothes might well have been added to the list.

The whole place swarmed with rats of an enormous size; one could hardly walk at night without treading on them. They destroyed an immense deal of property, and a good ratting terrier was worth his weight in gold dust. I knew instances, however, of first-rate terriers in Sacramento City (which for rats beat San Francisco hollow) becoming at last so utterly disgusted with killing rats, that they ceased to consider it any sport at all, and allowed the rats to run under their noses without deigning to look at them.

As for the other industrious little animals, they were a terrible nuisance. I suppose they were indigenous to the sandy soil. It was quite a common thing to see a gentleman suddenly pull up the sleeve of his coat, or the leg of his trousers, and smile in triumph when he caught his little tormentor. After a few weeks' residence in San Francisco, one became naturally very expert at this sort of thing.

Of the last article – the empty bottles – the enormous heaps of them, piled up in all sorts of out-of-the-way places, suggested a consumption of liquor which was truly awful. Empty bottles were as plentiful as bricks – and a large city might have been built with them.

The appearance of the people, being, as they were, a sort of world's show of humanity, was extremely curious and diversified. There were Chinamen in all the splendor of sky-blue or purple figured silk jackets, and tight yellow satin continuations, black satin shoes with thick white soles, and white gaiters; a fan in the hand, and a beautifully plaited glossy pigtail hanging down to the heels from under a scarlet skull-cap, with a gold knob on the top of it. These were the swell Chinamen ; the lower orders of Celestials were generally dressed in immensely wide blue calico jackets and bags, for they really could not be called trousers, and on their heads they wore enormous wickerwork extinguishers, which would have made very good family clothes-baskets.

The Mexicans were very numerous, and wore their national costume – the bright-colored sérape thrown gracefully over the left shoulder, with rows of silver buttons down the outside of their trousers, which were generally left open, so as to show the loose white drawers underneath, and the silver-handled bowie-knife in the stamped leather leggins.

Englishmen seemed to adhere to the shooting-coat style of dress, and the down-east Yankees to their eternal black dress-coat, black pantaloons, and black satin waistcoat; while New Yorkers, Southerners, and Frenchmen, came out in the latest Paris fashions.

Those who did not stick to their former style of dress, indulged in all the extravagant license of California costume, which was of every variety that caprice could suggest. No man could make his appearance sufficiently *bizarre* to attract any attention. The prevailing fashion among the rag-tag and bobtail was a red or blue flannel shirt, wide-awake hats of every conceivable shape and color, and trousers stuffed into a big pair of boots.

Pistols and knives were usually worn in the belt at the back, and to be without either was the exception to the rule.

The few ladies who were already in San Francisco, very naturally avoided appearing in public; but numbers of female toilettes, of the most extravagantly rich and gorgeous materials, swept the muddy streets, and added not a little to the incongruous variety of the scene.

To a cursory visitor, auction-sales and gambling would have appeared two of the principal features of the city.

The gambling-saloons were very numerous, occupying the most prominent positions in the leading thoroughfares, and all of them presenting a more conspicuous appearance than the generality of houses around them. They were thronged day and night, and in each was a very good band of music, the performers being usually German or French.

On entering a first-class gambling-room, one found a large well-proportioned saloon sixty or seventy feet long, brilliantly lighted up by several very fine chandeliers, the walls decorated with ornamental painting and gilding, and hung with large mirrors and showy pictures, while in an elevated projecting orchestra half-a-dozen Germans were playing operatic music. There were a dozen or more tables in the room, each with a compact crowd of eager betters around it, and the whole room was so filled with men that elbowing one's way between the tables was a matter of difficulty. The atmosphere was quite hazy with the quantity of tobacco smoke, and was strongly impregnated with the fumes of brandy. If one happened to enter while the musicians were taking a rest, the quiet and stillness were remarkable. Nothing was heard but a slight hum of voices, and the constant clinking of money; for it was the fashion, while standing betting at a table, to have a lot of dollars in one's hands, and to keep shuffling them backwards and forwards like so many cards.

The people composing the crowd were men of every class, from the highest to the lowest, and, though the same as might be seen elsewhere, their extraordinary variety of character and of dress appeared still more curious from their being brought into such close juxtaposition, and apparently placed upon an equality. Seated round the same table might be seen well-dressed, respectable-looking men, and, alongside of them, rough miners fresh from the diggings, with well-filled buckskin purses, dirty old flannel shirts, and shapeless hats; jolly tars half-seas over, not understanding anything about the game, nor apparently taking any interest in it, but having their spree out at the gaming-table because it was the fashion, and good-humoredly losing their pile of five or six hundred or a thousand dollars; Mexicans wrapped up in their blankets smoking cigaritas, and watching the game intently from under their broad-brimmed hats; Frenchmen in their blouses smoking black pipes; and little urchins, or little old scamps rather, ten or twelve years of age, smoking cigars as big as themselves, with the air of men who were quite up to all the hooks and crooks of this wicked world (as indeed they were), and losing their hundred dollars at a pop with all the nonchalance of an old gambler; while crowds of men, some dressed like gentlemen, and mixed with all sorts of nondescript ragamuffins, crowded round, and stretched over those seated at the tables, in order to make their bets.

There were dirty, squalid, villainous-looking scoundrels, who never looked straight out of their eyes, but still were always looking at something, as if they were "making a note of it," and who could have made their faces their fortunes in some parts of the world, by "sitting" for murderers, or ruffians generally.

Occasionally one saw, jostled about unresistingly by the crowd, and as if the crowd ignored its existence, the live carcass of some wretched, dazed, woe-begone man, clad in the worn-out greasy habiliments of quondam gentility; the glassy unintelligent eye looking as if no focus could be found for it, but as if it saw a dim misty vision of everything all at once; the only meaning in the face being about the lips, where still lingered the smack of grateful enjoyment of the last mouthful of whisky, blended with a longing humble sigh for the speedy recurrence of any opportunity of again experiencing such an awakening bliss, and forcibly expressing an unquenchable thirst for strong drinks, together with the total absence of all power to do anything towards relieving it, while the whole appearance of the man spoke of bitter disappointment and reverses, without the force to bear up under them. He was the picture of sottish despair, and the name of his duplicates was legion.

There was in the crowd a large proportion of sleek well-shaven men, in stove-pipe hats and broadcloth; but, however nearly a man might approach in appearance to the conventional idea of a gentleman, it is not to be supposed, on that account, that he either was, or got the credit of being, a bit better than his neighbors. The man standing next him, in the guise of a laboring man, was perhaps his superior in wealth, character, and education. Appearances, at least as far as dress was concerned, went for nothing at all. A man was judged by the amount of money in his purse, and frequently the man to be most courted for his dollars was the most to be despised for his looks.

One element of mixed crowds of people, in the States and in this country, was very poorly represented. There were scarcely any of the lower order of Irish; the cost of emigration to California was at that time too great for the majority of that class, although now the Irish population of San Francisco is nearly equal in proportion to that in the large cities of the Union.

The Spanish game of monte, which was introduced into California by the crowds of Mexicans who came there, was at this time the most popular game, and was dealt almost exclusively by Mexicans. It is played on a table about six feet by four, on each side of which sits a dealer, and between them is the bank of gold and silver coin, to the amount of five or ten thousand dollars, piled up in rows covering a space of a couple of square feet. The game is played with Spanish cards, which are differently figured from the usual play-ing-cards, and have only forty-eight in the pack, the ten being wanting. At either end of the table two compartments, are marked on the cloth, on each of which the dealer lays out a card. Bets are then made by placing one's stake on the card betted on; and are decided according to which of those laid out first makes its appearance, as the dealer draws card after card from the top of the pack. It is a game at which the dealer has such advantages, and which, at the same time, gives him such facilities for cheating, that any one who continues to bet at it is sure to be fleeced.

Faro, which was the more favorite game for heavy betting, and was dealt chiefly by Americans, is played on a table the same size as a monte table. Laid out upon it are all the thirteen cards of a suit, on any of which one makes his bets, to be decided according as the same card appears first or second as the dealer draws them two by two off the top of the pack.

Faro was generally played by systematic gamblers, who knew, or thought they knew, what they were about; while monte, from its being apparently more simple, was patronized by novices. There were also roulette and rouge-et-noir tables, and an infinite variety of small games played with dice, and classed under the general appellation of "chuck-a-luck."

I should mention that in California the word gambler is not used in exactly the same abstract sense as with us. An individual might spend all his time, and gain his living, in betting at public gaming-tables, but that would not entitle him to the distinctive appellation of a gambler; it would only be said of him that he gambled.

The gamblers were only the professionals, the men who laid out their banks in public rooms, and invited all and sundry to bet against them. They were a distinct and numerous class of the community, who followed their profession for the accommodation of the public; and any one who did business with them was no more a "gambler" than a man who bought a pound of tea was a grocer.

At this time the gamblers were, as a general thing, the best-dressed men in San Francisco. Many of them were very gentlemanly in appearance, but there was a peculiar air about them which denoted their profession – so much so, that one might frequently hear the remark, that such a person "looked like a gambler." They had a haggard, careworn look (though that was nothing uncommon in California), and as they sat dealing at their tables, no fluctuation of fortune caused the slightest change in the expression of their face, which was that of being intently occupied with their game, but at the same time totally indifferent as to the result. Even among the betters the same thing was remarkable, though in a less degree, for the struggle to appear unconcerned when a man lost his all, was often too plainly evident with them.

The Mexicans showed the most admirable impassibility. I have seen one betting so high at a monte table that a crowd collected round to watch the result. After winning a large sum of money, he finally staked it all on one card, and lost, when he exhibited less concern than many of the bystanders, for he merely condescended to give a slight shrug of his shoulders as he lighted his cigarita and strolled slowly off.

In the forenoon, when gambling was slack, the gamblers would get up from their tables, and, leaving exposed upon them, at the mercy of the heterogeneous crowd circulating through the room, piles of gold and silver, they would walk away, seemingly as little anxious for the safety of their money as if it were under lock and key in an iron chest. It was strange to see so much apparent confidence in the honesty of human nature, and – in a city where robberies and violence were so rife, that, when out at night in unfrequented quarters, one walked pistol in hand in the middle of the street – to see money exposed in such a way as would be thought madness in any other part of the world. But here the summary justice likely to be dispensed by the crowd, was sufficient to insure a due observance of the law of *meum* and *tuum*.

These saloons were not by any means frequented exclusively by persons who went there for the purpose of gambling. Few men had much inducement to pass their evenings in their miserable homes, and the gambling-rooms were a favorite public resort, the music alone offering sufficient attraction to many who never thought of staking a dollar at any of the tables.

Another very attractive feature is the bar, a long polished mahogany or marble counter, at which two or three smart young men officiated, having behind them long rows of ornamental bottles, containing all the numerous ingredients necessary for concocting the hundred and one different "drinks" which were called for. This was also the most elaborately-decorated part of the room, the wall being completely covered with mirrors and gilding, and further ornamented with china vases, bouquets of flowers, and gold clocks.

Hither small parties of men are continually repairing to "take a drink." Perhaps they each choose a different kind of punch, or sling, or cocktail, requiring various combinations, in different proportions, of whisky, brandy, or gin, with sugar, bitters, peppermint, absinthe, curaçoa, lemon-peel, mint, and what not ; but the bar-keeper mixes them all as if by magic, when each man, taking his glass, and tipping those of all the rest as he mutters some sentiment, swallows the compound and wipes his moustache. The party then move off to make way for others, the whole operation from beginning to end not occupying more than a couple of minutes.

CHAPTER IV

LIFE AT HIGH SPEED

A MOST useful quality for a California emigrant was one which the Americans possess in a preeminent degree – a natural versatility of disposition and adaptability to every description of pursuit or occupation.

The numbers of the different classes forming the community were not in the proportion requisite to preserve its equilibrium. Transplanting oneself to California from any part of the world involved an outlay beyond the means of the bulk of the laboring classes; and to those who did come to the country, the mines were of course the great point of attraction; so that in San Francisco the numbers of the laboring and of the working classes generally, were not nearly equal to the demand. The consequence was that laborers' and mechanics' wages were ridiculously high; and, as a general thing, the lower the description of labor, or of service, required, the more extravagant in proportion were the wages paid. Sailors' wages were two and three hundred dollars per month, and there were hundreds of ships lying idle in the bay for want of crews to man them even at these rates. Every ship, on her arrival, was immediately deserted by all hands; for, of all people, sailors were the most unrestrainable in their determination to go to the diggings; and it was there a common saying, of the truth of which I saw myself many examples, that sailors, niggers, and Dutchmen, were the luckiest men in the mines: a very drunken old salt was always particularly lucky.

There was a great overplus of young men of education, who had never dreamed of manual labor, and who found that their services in their wonted capacities were not required in such a rough-and-ready, every-man-for-himself sort of place. Hard work, however, was generally better paid than head work, and men employed themselves in any way, quite regardless of preconceived ideas of their own dignity. It was one intense scramble for dollars – the man who got most was the best man – how he got them had nothing to do with it. No occupation was considered at all derogatory, and, in fact, every one was too much occupied with his own affairs to trouble himself in the smallest degree about his neighbor.

A man's actions and conduct were totally unrestrained by the ordinary conventionalities of civilized life, and, so long as he did not interfere with the rights of others, he could follow his own course, for good or for evil, with utmost freedom.

Among so many temptations to err, thrust prominently in one's way, without any social restraint to counteract them, it was not surprising that many men were too weak for such a trial and, to use an expressive, though not very elegant phrase, went to the devil. The community was composed of isolated individuals, each quite regardless of the good opinion of his neighbors; and, the outside pressure of society being removed, men assumed their natural shape, and showed what they really were, following their unchecked impulses and inclinations. The human nature of ordinary life appeared in a bald and naked state, and the natural bad passions of men, with all the vices and depravities of civilization, were indulged with the same freedom which characterizes the life of a wild savage.

There were, however, bright examples of the contrary. If there was a lavish expenditure in ministering to vice, there was also munificence in the bestowing of charity. Though there were gorgeous temples for the worship of mammon, there was a sufficiency of schools and churches for every denomination ; while, under the influence of the constantly increasing numbers of virtuous women, the standard of morals was steadily improving, and society, as it assumed a shape and a form, began to assert its claims to respect.

Although employment, of one sort or another, and good pay, were to be had by all who were able and willing to work, there was nevertheless a vast amount of misery and destitution. Many men had come to the country with their expectations raised to an unwarrantable pitch, imagining that the mere fact of emigration to California would insure them a rapid fortune; but when they came to experience the severe competition in every branch of trade, their hopes were gradually destroyed by the difficulties of the reality.

Every kind of business, custom, and employment, was solicited with an importunity little known in old countries, where the course of all such things is in so well-worn a channel, that it is not easily diverted. But here the field was open, and every one was striving for what seemed to be within the reach of all – a foremost rank in his own sphere. To keep one's place in the crowd required an unremitted exercise of the same vigor and energy which were necessary to obtain it; and many a man, though possessed of qualities which would have enabled him to distinguish himself in the quiet routine life of old countries, was crowded out of his place by the multitude of competitors, whose deficiency of merit in other respects was more than counterbalanced by an excess of unscrupulous boldness and physical energy. A polished education was of little service, unless accompanied by an unwonted amount of democratic feeling; for the extreme sensitiveness which it is otherwise apt to produce, unfitted a man for taking part in such a hand-to-hand struggle with his fellow-men.

Drinking was the great consolation for those who had not moral strength to bear up under their disappointments. Some men gradually obscured their intellects by increased habits of drinking, and, equally gradually, reached the lowest stage of misery and want; while others went at it with more force, and drank themselves into *delirium tremens* before they knew where they were. This is a very common disease in California: there is something in the climate which superinduces it with less provocation than in other countries.

But, though drunkenness was common enough, the number of drunken men one saw was small, considering the enormous consumption of liquor.

The American style of drinking is so different from that in fashion in the Old World, and forms such an important part of social intercourse, that it certainly deserves to be considered one of the peculiar institutions of the country.

In England a man reserves his drinking capacities to enhance the enjoyment of the great event of the day, and to increase the comfortable feeling of repletion which he experiences while ruminating over it. Dinner divides his day into two separate existences, and drinking in the forenoon suggests the idea of a man slinking off into out-of-the-way, mysterious places, and boozily muddling himself in private with quart pots of ale or numerous glasses of brandy-and-water.

With Americans, however, the case is very different. Dinner with them forms no such comfortable epoch in their daily life: it brings not even the hour of rest which is allowed to the laboring man – but it is one of the necessities of human existence, and, as it precludes all other occupations for the time being, it is despatched as quickly as possible. They do not drink during dinner, nor immediately afterwards. The most common excuse for declining the invitation of a friend to "take a drink," is "Thank you, I've just dined." They make the voyage through life under a full head of steam all the time; they live more in a given time than other people, and naturally have recourse to constant stimulants to make up for the want of intervals of *abandon* and repose. The necessary amount of food they eat at stated hours, but their allowance of stimulants is divided into a number of small doses, to be taken at short intervals throughout the day.

So it is that a style of drinking, which would ruin a man's character in this or any other country where eating and drinking go together, is in the States carried on publicly and openly. The bars are the most favorite resort, being situated in the most frequented and conspicuous places; and here, at all hours of the day, men are gulping down fiery mouthfuls of brandy or gin, rendered still more pungent by the addition of other ingredients, and softened down with a little sugar and water.

No one ever thinks of drinking at a bar alone: he looks round for some friend whom he can ask to join him; it is not etiquette to refuse, and it is expected that the civility will be returned: so that the system gives the idea of being a mere interchange of compliments; and many men, in submitting to it, are actuated chiefly by a desire to show a due amount of courtesy to their friends.

In San Francisco, where the ordinary rate of existence was even faster than in the Atlantic States, men required an extra amount of stimulant to keep it up, and this fashion of drinking was carried to excess. The saloons were crowded from early morning till late at night; and in each, two or three bar-keepers were kept unceasingly at work, mixing drinks for expectant groups of customers. They had no time even to sell cigars, which were most frequently dispensed at a miniature tobacconist's shop in another part of the saloon.

Among the proprietors of saloons, or bars, the competition was so great, that, from having, as is usual, merely a plate of crackers and cheese on the counter, they got the length of laying out, for several hours in the forenoon, and again in the evening, a table covered with a most sumptuous lunch of soups, cold meats, fish, and so on, – with two or three waiters to attend to it. This was all free – there was nothing to pay for it: it was only expected that no one would partake of the good things without taking a "drink" afterwards.

This sort of thing is common enough in New Orleans; but in a place like San Francisco, where the plainest dinner any man could eat cost a dollar, it did seem strange that such goodly fare should be provided gratuitously for all and sundry. It showed, however, what immense profits were made at the bars to allow of such an outlay, and gave an idea of the rivalry which existed even in that line of business.

Another part of the economy of the American bar is an instance of the confidence placed in the discretion of the public – namely, the mode of dispensing liquors. When you ask for brandy, the bar-keeper hands you a tumbler and a decanter of brandy, and you help yourself to as much as you please: the price is all the same; it does not matter what or how big a dose one takes: and in the case of cocktails, and such drinks as the bar-keeper mixes, you tell him to make it as light, or stiff, as you wish. This is the custom even at the very lowest class of grogshops. They have a story in the States connected with this, so awfully old that I am almost ashamed to repeat it. I have heard it told a thousand times, and always located in the bar of the Astor House in New York; so we may suppose it to have happened there.

A man came up to the bar, and asking for brandy, was handed a decanter of brandy accordingly. Filling a tumbler nearly full, he drank it off, and, laying his shilling on the counter, was walking away, when the bar-keeper called after him, "Saay, stranger! you've forgot your change – there's sixpence." "No," he said, "I only gave you a shilling; is not it a shilling a drink?" "Yes," said the bar-keeper; "selling it retail we charge a shilling, but a fellow like you taking it wholesale we only charge sixpence."

The American bar-keeper is quite an institution of himself. He is a superior class of man to those engaged in a similar capacity in this country, and has no counterpart here. In fact, bar-keeping is a profession, in which individuals rise to eminence, and become celebrated for their cocktails, and for their address in serving customers. The rapidity and dexterity with which they mix half-a-dozen different kinds of drinks all at once is perfectly wonderful; one sees nothing but a confusion of bottles and tumblers and cascades of fluids as he pours them from glass to glass at arm's length for the better amalgamation of the ingredients; and in the time it would take an ordinary man to pour out a glass of wine, the mixtures are ready, each prepared as accurately as an apothecary makes up a prescription.

The bar-keepers in San Francisco exercised their ingenuity in devising new drinks to suit the popular taste. The most simple and the best that I know of is a champagne cocktail, which is very easily made by putting a few drops of bitters in a tumbler and filling it up with champagne.

The immigration of Frenchmen had been so large that some parts of the city were completely French in appearance ; the shops, restaurants, and estaminets, being painted according to French taste, and exhibiting French signs, the very letters of which had a French look about them. The names of some of the restaurants were rather ambitious – as the Trois Frères, the Café de Paris, and suchlike; but these were second and third-rate places ; those which courted the patronage of the upper classes of all nations, assumed names more calculated to tickle the American ear, – such as the Jackson House and the Lafayette. They were presided over by elegantly dressed *dames du comptoir,* and all the arrangements were in Parisian style.

The principal American houses were equally good; and there was also an abundance of places where those who delighted in corn-bread, buckwheat cakes, pickles, grease, molasses, apple-sauce, and pumpkin pie, could gratify their taste to the fullest extent.

There was nothing particularly English about any of the eating-houses ; but there were numbers of second-rate English drinking-shops, where John Bull could smoke his pipe and swig his ale coolly and calmly, without having to gulp it down and move off to make way for others, as at the bars of the American saloons.

The Germans too had their lager-beer cellars, but the noise and smoke which came up from them was enough to deter any one but a German from venturing in.

There was also a Mexican quarter of the town, where there were greasy-looking Mexican *fondas,* and crowds of lazy Mexicans lying about, wrapped up in their blankets, smoking cigaritas.

In another quarter the Chinese most did congregate. Here the majority of the houses were of Chinese importation, and were stores, stocked with hams, tea, dried fish, dried ducks, and other very nasty-looking Chinese eatables, besides copper pots and kettles, fans, shawls, chessmen, and all sorts of curiosities. Suspended over the doors were brilliantly colored boards, about the size and shape of a headboard over a grave, covered with Chinese characters, and with several yards of red ribbon streaming from them; while the streets were thronged with longtailed Celestials, chattering vociferously as they rushed about from store to store, or standing in groups studying the Chinese bills posted up in the shop windows, which may have been play-bills, – for there was a

Chinese theatre, – or perhaps advertisements informing the public where the best rat-pies were to be had. A peculiarly nasty smell pervaded this locality, and it was generally believed that rats were not so numerous here as elsewhere.

Owing to the great scarcity of washerwomen, Chinese energy had ample room to display itself in the washing and ironing business. Throughout the town might be seen occasionally over some small house a large American sign, intimating that Ching Sing, Wong Choo, or Ki-chong did washing and ironing at five dollars a-dozen. Inside these places one found two or three Chinamen ironing shirts with large flat-bottomed copper pots full of burning charcoal, and, buried in heaps of dirty clothes, half-a-dozen more, smoking, and drinking tea.

The Chinese tried to keep pace with the rest of the world. They had their theatre and their gambling rooms, the latter being small dirty places, badly lighted with Chinese paper lamps. They played a peculiar game. The dealer placed on the table several handfuls of small copper coins, with square holes in them. Bets were made by placing the stake on one of four divisions, marked in the middle of the table, and the dealer, drawing the coins away from the heap, four at a time, the bets were decided according to whether one, two, three, or four remained at the last. They are great gamblers, and, when their last dollar is gone, will stake anything they possess: numbers of watches, rings, and such articles, were always lying in pawn on the table.

The Chinese theatre was a curious pagoda-looking edifice, built by them expressly for theatrical purposes, and painted, outside and in, in an extraordinary manner. The performances went on day and night, without intermission, and consisted principally of juggling and feats of dexterity. The most exciting part of the exhibition was when one man, and decidedly a man of some little nerve, made a spread eagle of himself and stood up against a door, while half-a-dozen others, at a distance of fifteen or twenty feet, pelted the door with sharp-pointed bowie-knives, putting a knife into every square inch of the door, but never touching the man. It was very pleasant to see, from the unflinching way in which the fellow stood it out, the confidence he placed in the infallibility of his brethren. They had also short dramatic performances, which were quite unintelligible to outside barbarians. The only point of interest about them was the extraordinary gorgeous dresses of the actors; but the incessant noise they made with gongs and kettle-drums was so discordant and deafening that a few minutes at a time was as long as any one could stay in the place.

There were several very good American theatres, a French theatre, and an Italian opera, besides concerts, masquerades, a circus, and other public amusements. The most curious were certainly the masquerades. They were generally given in one of the large gambling saloons, and in the placards announcing that they were to come off, appeared conspicuously also the intimation of "No weapons admitted"; "A strong police will be in attendance." The company was just such as might be seen in any gambling room; and, beyond the presence of half-a-dozen masks in female attire, there was nothing to carry out the idea of a ball or a masquerade at all; but it was worth while to go, if only to watch the company arrive, and to see the practical enforcement of the weapon clause in the announcements. Several doorkeepers were in attendance, to whom each man as he entered delivered up his knife or his pistol, receiving a check for it, just as one does for his cane or umbrella at the door of a picture-gallery. Most men drew a pistol from behind their back, and very often a knife along with it; some carried their bowie-knife down the back of their neck, or in their breast; demure, pious-looking men, in white neckcloths, lifted up the bottom of their waistcoat, and revealed the butt of a revolver; others, after having already disgorged a pistol, pulled up the leg of their trousers, and abstracted a huge bowie-knife from their boot; and there were men, terrible fellows, no doubt, but who were more likely to frighten themselves than any one else, who produced a revolver from each trouser-pocket, and a bowie-knife from their belt. If any man declared that he had no weapon, the statement was so incredible that he had to submit to be searched; an operation which was performed by the doorkeepers, who, I observed, were occasionally rewarded for their diligence by the discovery of a pistol secreted in some unusual part of the dress.

Some of the shops were very magnificently got up, and would not have been amiss in Regent Street. The watchmakers' and jewelers' shops especially were very numerous, and made a great display of immense gold watches, enormous gold rings and chains, with gold-headed canes, and diamond pins and brooches of a most formidable size. With numbers of men who found themselves possessed of an amount of money which they had never before dreamed of, and which they had no idea what to do with, the purchase of gold watches and diamond pins was a very favorite mode of getting rid of their spare cash. Laboring men fastened their coarse dirty shirts with a cluster of diamonds the size of a shilling, wore colossal gold rings on their fingers, and displayed a massive gold chain and seals from their watch-pocket; while hardly a man of any consequence returned to the Atlantic States without receiving from some one of his friends a huge gold-headed cane, with all his virtues and good qualities engraved upon it.

A large business was also done in Chinese shawls, and various Chinese curiosities. It was greatly the fashion for men, returning home, to take with them a quantity of such articles, as presents for their friends. In fact, a gorgeous Chinese shawl seemed to be as necessary for the returning Californian as a revolver and bowie-knife for the California emigrant. There was one large bazaar in particular where was exhibited such a stock of the costliest shawls, cabinets, workboxes, vases, and other articles of Chinese manufacture, with clocks, bronzes, and all sorts of drawingroom ornaments, that one would have thought it an establishment which could only be supported in a city like London or Paris.

Some of the streets in the upper part of the city presented a very singular appearance. The houses had been built before the grade of the different streets had been fixed by the corporation, and there were places where the streets, having been cut down through the hills to their proper level, were nothing more than wide trenches, with a perpendicular bank on either side, perhaps forty or fifty feet high, and on the brink of these stood the houses, to which access was gained by ladders and temporary wooden stairs, the unfortunate proprietor being obliged to go to the expense of grading his own lot, and so bringing himself down to a level with the rest of the world. In other places, where the street crossed a deep hollow, it formed a high embankment, with a row of houses at the foot of it, some nearly buried, and others already raised to the level of the street, resting on a sort of scaffolding, while the foundation was being filled in under them.

The soil was so sandy that the hills were easily cut down, and for this purpose a contrivance was used called a Steam Paddy, which did immense execution. It was worked by steam, and was somewhat on the principle of a dredging-machine, but with only one large bucket, which cut down about two tons of earth at a time and emptied itself into a truck placed alongside. From the spot where the Paddy was thus walking into the hills a railway was laid, extending to the shore, and trains of cars were continually rattling down across the streets, taking the earth to fill up those parts of the city which were as yet under water.

Two or three years later, in '54, when an alteration was made in the grade of some of the streets, large brick and stone houses were raised several feet, by means of a most ingenious application of hydraulic pressure. Excavations were made, and under the foundation-walls of the houses were inserted a number of cylinders about two feet in height, so that the building rested entirely on the heads of the pistons. The cylinders were all connected by pipes with a force-pump, worked by a couple of men, who in this way could pump up a five-story brick building three or four inches in the course of the day. As the house grew up, props were inserted in case of accidents; and when it had been raised as far as the length of the pistons would allow, the whole apparatus was readjusted, and the operation was repeated till the required height was obtained. I went to witness the process when it was being applied to a large corner brick building, five stories high, with about sixty feet frontage each way. The flagged sidewalk was being raised along with it; but there was no interruption of the business going on in the premises, or anything whatever to indicate to the passer-by that the ground was growing under his feet. On going down under the house, one saw that the building was detached from the surrounding ground, and rested on a number of cylinders; but the only appearance of work being done was by two men quietly working a pump amid a ramification of small iron pipes. The apparatus had of course to be of an immense strength to withstand the pressure to which it was subjected, and the utmost nicety was required in its adjustment, to avoid straining and cracking the walls; but numbers of large buildings were raised most successfully in this way without receiving the slightest injury.

The hackney carriages of San Francisco were infinitely superior to those of any other city in the world. One might have supposed that any old cab which would hold together would have been good enough for such a place; but, on the contrary, the cabs – if cabs they could be called – were large handsome carriages, lined with silk, and brightly painted and polished, drawn by pairs of magnificent horses, in harness, which, like the carriages, was loaded with silver. They would have passed anywhere for showy private equipages, had the drivers only been in livery, instead of being fashionably dressed individuals in kid gloves. A London cabby would have stared in astonishment at an apparition of a stand of such cabs, and also at the fares which were charged. One could not cross the street in them under five dollars. The scale of cab-fares, however, was not out of proportion to the extravagance of other ordinary expenses. The drivers probably received two or three hundred dollars a month (about £700 a year), and the horses alone were worth from a thousand to fifteen hundred dollars each.

None of the private carriages came at all near the hacks in splendor. They were mostly of the American "buggy" character, and were drawn by fast-trotting horses. The Americans have a style and taste in driving peculiarly their own ; they study neither grace nor comfort in their attitudes; speed is the only source of pleasure; and a "three-minute horse" – that is to say, one which trots his mile in three minutes – is the only horse worth driving; while anything slower than a "two-forty (*2m.* 40r.) horse" is not considered really fast.

A great many very fine horses had been imported from Sydney, but these were chiefly used in drays and under the saddle. The buggy horses were all American, and had made the journey across the plains. The native Californian horses are small, with great powers of endurance, but are generally not very tractable in harness.

On the arrival of the fortnightly steamer from Panama with the mails from the Atlantic States and from Europe, the distribution of letters at the post-office occasioned a very singular scene. In the United States the system of delivering letters by postmen is not carried to the same extent as in this country. In San Francisco no such thing existed as a postman; every one had to call at the post-office for his letters. The mail usually consisted of several wagon-loads of letter-bags; and on its being received, notice was given at the post-office at what hour the delivery would commence, a whole day being frequently required to sort the letters, which were then delivered from a row of half-a-dozen windows, lettered A to E, F to K, and so on through the alphabet. Independently of the immense mercantile correspondence, of course every man in the city was anxiously expecting letters from home ; and for hours before the appointed time for opening the windows, a dense crowd of people collected, almost blocking up the two streets which gave access to the post-office, and having the appearance at a distance of being a mob; but on coming up to it, one would find that, though closely packed together, the people were all in six strings, twisted up and down in all directions, the commencement of them being the lucky individuals who had been first on the ground, and taken up their position at their respective windows, while each new-comer had to fall in behind those already waiting. Notwithstanding the value of time, and the impatience felt by every individual, the most perfect order prevailed : there was no such thing as a man attempting to push himself in ahead of those already waiting, nor was there the slightest respect of persons ; every new-comer quietly took his position, and had to make the best of it, with the prospect of waiting for hours before he could hope to reach the window. Smoking and chewing tobacco were great aids in passing the time, and many came provided with books and newspapers, which they could read in perfect tranquillity, as there was no unnecessary crowding or jostling. The principle of "first come first served" was strictly adhered to, and any attempt to infringe the established rule would have been promptly put down by the omnipotent majority.

A man's place in the line was his individual property, more or less valuable according to his distance from the window, and, like any other piece of property, it was bought and sold, and converted into cash. Those who had plenty of dollars to spare, but could not afford much time, could buy out some one who had already spent several hours in keeping his place. Ten or fifteen dollars were frequently paid for a good position, and some men went there early, and waited patiently, without any expectation of getting letters, but for the chance of turning their acquired advantage into cash.

The post-office clerks got through their work briskly enough when once they commenced the delivery, the alphabetical system of arrangement enabling them to produce the letters immediately on the name being given. One was not kept long in suspense, and many a poor fellow's face lengthened out into a doleful expression of disbelief and disappointment, as, scarcely had he uttered his name, when he was promptly told there was nothing for him. This was a sentence from which there was no appeal, however incredulous one might be; and every man was incredulous; for during the hour or two he had been waiting, he had become firmly convinced in his own mind that there must be a letter for him; and it was no satisfaction at all to see the clerk, surrounded as he was by thousands of letters, take only a packet of a dozen or so in which to look for it: one would like to have had the post-office searched all over, and if without success, would still have thought there was something wrong. I was myself upon one occasion deeply impressed with this spirit of unbelief in the infallibility of the post-office oracle, and tried the effect of another application the next day, when my perseverance was crowned with success.

There was one window devoted exclusively to the use of foreigners, among whom English were not included; and here a polyglot individual, who would have been a useful member of society of the Tower of Babel, answered the demands of all European nations, and held communication with Chinamen, Sandwich Islanders, and all the stray specimens of humanity from unknown parts of the earth.

One reason why men went to little trouble or expense in making themselves comfortable in their homes, if homes they could be called, was the constant danger of fire.

The city was a mass of wooden and canvas buildings, the very look of which suggested the idea of a conflagration. A room was a mere partitioned-off place, the walls of which were sometimes only of canvas, though generally of boards, loosely put together, and covered with any sort of material which happened to be most convenient – cotton cloth, printed calico, or drugget, frequently papered, as if to render it more inflammable. Floors and walls were by no means so exclusive as one is accustomed to think them; they were not transparent certainly, but otherwise they insured little privacy : a general conversation could be very easily carried on by all the dwellers in a house, while, at the same time, each of them was enjoying the seclusion, such as it was, of his own apartment. A young lady, who was boarding at one of the hotels, very feelingly remarked that it was a most disagreeable place to live in, because, if any gentleman was to pop the question to her, the report would be audible in every part of the house, and all the other inmates would be waiting to hear the answer she might give.

The cry of fire is dreadful enough anywhere, but to any one who lived in San Francisco in those days it must ever be more exciting and more suggestive of disaster and destruction of property than it can be to those who have been all their lives surrounded by brick and stone, and insurance companies.

In other countries, when a fire occurs and a large amount of property is destroyed, the loss falls on a company – a body without a soul, having no individual identity, and for which no one, save perhaps a few of the shareholders, has the slightest sympathy. The loss, being sustained by an unknown quantity, as it were, is not appreciated; but in San Francisco no such institution as insurance against fire as yet existed. To insure a house there would have been as great a risk as to insure a New York steamer two or three weeks overdue. By degrees, brick buildings were superseding those of wood and pasteboard; but still, for the whole city, destruction by fire, sooner or later, was the dreaded and fully-expected doom. When such a combustible town once ignited in any one spot, the flames, of course, spread so rapidly that every part, however distant, stood nearly an equal chance of being consumed. The alarm of fire acted like the touch of a magician's wand. The vitality of the whole city was in an instant arrested and turned from its course. Theatres, saloons, and all public places, were emptied as quickly as if the buildings themselves were on fire; the business of the moment, whatever it was, was at once abandoned, and the streets became filled with people rushing frantically in every direction – not all towards the fire by any means; few thought it worth while to ask even where it was. To know there was fire somewhere was quite sufficient, and they made at once for their house or their store, or wherever they had any property that might be saved; while, as soon as the alarm was given, the engines were heard thundering along the streets, amid the ringing of the fire-bells and the shouts of the excited crowd.

The fire-companies, of which several were already organized, were on the usual American system – volunteer companies of citizens, who receive no pay, but are exempt from serving on juries and from some other citizens' duties. They have crack fire-companies just as we have crack regiments, and of these the fast young men of the upper classes are frequently the most enthusiastic members. Each company has its own officers; but they are all under control of a "chief engineer;" who is appointed by the city, and who directs the general plan of operations at a fire. There is great rivalry among the different companies, who vie with each other in making their turn-out as handsome as possible. They each have their own uniform, but the nature of their duties does not admit of much finery in their dress; red shirts and helmets are the principal features in it. Their engines, however, are got up in very magnificent style, being most elaborately painted, all the iron-work shining like polished steel, and heavily mounted with brass or silver. They are never drawn by horses, but by the firemen themselves. A long double coil of rope is attached to the engine, and is paid out as the crowd increases, till the engine appears to be tearing and bumping along in pursuit of a long narrow mob of men, who run as if the very devil himself were after them.

Their *esprit de corps* is very strong, and connected with the different engine-houses are reading-rooms, saloons, and so on, for the use of the members of the company, many of these places being in the same style of luxurious magnificence as the most fashionable hotels. On holidays, and on every possible occasion which offers an excuse for so doing, the whole fire brigade parade the streets in full dress, each company dragging their engine after them, decked out in flags and flowers, which are presented to them by their lady-admirers, in return for the balls given by the firemen for their entertainment. They also have field-days, when they all turn out, and in some open part of the city have a trial of strength, seeing which can throw a stream of water to the greatest height, or which can flood the other, by pumping water into each other's engines.

As firemen they are most prompt and efficient, performing their perilous duties with the greatest zeal and intrepidity – as might indeed be expected of men who undertake such a service for no hope of reward, but for their own love of the danger and excitement attending upon it, actuated, at the same time, by a chivalrous desire to save either life or property, in trying to accomplish which they gallantly risk, and frequently lose, their own lives. This feeling is kept alive by the readiness with which the public pay honor to any individual who conspicuously distinguishes himself – generally by presenting him with a gold or silver speaking-trumpet (that article being in the States as much the badge of office of a captain of a fire-company as with us of a captain of a man-of-war), while any fireman who is killed in discharge of his duties is buried with all pomp and ceremony by the whole fire-brigade.

Two miles above San Francisco, on the shore of the bay, is the Mission Dolores, one of those which were established in different parts of the country by the Spaniards. It was a very small village of a few adobe houses and a church, adjoining which stood a large building, the abode of the priests. The land in the neighborhood is flat and fertile, and was being rapidly converted into market-gardens ; but the village itself was as yet but little changed. It had a look of antiquity and completeness, as if it had been finished long ago, and as if nothing more was ever likely to be done with it. As is the case with all Spanish-American towns, the very style of the architecture communicated an oppressive feeling of stillness, and its gloomy solitude was only relieved by a few listless unoccupied-looking Mexicans and native Californians.

The contrast to San Francisco was so great that on coming out here one could almost think that the noisy city he had left but half an hour before had existence only in his imagination; for San Francisco presented a picture of universal human nature boiling over, while here was nothing but human stagnation – a more violent extreme than would have been the wilderness as yet untrodden by man. Being but a slightly reduced counterpart of what San Francisco was a year or two before, it offered a good point of view from which to contemplate the miraculous growth of that city, still not only increasing in extent but improving in beauty and in excellence in all its parts, and progressing so rapidly that, almost from day to day, one could mark its steady advancement in everything which denotes the presence of a wealthy and prosperous community.

The "Mission," however, was not suffered to remain long in a state of torpor. A plank road was built to it from San Francisco. Numbers of villas sprang up around it, – and good hotels, a race-course, and other attractions soon made it the favorite resort for all who sought an hour's relief from the excitement of the city.

At the very head of the bay, some sixty miles from San Francisco, is the town of San José, situated in an extensive and most fertile valley, which was all being brought under cultivation, and where some farmers had already made large fortunes by their onions and potatoes, for the growth of which the soil is peculiarly adapted. San José was the headquarters of the native Californians, many of whom were wealthy men, at least in so far as they owned immense estates and thousands of wild cattle. They did not "hold their own," however, with the more enterprising people who were now effecting such a complete revolution in the country. Their property became a thousandfold more valuable, and they had every chance to benefit by the new order of things; but men who had passed their lives in that sparsely populated and secluded part of the world, directing a few half-savage Indians in herding wild cattle, were not exactly calculated to foresee, or to speculate upon, the effects of an overwhelming influx of men so different in all respects from themselves; and even when occasions of enriching themselves were forced upon them, they were ignorant of their own advantages, and were inferior in smartness to the men with whom they had to deal. Still, although too slow to keep up with the pace at which the country was now going ahead, many of them were, nevertheless, men of considerable sagacity, and appeared to no disadvantage as members of the legislature, to which they were returned from parts of the State remote from the mines, and where as yet there were few American settlers.

San José was quite out of the way of gold-hunters, and there was consequently about the place a good deal of the California of other days. It was
at that time, however, the seat of government; and, consequently, a large
number of Americans were here assembled, and gave some life to the town,
which had also been improved by the addition of several new streets of more
modern-looking houses than the old mud and tile concerns of the native Californians.

Small steamers plied to within a mile or two of the town from San Francisco, and there were also four-horse coaches which did the sixty miles in about
five hours. The drive down the valley of the San José is in some parts very
beautiful. The country is smooth and open – not so flat as to appear monoto-
nous – and is sufficiently wooded with fine oaks ; but towards San Francisco it
becomes more hilly and bleak. The soil is sandy; indeed, excepting a few spots
here and there, it is nothing but sand, and there is hardly a tree ten feet high
within as many miles of the city.

CHAPTER V

OFF FOR THE MINES

I REMAINED in San Francisco till the worst of the rainy season was over, when I determined to go and try my luck in the mines; so, leaving my valuables in charge of a friend in San Francisco, I equipped myself in my worst suit of old clothes, and, with my blankets slung over my shoulder, I put myself on board the steamer for Sacramento.

As we did not start till five o'clock in the afternoon, we had not an opportunity of seeing very much of the scenery on the river. As long as daylight lasted, we were among smooth grassy hills and valleys, with but little brushwood, and only here and there a few stunted trees. Some of the valleys are exceedingly fertile, and* all those sufficiently watered to render them available for cultivation had already been "taken up."

We soon, however, left the hilly country behind us, and came upon the vast plains which extend the whole length of California, bounded on one side by the range of mountains which runs along the coast, and on the other side by the mountains which constitute the mining districts. Through these plains flows the Sacramento river, receiving as tributaries all the rivers flowing down from the mountains on either side.

The steamer – which was a very fair specimen of the usual style of New York river-boat – was crowded with passengers and merchandise. There were not berths for one-half of the people on board; and so, in company with many others, I lay down and slept very comfortably on the deck of the saloon till about three o'clock in the morning, when we were awakened by the noise of letting off the steam on our arrival at Sacramento.

One of not the least striking wonders of California was the number of these magnificent river steamboats which, even at that early period of its history, had steamed round Cape Horn from New York, and now, gliding along the California rivers at the rate of twenty-two miles an hour, afforded the same rapid and comfortable means of traveling, and sometimes at as cheap rates, as when they plied between New York and Albany. Every traveler in the United States has described the river steamboats; suffice it to say here, that they lost none of their characteristics in California; and, looking at these long, white, narrow, two-story houses, floating apparently on nothing, so little of the hull of the boat appears above water, and showing none of the lines which, in a ship, convey an idea of buoyancy and power of resistance, but, on the contrary, suggesting only the idea of how easy it would be to smash them to pieces – following in imagination these fragile-looking fabrics over the seventeen thousand miles of stormy ocean over which they had been brought in safety, one could not help feeling a degree of admiration and respect for the daring and skill of the men by whom such perilous undertakings had been accomplished. In preparing these steamboats for their long voyage to California, the lower story was strengthened with thick planking, and on the forward part of the deck was built a strong wedge-shaped screen, to break the force of the waves, which might otherwise wash the whole house overboard. They crept along the coast, having to touch at most of the ports on the way for fuel; and passing through the Straits of Magellan, they escaped to a certain extent the dangers of Cape Horn, although equal dangers might be encountered on any part of the voyage.

But besides the question of nautical skill and individual daring, as a commercial undertaking the sending such steamers round to California was a very bold speculation. Their value in New York is about a hundred thousand dollars, and to take them round to San Francisco costs about thirty thousand more. Insurance is, of course, out of the question (I do not think 99 per cent would insure them in this country from Dover to Calais) ; so the owners had to play a neck-or-nothing game. Their enterprise was in most cases duly rewarded. I only know of one instance – though doubtless others have occurred – in which such vessels did not get round in safety: it was an old Long Island Sound boat; she was rotten before ever she left New York, and foundered somewhere about the Bermudas, all hands on board escaping in the boats.

The profits of the first few steamers which arrived out were of course enormous ; but, after a while, competition was so keen that for some time cabin fare between San Francisco and Sacramento was only one dollar; a ridiculously small sum to pay, in any part of the world, for being carried in such boats two hundred miles in ten hours; but, in California at that time, the wages of the common deck hands on board these same boats were about a hundred dollars a-month; and ten dollars were there, to the generality of men, a sum of much less consequence than ten shillings are here.

These low fares did not last long, however; the owners of steamers came to an understanding, and the average rate of fare from San Francisco to Sacramento was from five to eight dollars. I have only alluded to the one-dollar fares for the purpose of giving an idea of the competition which existed in such a business as "steamboating," which requires a large capital; and from that it may be imagined what intense rivalry there was among those engaged in less important lines of business, which engrossed their whole time and labor, and required the employment of all the means at their command.

Looking at the map of California, it will be seen that the "mines" occupy a long strip of mountainous country, which commences many miles to the eastward of San Francisco, and stretches northward several hundred miles. The Sacramento river running parallel with the mines, the San Joaquin joining it from the southward and eastward, and the Feather river continuing a northward course from the Sacramento – all of them being navigable – present the natural means of communication between San Francisco and the "mines." Accordingly, the city of Sacramento – about two hundred miles north of San Francisco – sprang up as the depot for all the middle part of the mines, with roads radiating from it across the plains to the various settlements in the mountains. In like manner the city of Marysville, being at the extreme northern point of navigation of the Feather river, became the starting-place and the depot for the mining districts in the northern section of the State; and Stockton, named after Commodore Stockton, of the United States Navy, who had command of the Pacific squadron during the Mexican war, being situated at the head of navigation of the San Joaquin, forms the intermediate station between San Francisco and all the "southern mines."

Seeing the facilities that California thus presented for inland navigation, it is not surprising that the Americans, so pre-eminent as they are in that branch of commercial enterprise, should so soon have taken advantage of them. But though the prospective profits were great, still the enormous risk attending the sending of steamboats round the Horn might have seemed sufficient to deter most men from entering into such a hazardous speculation. It must be remembered that many of these river steamboats were despatched from New York, on an ocean voyage of seventeen thousand miles, to a place of which one-half the world as yet even doubted the existence, and when people were looking up their atlases to see in what part of the world California was. The risk of taking a steamboat of this kind to what was then such an out-of-the-way part of the world, did not end with her arrival in San Francisco by any means. The slightest accident to her machinery, which there was at that time no possibility of repairing in California, or even the extreme fluctuations in the price of coal, might have rendered her at any moment so much useless lumber.

In ocean navigation the same adventurous energy was manifest. Hardly had the news of the discovery of gold in California been received in New York, when numbers of steamers were despatched, at an expense equal to one-half their value, to take their place on the Pacific in forming a line between the United States and San Francisco *via* Panama; so that almost from the commencement of the existence of California as a gold-bearing country, steam-communication was established between New York and San Francisco, bringing the two places within twenty to twenty-five days of each other. It is true the mail line had the advantage of a mail contract from the United States government; but other lines, without any such fostering influence, ran them close in competition for public patronage.

The Americans are often accused of boasting – perhaps deservedly so; but there certainly are many things in the history of California of which they may justly be proud, having transformed her, as they did so suddenly, from a wilderness into a country in which most of the luxuries of life were procurable; and a fair instance of the bold and prompt spirit of commercial enterprise by which this was accomplished was seen in the fact that, from the earliest days of her settlement, California had as good means of both ocean and inland steam-communication as any of the oldest countries in the world.

Sacramento City is next in size and importance to San Francisco. Many large commercial houses had there established their headquarters, and imported direct from the Atlantic States. The river is navigable so far by vessels of six or eight hundred tons, and in the early days of California, many ships cleared directly for Sacramento from the different ports on the Atlantic; but as the course of trade by degrees found its proper channel, San Francisco became exclusively the emporium for the whole of California, and even at the time I write of, sea-going vessels were rarely seen so far in the interior of the country as Sacramento.

The plains are but very little above the average level of the river, and a levee had been built all along the front of the city eight or ten feet high, to save it from inundation by the high waters of the rainy season. With the exception of a few handsome blocks of brick buildings, the houses were all of wood, and had an unmistakably Yankee appearance, being all painted white turned up with green, and covered from top to bottom with enormous signs.

The streets are wide, perfectly straight, and cross each other at right angles at equal distances, like the lines of latitude and longitude on a chart. The street nomenclature is unique – very democratic, inasmuch as it does not immortalize the names of prominent individuals – and admirably adapted to such a rectangular city. The streets running parallel with the river are numbered First, Second, Third Street, and so on to infinity, and the cross streets are designated by the letters of the alphabet. J Street was the great central street, and was nearly a mile long; so the reader may reckon the number of parallel streets on each side of it, and get an idea of the extent of the city. This system of lettering and numbering the streets was very convenient, as, the latitude and longitude of a house being given, it could be found at once. A stranger could navigate all over the town without ever having to ask his way, as he could take an observation for himself at the corner of every street.

My stay in Sacramento on this occasion was limited to a few hours. I went to a large hotel, which was also the great staging-house, and here I snoozed till about five o'clock, when, it being still quite dark, the whole house woke up into active life. About a hundred of us breakfasted by candle-light, and, going out into the bar-room while day was just dawning, we found, turned out in front of the hotel, about four-and-twenty four-horse coaches, all bound for different places in the mines. The street was completely blocked up with them, and crowds of men were taking their seats, while others were fortifying themselves for their journey at the bar.

The coaches were of various kinds. Some were light spring-wagons – mere oblong boxes, with four or five seats placed across them; others were of the same build, but better finished, and covered by an awning; and there were also numbers of regular American stage-coaches, huge high-hung things which carry nine inside upon three seats, the middle one of which is between the two doors.

The place which I had intended should be the scene of my first mining exploits, was a village rejoicing in the suggestive appellation of Hangtown; designated, however, in official documents as Placer-ville. It received its name of Hangtown while yet in its infancy from the number of malefactors who had there expiated their crimes at the hands of Judge Lynch. I soon found the stage for that place – it happened to be one of the oblong boxes – and, pitching in my roll of blankets, I took my seat and lighted my pipe that I might the more fully enjoy the scene around me. And a scene it was, such as few parts of the world can now show, and which would have gladdened the hearts of those who mourn over the degeneracy of the present age, and sigh for the good old days of stage-coaches.

Here, certainly, the genuine old mail-coach, the guard with his tin horn, and the jolly old coachman with his red face, were not to be found; but the horses were as good as ever galloped with Her Majesty's mail. The teams were all headed the same way, and with their stages, four or five abreast, occupied the whole of the wide street for a distance of sixty or seventy yards. The horses were restive, and pawing, and snorting, and kicking; and passengers were try-ing to navigate to their proper stages through the labyrinth of wheels and hors-es, and frequently climbing over half-a-dozen wagons to shorten their journey. Grooms were standing at the leaders' heads, trying to keep them quiet, and the drivers were sitting on their boxes, or seats rather, for they scorn a high seat, and were swearing at each other in a very shocking manner, as wheels got locked, and wagons were backed into the teams behind them, to the discom-fiture of the passengers on the back-seats, who found horses* heads knocking the pipes out of their mouths. In the intervals of their little private battles, the drivers were shouting to the crowds of passengers who loitered about the front of the hotel; for there, as elsewhere, people will wait till the last moment; and though it is more comfortable to sit than to stand, men like to enjoy their free-dom as long as possible, before resigning all control over their motions, and charging with their precious persons a coach or a train, on full cock, and ready to go off, and shoot them out upon some remote part of creation.

On each wagon was painted the name of the place to which it ran; the drivers were also bellowing it out to the crowd, and even among such a con-fusion of coaches a man could have no difficulty in finding the one he wanted. One would have thought that the individual will and locomotive power of a man would have been sufficient to start him on his journey; but in this go-ahead country, people who had to go were not allowed to remain inert till the spirit moved them to go; they had to be "hurried up;" and of the whole crowd of men who were standing about the hotel, or struggling through the maze of wagons, only one half were passengers, the rest were "runners" for the various stages, who were exhausting all their persuasive eloquence in entreating the passengers to take their seats and go. They were all mixed up with the crowd, and each was exerting his lungs to the utmost. "Now then, gentlemen," shouts one of them, "all aboard for Nevada City. Who's agoin'? only three seats left – the last chance to-day for Nevada City – take you there in five hours. Who's there for Nevada City?" Then catching sight of some man who betrays the very slightest appearance of helplessness, or of not knowing what he is about, he pounces upon him, saying, "Nevada City, sir? – this way – just in time," and seizing him by the arm, he drags him into the crowd of stages, and almost has him bundled into that for Nevada City before the poor devil can make it understood that it is Caloma he wants to go to, and not Nevada City. His captor then calls out to some one of his brother runners who is collecting passengers for Caloma – "Oh Bill! – oh Bill! where the are you?" "Hullo!" says Bill from the other end of the crowd. "Here's a man for Caloma!" shouts the other, still holding on to his prize in case he should escape before Bill comes up to take charge of him.

This sort of thing was going on all the time. It was very ridiculous. Apparently, if a hundred men wanted to go anywhere, it required a hundred more to despatch them. There was certainly no danger of any one being left behind; on the contrary, the probability was, that any weak-minded man who happened to be passing by, would be shipped off to parts unknown before he could collect his ideas.

There were few opposition stages, excepting for Marysville, and one or two of the larger places; they were all crammed full – and of what use these "runners" or "tooters" were to anybody, was not very apparent, at least to the uninitiated. But they are a common institution with the Americans, who are not very likely to support such a corps of men if their services bring no return. In fact, it is merely part of the American system of advertising, and forcing the public to avail themselves of certain opportunities, by repeatedly and pertinaciously representing to them that they have it in their power to do so. In the States, to blow your own horn, and to make as much noise as possible with it, is the fundamental principle of all business. The most eminent lawyers and doctors advertise, and the names of the first merchants appear in the newspapers every day. A man's own personal exertions are not sufficient to keep the world aware of his existence, and without advertising he would be to all intents and purposes dead. Modest merit does not wait for its reward – it is rather too smart for that – it clamors for it, and consequently gets it all the sooner.

However, I was not thinking of this while sitting on the Hangtown stage. I had too much to look at, and some of my neighbors also took up my attention. I found seated around me a varied assortment of human nature. A New Yorker, a Yankee, and an English Jack-tar were my immediate neighbors, and a general conversation helped to beguile the time till the "runners" had succeeded in placing a passenger upon every available spot of every wagon. There was no trouble about luggage – that is an article not much known in California. Some stray individuals might have had a small carpet-bag – almost every man had his blankets – and the western men were further encumbered with their long rifles, the barrels poking into everybody's eyes, and the butts in the way of everybody's toes.

At last the solid mass of four-horse coaches began to dissolve. The drivers gathered up their reins and settled themselves down in their seats, cracked their whips, and swore at their horses; the grooms cleared out the best way they could; the passengers shouted and hurrahed; the teams in front set off at a gallop; the rest followed them as soon as they got room to start, and chevied them up the street, all in a body, for about half a mile, when, as soon as we got out of town, we spread out in all directions to every point of a semicircle, and in a few minutes I found myself one of a small isolated community, with which four splendid horses were galloping over the plains like mad. No hedges, no ditches, no houses, no road in fact – it was all a vast open plain, as smooth as à calm ocean. We might have been steering by compass, and it was like going to sea; for we emerged from the city as from a landlocked harbor, and followed our own course over the wide wide world. The transition from the confinement of the city to the vastness of space was instantaneous; and our late neighbors, rapidly diminishing around us, and getting hull down on the horizon, might have been bound for the uttermost parts of the earth, for all we could see that was to stop them.

To sit behind four horses tearing along a good road is delightful at any time, but the mere fact of such rapid locomotion formed only a small part of the pleasure of our journey.

The atmosphere was so soft and balmy that it was a positive enjoyment to feel it brushing over one's face like the finest floss silk. The sky was clear and cloudless, the bright sunshine warmed us up to a comfortable temperature; and we were traveling over such an expanse of nature that our progress, rapid as it was, seemed hardly perceptible, unless measured by the fast disappearing chimney tops of the city, or by the occasional clumps of trees we left behind us. The scene all round us was magnificent, and impressed one as much with his own insignificance as though he beheld the countries of the earth from the summit of a high mountain.

Out of sight of land at sea one experiences a certain feeling of isolation: there is nothing to connect one's ideas with the habitable globe but the ship on which one stands; but there is also nothing to carry the imagination beyond what one does see, and the view is limited to a few miles. But here, we were upon an ocean of grass-covered earth, dotted with trees, and sparkling in the sunshine with the gorgeous hues of the dense patches of wild flowers; while far beyond the horizon of the plains there rose mountains beyond mountains, all so distinctly seen as to leave no uncertainty as to the shape or the relative position of any one of them, and fading away in regular graduation till the most distant, though clearly defined, seemed still to be the most natural and satisfactory point at which the view should terminate. It was as if the circumference of the earth had been lifted up to the utmost range of vision, and there melted into air.

Such was the view ahead of us as we traveled towards the mines, where wavy outlines of mountains appeared one above another, drawing together as they vanished, and at last indenting the sky with the snowy peaks of the Sierra Nevada. On either side of us the mountains, appearing above the horizon, were hundreds of miles distant, and the view behind us was more abruptly terminated by the Coast Range, which lies between the Sacramento river and the Pacific.

It was the commencement of spring, and at that season the plains are seen to advantage. But after a few weeks of dry weather the hot sun bums up every blade of vegetation, the ground presents a cracked surface of hard-baked earth, and the roads are ankle-deep in the finest and most penetrating kind of dust, which rises in clouds like clouds of smoke, saturating one's clothes, and impregnating one's whole system.

We made a straight course of it across the plains for about thirty miles, changing horses occasionally at some of the numerous wayside inns, and passing numbers of wagons drawn by teams of six or eight mules or oxen, and laden with supplies for the mines.

The ascent from the plains was very gradual, over a hilly country, well wooded with oaks and pines. Our pace here was not so killing as it had been. We had frequently long hills to climb, where all hands were obliged to get out and walk ; but we made up for the delay by galloping down the descent on the other side.

The road, which, though in some places very narrow, for the most part spread out to two or three times the width of an ordinary road, was covered with stumps and large rocks; it was full of deep ruts and hollows, and roots of trees spread all over it.

To any one not used to such roads or to such driving, an upset would have seemed inevitable. If there was safety in speed, however, we were safe enough, and all sense of danger was lost in admiration of the coolness and dexterity of the driver as he circumvented every obstacle, but without going one inch farther than necessary out of his way to save us from perdition. He went through extraordinary bodily contortions, which would have shocked an English coachman out of his propriety; but, at the same time, he performed such feats as no one would have dared to attempt who had never been used to anything worse than an English road. With his right foot he managed a brake, and, clawing at the reins with both hands, he swayed his body from side to side to preserve his equilibrium, as now on the right pair of wheels, now on the left, he cut the "outside edge" round a stump or a rock; and when coming to a spot where he was going to execute a difficult maneuver on a piece of road which slanted violently down to one side, he trimmed the wagon as one would a small boat in a squall, and made us all crowd up to the weather side to prevent a capsize.

When about ten miles from the plains, I first saw the actual reality of gold-digging. Four or five men were working in a ravine by the roadside, digging holes like so many grave-diggers. I then considered myself fairly in "the mines," and experienced a disagreeable consciousness that we might be passing over huge masses of gold, only concealed from us by an inch or two of earth.

As we traveled onwards, we passed at intervals numerous parties of miners, and the country assumed a more inhabited appearance. Log-cabins and clapboard shanties were to be seen among the trees; and occasionally we found about a dozen of such houses grouped together by the roadside, and dignified with the name of a town.

For several miles again the country would seem to have been deserted. That it had once been a busy scene was evident from the uptorn earth in the ravines and hollows, and from the numbers of unoccupied cabins; but the cream of such diggings had already been taken, and they were not now sufficiently rich to suit the ambitious ideas of the miners.

After traveling about thirty miles over this mountainous region, ascending gradually all the while, we arrived at Hangtown in the afternoon, having accomplished the sixty miles from Sacramento city in about eight hours.

CHAPTER VI

LOOKING FOR GOLD

THE town of Placerville – or Hangtown, as it was commonly called – consisted of one long straggling street of clapboard houses and log cabins, built in a hollow at the side of a creek, and surrounded by high and steep hills.

The diggings here had been exceedingly rich – men used to pick the chunks of gold out of the crevices of the rocks in the ravines with no other tool than a bowie-knife; but these days had passed, and now the whole surface of the surrounding country showed the amount of real hard work which had been done. The beds of the numerous ravines which wrinkle the faces of the hills, the bed of the creek, and all the little flats alongside of it, were a confused mass of heaps of dirt and piles of stones lying around the innumerable holes, about six feet square and five or six feet deep, from which they had been thrown out. The original course of the creek was completely obliterated, its waters being distributed into numberless little ditches, and from them conducted into the "long toms" of the miners through canvas hoses, looking like immensely long slimy sea-serpents.

The number of bare stumps of what had once been gigantic pine trees, dotted over the naked hill-sides surrounding the town, showed how freely the ax had been used, and to what purpose was apparent in the extent of the town itself, and in the numerous log-cabins scattered over the hills, in situations apparently chosen at the caprice of the owners, but in reality with a view to be near to their diggings, and at the same time to be within a convenient distance of water and firewood.

Along the whole length of the creek, as far as one could see, on the banks of the creek, in the ravines, in the middle of the principal and only street of the town, and even inside some of the houses, were parties of miners, numbering from three or four to a dozen, all hard at work, some laying into it with picks, some shoveling the dirt into the "long toms," or with long-handled shovels washing the dirt thrown in, and throwing out the stones, while others were working pumps or baling water out of the holes with buckets. There was a continual noise and clatter, as mud, dirt, stones, and water were thrown about in all directions; and the men, dressed in ragged clothes and big boots, wielding picks and shovels, and rolling big rocks about, were all working as if for their lives, going into it with a will, and a degree of energy, not usually seen among laboring men. It was altogether a scene which conveyed the idea of hard work in the fullest sense of the words, and in comparison with which a gang of railway navvies would have seemed to be merely a party of gentlemen amateurs playing at working *pour passer le temps.*

A stroll through the village revealed the extent to which the ordinary comforts of life were attainable. The gambling-houses, of which there were three or four, were of course the largest and most conspicuous buildings; their mirrors, chandeliers, and other decorations, suggesting a style of life totally at variance with the outward indications of everything around them.

The street itself was in many places knee-deep in mud, and was plentifully strewed with old boots, hats, and shirts, old sardine-boxes, empty tins of preserved oysters, empty bottles, worn-out pots and kettles, old ham-bones, broken picks and shovels, and other rubbish too various to particularize. Here and there, in the middle of the street, was a square hole about six feet deep, in which one miner was digging, while another was baling the water out with a bucket, and a third, sitting alongside the heap of dirt which had been dug up, was washing it in a rocker. Wagons, drawn by six or eight mules or oxen, were navigating along the street, or discharging their strangely-assorted cargoes at the various stores; and men in picturesque rags, with large muddy boots, long beards, and brown faces, were the only inhabitants to be seen.

There were boarding-houses on the *table-d'hôte* principle, in each of which forty or fifty hungry miners sat down three times a day to an oilcloth-covered table, and in the course of about three minutes surfeited themselves on salt pork, greasy steaks, and pickles. There were also two or three "hotels," where much the same sort of fare was to be had, with the extra luxuries of a table-cloth and a superior quality of knives and forks.

The stores were curious places. There was no specialty about them – everything was to be found in them which it could be supposed that any one could possibly want, excepting fresh beef (there was a butcher who monopolized the sale of that article).

On entering a store, one would find the storekeeper in much the same style of costume as the miners, very probably sitting on an empty keg at a rickety little table, playing "seven up" for "the liquor" with one of his customers.

The counter served also the purpose of a bar, and behind it was the usual array of bottles and decanters, while on shelves above them was an ornamental display of boxes of sardines, and brightly-colored tins of preserved meats and vegetables with showy labels, interspersed with bottles of champagne and strangely-shaped bottles of exceedingly green pickles, the whole being arranged with some degree of taste.

Goods and provisions of every description were stowed away promiscuously all round the store, in the middle of which was invariably a small table with a bench, or some empty boxes and barrels for the miners to sit on while they played cards, spent their money in brandy and oysters, and occasionally got drunk.

The clothing trade was almost entirely in the hands of the Jews, who are very numerous in California, and devote their time and energies exclusively to supplying their Christian brethren with the necessary articles of wearing apparel.

In traveling through the mines from one end to the other, I never saw a Jew lift a pick or shovel to do a single stroke of work, or, in fact, occupy himself in any other way than in selling slops. While men of all classes and of every nation showed such versatility in betaking themselves to whatever business or occupation appeared at the time to be most advisable, without reference to their antecedents, and in a country where no man, to whatever class of society he belonged, was in the least degree ashamed to roll up his sleeves and dig in the mines for gold, or to engage in any other kind of manual labor, it was a very remarkable fact that the Jews were the only people among whom this was not observable.

They were very numerous – so much so, that the business to which they confined themselves could hardly have yielded to every individual a fair average California rate of remuneration. But they seemed to be proof against all temptation to move out of their own limited sphere of industry, and of course, concentrated upon one point as their energies were, they kept pace with the go-ahead spirit of the times. Clothing of all sorts could be bought in any part of the mines more cheaply than in San Francisco, where rents were so very high that retail prices of everything were most exorbitant; and scarcely did twenty or thirty miners collect in any out-of-the-way place, upon newly discovered diggings, before the inevitable Jew slop-seller also made his appearance, to play his allotted part in the newly-formed community.

The Jew slop-shops were generally rattletrap erections about the size of a bathing-machine, so small that one half of the stock had to be displayed suspended from projecting sticks outside. They were filled with red and blue flannel shirts, thick boots, and other articles suited to the wants of the miners, along with Colt's revolvers and bowie-knives, brass jewelry, and diamonds like young Koh-i-Noors.

Almost every man, after a short residence in California, became changed to a certain extent in his outward appearance. In the mines especially, to the great majority of men, the usual style of dress was one to which they had never been accustomed; and those to whom it might have been supposed such a costume was not so strange, or who were even wearing the old clothes they had brought with them to the country, acquired a certain California air, which would have made them remarkable in whatever part of the world they came from, had they been suddenly transplanted there. But to this rule also the Jews formed a very striking exception. In their appearance there was nothing at all suggestive of California; they were exactly the same unwashed-looking, slobbery, slipshod individuals that one sees in every seaport town.

During the week, and especially when the miners were all at work, Hangtown was comparatively quiet; but on Sundays it was a very different place. On that day the miners living within eight or ten miles all flocked in to buy provisions for the week – to spend their money in the gambling-rooms – to play cards – to get their letters from home – and to refresh themselves, after a week's labor and isolation in the mountains, in enjoying the excitement of the scene according to their tastes.

The gamblers on Sundays reaped a rich harvest; their tables were thronged with crowds of miners, betting eagerly, and of course losing their money. Many men came in, Sunday after Sunday, and gambled off all the gold they had dug during the week, having to get credit at a store for their next week's provisions, and returning to their diggings to work for six days in getting more gold, which would all be transferred the next Sunday to the gamblers, in the vain hope of recovering what had been already lost.

The street was crowded all day with miners loafing about from store to store, making their purchases and asking each other to drink, the effects of which began to be seen at an early hour in the number of drunken men, and the consequent frequency of rows and quarrels. Almost every man wore a pistol or a knife – many wore both – but they were rarely used. The liberal and prompt administration of Lynch law had done a great deal towards checking the wanton and indiscriminate use of these weapons on any slight occasion. The utmost latitude was allowed in the exercise of self-defence. In the case of a row, it was not necessary to wait till a pistol was actually leveled at one's head – if a man made even a motion towards drawing a weapon, it was considered perfectly justifiable to shoot him first, if possible. The very prevalence of the custom of carrying arms thus in a great measure was a cause of their being seldom used. They were never drawn out of bravado, for when a man once drew his pistol, he had to be prepared to use it, and to use it quickly, or he might expect to be laid low by a ball from his adversary; and again, if he shot a man without sufficient provocation, he was pretty sure of being accommodated with a hempen cravat by Judge Lynch.

The storekeepers did more business on Sundays than in all the rest of the week; and in the afternoon crowds of miners could be seen dispersing over the hills in every direction, laden with the provisions they had been purchasing, chiefly flour, pork and beans, and perhaps a lump of fresh beef.

There was only one place of public worship in Hangtown at that time, a very neat little wooden edifice, which belonged to some denomination of Methodists, and seemed to be well attended.

There was also a newspaper published two or three times a week, which kept the inhabitants "posted up" as to what was going on in the world.

The richest deposits of gold were found in the beds and banks of the rivers, creeks, and ravines, in the flats on the convex side of the bends of the streams, and in many of the flats and hollows high up in the mountains. The precious metal was also abstracted from the very hearts of the mountains, through tunnels drifted into them for several hundred yards; and in some places real mining was carried on in the bowels of the earth by means of shafts sunk to the depth of a couple of hundred feet.

The principal diggings in the neighborhood of Hangtown were surface diggings; but, with the exception of river diggings, every kind of mining operation was to be seen in full force.

The gold is found at various depths from the surface ; but the dirt on the bed-rock is the richest, as the gold naturally in time sinks through earth and gravel, till it is arrested in its downward progress by the solid rock.

The diggings here were from four to six or seven feet deep; the layer of "pay-dirt" being about a couple of feet thick on the top of the bed-rock.

I should mention that "dirt" is the word universally used in California to signify the substance dug, earth, clay, gravel, loose slate, or whatever other name might be more appropriate. The miners talk of rich dirt and poor dirt, and of "stripping off" so many feet of "top dirt" before getting to "pay-dirt," the latter meaning dirt with so much gold in it that it will pay to dig it up and wash it.

The apparatus generally used for washing was a "long tom," which was nothing more than a wooden trough from twelve to twenty-five feet long, and about a foot wide. At the lower end it widens considerably, and on the floor there is a sheet of iron pierced with holes half an inch in diameter, under which is placed a flat box a couple of inches deep. The long tom is set at a slight inclination over the place which is to be worked, and a stream of water is kept running through it by means of a hose, the mouth of which is inserted in a dam built for the purpose high enough up the stream to gain the requisite elevation ; and while some of the party shovel the dirt into the tom as fast as they can dig it up, one man stands at the lower end stirring up the dirt as it is washed down, separating the stones and throwing them out, while the earth and small gravel falls with the water through the sieve into the "ripple-box." This box is about five feet long, and is crossed by two partitions. It is also placed at an inclination, so that the water falling into it keeps the dirt loose, allowing the gold and heavy particles to settle to the bottom, while all the lighter stuff washes over the end of the box along with the water. When the day's work is over, the dirt is taken from the "ripple-box" and is "washed out" in a "wash-pan," a round tin dish, eighteen inches in diameter, with shelving sides three or four inches deep. In washing out a panful of dirt, it has to be placed in water deep enough to cover it over; the dirt is stirred up with the hands, and the gravel thrown out; the

pan is then taken in both hands, and by an indescribable series of maneuvers all
the dirt is gradually washed out of it, leaving nothing but the gold and a small
quantity of black sand. This black sand is mineral (some oxide or other salt of
iron), and is so heavy that it is not possible to wash it all out; it has to be blown
out of the gold afterwards when dry.

Another mode of washing dirt, but much more tedious, and consequently
only resorted to where a sufficient supply of water for a long tom could not
be obtained, was by means of an apparatus called a "rocker" or "cradle." This
was merely a wooden cradle, on the top of which was a sieve. The dirt was
put into this, and a miner, sitting alongside of it, rocked the cradle with one
hand, while with a dipper in the other he kept baling water on to the dirt. This
acted on the same principle as the "tom," and had formerly been the only
contrivance in use; but it was now seldom seen, as the long tom effected such
a saving of time and labor. The latter was set immediately over the claim, and
the dirt was shoveled into it at once, while a rocker had to be set alongside
of the water, and the dirt was carried to it in buckets from the place which
was being worked. Three men working together with a rocker – one digging,
another carrying the dirt in buckets, and the third rocking the cradle – would
wash on an average a hundred bucketfuls of dirt to the man in the course of
the day. With a "long tom" the dirt was so easily washed that parties of six or
eight could work together to advantage, and four or five hundred bucketfuls
of dirt a day to each one of the party was a usual day's work.

I met a San Francisco friend in Hangtown practising his profession as a
doctor, who very hospitably offered me quarters in his cabin, which I gladly
accepted. The accommodation was not very luxurious, being merely six feet
of the floor on which to spread my blankets. My host, however, had no better
bed himself, and indeed it was as much as most men cared about. Those who
were very particular preferred sleeping on a table or a bench when they were
to be had ; bunks and shelves were also much in fashion ; but the difference
in comfort was a mere matter of imagination, for mattresses were not known,
and an earthen floor was quite as soft as any wooden board. Three or four miners were also inmates of the doctor's cabin. They were quondam New South
Wales squatters, who had been mining for several months in a distant part of
the country, and were now going to work a claim about two miles up the creek
from Hangtown. As they wanted another hand to work their long tom with
them, I very readily joined their party. For several days we worked this place,

trudging out to it when it was hardly daylight, taking with us our dinner, which consisted of beefsteaks and bread, and returning to Hangtown about dark; but the claim did not prove rich enough to satisfy us, so we abandoned it, and went "prospecting," which means looking about for a more likely place.

A "prospector" goes out with a pick and shovel, and a wash-pan; and to test the richness of a place he digs down till he reaches the dirt in which it may be expected that the gold will be found; and washing out a panful of this, he can easily calculate, from the amount of gold which he finds in it, how much could be taken out in a day's work. An old miner, looking at the few specks of gold in the bottom of his pan, can tell their value within a few cents; calling it a twelve or a twenty cent "prospect," as it may be. If, on washing out a panful of dirt, a mere speck of gold remained, just enough to swear by, such dirt was said to have only "the color," and was not worth digging. A twelve-cent prospect was considered a pretty good one; but in estimating the probable result of a day's work, allowance had to be made for the time and labor to be expended in removing top-dirt, and in otherwise preparing the claim for being worked.

To establish one's claim to a piece of ground, all that was requisite was to leave upon it a pick or shovel, or other mining tool. The extent of ground allowed to each individual varied in different diggings from ten to thirty feet square, and was fixed by the miners themselves, who also made their own laws, defining the rights and duties of those holding claims; and any dispute on such subjects was settled by calling together a few of the neighboring miners, who would enforce the due observance of the laws of the diggings. After prospecting for two or three days we concluded to take up a claim near a small settlement called Middletown, two or three miles distant from Hangtown. It was situated by the side of a small creek, in a rolling hilly country, and consisted of about a dozen cabins, one of which was a store supplied with flour, pork, tobacco, and other necessaries.

We found near our claim a very comfortable cabin, which the owner had deserted, and in which we established ourselves. We had plenty of firewood and water close to us, and being only two miles from Hangtown, we kept ourselves well supplied with fresh beef. We cooked our "dampers" in New South Wales fashion, and lived on the fat of the land, our bill of fare being beefsteaks, damper, and tea for breakfast, dinner, and supper. A damper is a very good thing, but not commonly seen in California, excepting among men from New

South Wales. A quantity of flour and water, with a pinch or two of salt, is worked into a dough, and, raking down a good hardwood fire, it is placed on the hot ashes, and then smothered in more hot ashes to the depth of two or three inches, on the top of which is placed a quantity of the still burning embers. A very little practice enables one to judge from the feel of the crust when it is sufficiently cooked. The great advantage of a damper is, that it retains a certain amount of moisture, and is as good when a week old as when fresh baked. It is very solid and heavy, and a little of it goes a great way, which of itself is no small recommendation when one eats only to live.

Another sort of bread we very frequently made by filling a frying-pan with dough, and sticking it upon end to roast before the fire.

The Americans do not understand dampers. They either bake bread, using saleratus to make it rise, or else they make flapjacks, which are nothing more than pancakes made of flour and water, and are a very good substitute for bread when one is in a hurry, as they are made in a moment.

As for our beefsteaks, they could not be beat anywhere. A piece of an old iron-hoop, twisted into a serpentine form and laid on the fire, made a first-rate gridiron, on which every man cooked his steak to his own taste. In the matter of tea I am afraid we were dreadfully extravagant, throwing it into the pot in hand-fuls. It is a favorite beverage in the mines – morning, noon, and night – and at no time is it more refreshing than in the extreme heat of midday.

In the cabin two bunks had been fitted up, one above the other, made of clapboards laid crossways, but they were all loose and warped. I tried to sleep on them one night, but it was like sleeping on a gridiron; the smooth earthen floor was a much more easy couch.

CHAPTER VII

INDIANS AND CHINAMEN

WITHIN a few miles of us there was camped a large tribe of Indians, who were generally quite peaceable, and showed no hostility to the whites.

Small parties of them were constantly to be seen in Hangtown, wandering listlessly about the street, begging for bread, meat, or old clothes. These Digger Indians, as they are called, from the fact of their digging for themselves a sort of subterranean abode in which they pass the winter, are most repulsive-looking wretches, and seem to be very little less degraded and uncivilizable than the blacks of New South Wales.

They are nearly black, and are exceedingly ugly, with long hair, which they cut straight across the forehead just above the eyes. They had learned the value of gold, and might be seen occasionally in unfrequented places washing out a panful of dirt, but they had no idea of systematic work. What little gold they got, they spent in buying fresh beef and clothes. They dress very fantastically. Some, with no other garment than an old dress-coat buttoned up to the throat, or perhaps with only a hat and a pair of boots, think themselves very well got up, and look with great contempt on their neighbors whose wardrobe is not so extensive. A coat with showy linings to the sleeves is a great prize; it is worn inside out to produce a better effect, and pantaloons are frequently worn, or rather carried, with the legs tied around the waist. They seemed to think it impossible to have too much of a good thing; and any man so fortunate as to be the possessor of duplicates of any article of clothing, puts them on one over the other, piling hat upon hat after the manner of "Old clo."

The men are very tenacious of their dignity, and carry nothing but their bows and arrows, while the attendant squaws are loaded down with a large creel on the back, which is supported by a band passing across the forehead, and is the receptacle for all the rubbish they pick up. The squaws have also, of course, to carry the babies; which, however, are not very troublesome, as they are wrapped up in papoose-frames like those of the North American Indians, though of infinitely inferior workmanship.

They are very fond of dogs, and have always at their heels a number of the most wretchedly thin, mangy, starved-looking curs, of dirty brindle color, something the shape of a greyhound, but only about half his size. A strong mutual attachment exists between the dogs and their masters; but the affection of the latter does not move them to bestow much food on their canine friends, who live in a state of chronic starvation; every bone seems ready to break through the confinement of the skin, and their whole life is merely a slow death from inanition. They have none of the life or spirit of other dogs, but crawl along as if every step was to be their last, with a look of most humble resignation, and so conscious of their degradation that they never presume to hold any communion with their civilized fellow-creatures. It is very likely that canine nature cannot stand such food as the Indians are content to live upon, and of which acorns and grasshoppers are the staple articles. There are plenty of small animals on which one would think that a dog could live very well, if he would only take the trouble to catch them; but it would seem that a dog, as long as he remains a companion of man, is an animal quite incapable of providing for himself.

A failure of the acorn crop is to the Indians a national calamity, as they depend on it in a great measure for their subsistence during the winter. In the fall of the year the squaws are busily employed in gathering acorns, to be afterwards stored in small conical stacks, and covered with a sort of wicker-work. They are prepared for food by being made into a paste, very much of the color and consistency of opium. Such horrid-looking stuff it is, that I never ventured to taste it; but I believe that the bitter and astringent taste of the raw material is in no way modified by the process of manufacture.*

As is the case with most savages, the Digger Indians show remarkable instances of ingenuity in some of their contrivances, and great skill in the manufacture of their weapons. Their bows and arrows are very good specimens of workmanship. The former are shorter than the bows used in this country, but resemble them in every other particular, even in the shape of the pieces of horn at the ends. The head of the arrow is of the orthodox cut, the three feathers being placed in the usual position; the point, however, is the most elaborate part. About three inches of the end is of a heavier wood than the rest of the arrow, being very neatly spliced in with thin tendons. The point itself is a piece of flint chipped down into a flat diamond shape, about the size of a diamond on a playing-card; the edges are very sharp, and are notched to receive the tendons with which it is firmly secured to the arrow.

The women make a kind of wicker-work basket of a conical form, so closely woven as to be perfectly water-tight, and in these they have an ingenious method of boiling water, by heating a number of stones in the fire, and throwing a succession of them into the water till the temperature is raised to boiling point.

We had a visit at our cabin one Sunday from an Indian and his squaw. She was such a particularly ugly specimen of human nature that I made her sit down, and proceeded to take a sketch of her, to the great delight of her dutiful husband, who looked over my shoulder and reported progress to her. I offered her the sketch when I had finished, but after admiring herself in the bottom of a new tin pannikin, the only substitute for a looking-glass which I could find, and comparing her own beautiful face with her portrait, she was by no means pleased, and would have nothing to do with it. I suppose she thought I had not done her justice; which was very likely, for no doubt our ideas of female beauty must have differed very materially.

Not many days after we had settled ourselves at Middletown, news was brought into Hangtown that a white man had been killed by Indians at a place called Johnson's Ranch, about twelve miles distant. A party of three or four men immediately went out to recover the body, and to "hunt" the Indians. They found the half-burned remains of the murdered man ; but were attacked by a large number of Indians, and had to retire, one of the party being wounded by an Indian arrow. On their return to Hangtown there was great excitement; about thirty men, mostly from the Western States, turned out with their long rifles, intending, in the first place, to visit the camp of the Middletown tribe, and to take from them their rifles, which they were reported to have bought from the storekeeper there, and after that to lynch the storekeeper himself for selling arms to the Indians, which is against the law; for however friendly the Indians may be, they trade them off to hostile tribes.

It happened, however, that on this particular day a neighboring tribe had come over to the camp of the Middletown Indians for the purpose of having a *fandango* together; and when they saw this armed party coming upon them, they immediately saluted them with a shower of arrows and rifle-balls, which damaged a good many hats and shirts, without wounding any one. The miners returned their fire, killing a few of the Indians; but their party being too small to fight against such odds, they were compelled to retreat; and as the storekeeper, having got a hint of their kind intentions towards him, had made himself scarce, they marched back to Hangtown without having done much to boast of.

When the result of their expedition was made known, the excitement in Hangtown was of course greater than ever. The next day crowds of miners flocked in from all quarters, each man equipped with a long rifle in addition to his bowie-knife and revolver, while two men, playing a drum and a fife, marched up and down the street to give a military air to the occasion. A public meeting was held in one of the gambling-rooms, at which the governor, the sheriff of the county, and other big men of the place, were present. The miners about Hangtown were mostly all Americans, and a large proportion of them were men from the Western States, who had come by the overland route across the plains – men who had all their lives been used to Indian wiles and treachery, and thought about as much of shooting an Indian as of killing a rattlesnake. They were a rough-looking crowd; long, gaunt, wiry men, dressed in the usual old-flannel-shirt costume of the mines, with shaggy beards, their faces, hands, and arms as brown as mahogany, and with an expression about their eyes which boded no good to any Indian who should come within range of their rifles.

There were some very good speeches made at the meeting; that of a young Kentuckian doctor was quite a treat. He spoke very well, but from the fuss he made it might have been supposed that the whole country was in the hands of the enemy. The eyes of the thirty States of the Union, he said, were upon them; and it was for them, the thirty-first, to avenge this insult to the Anglo-Saxon race, and to show the wily savage that the American nation, which could dictate terms of peace or war to every other nation on the face of the globe, was not to be trifled with. He tried to rouse their courage, and excite their animosity against the Indians, though it was quite unnecessary, by drawing a vivid picture of the unburied bones of poor Brown, or Jones, the unfortunate individual who had been murdered, bleaching on the mountains of the Sierra Nevada, while his death was still unavenged. If they were cowardly enough not to go out and whip the savage Indians, their wives would spurn them, their sweethearts would reject them, and the whole world would look upon them with scorn. The most common-sense argument in his speech, however, was, that unless the Indians were taught a lesson, there would be no safety for the straggling miners in the mountains at any distance from a settlement. Altogether he spoke very well, considering the sort of crowd he was addressing; and judging from the enthusiastic applause, and from the remarks I heard made by the men around me, he could not have spoken with better effect.

The Governor also made a short speech, saying that he would take the responsibility of raising a company of one hundred men, at five dollars a day, to go and whip the Indians.

The Sheriff followed. He "cal'lated" to raise out of that crowd one hundred men, but wanted no man to put down his name who would not stand up in his boots, and he would ask no man to go any further than he would go himself.

Those who wished to enlist were then told to come round to the other end of the room, when nearly the whole crowd rushed eagerly forward, and the required number were at once enrolled. They started the next day, but the Indians retreating before them, they followed them far up into the mountains, where they remained for a couple of months, by which time the wily savages, it is to be hoped, got properly whipped, and were taught the respect due to white men.

We continued working our claim at Middletown, having taken into partnership an old sea-captain whom we found there working alone. It paid us very well for about three weeks, when, from the continued dry weather, the water began to fail, and we were obliged to think of moving off to other diggings.

It was now time to commence preparatory operations before working the beds of the creeks and rivers, as their waters were falling rapidly; and as most of our party owned shares in claims on different rivers, we became dispersed. A young Englishman and myself alone remained, uncertain as yet where we should go.

We had gone into Hangtown one night for provisions, when we heard that a great strike had been made at a place called 'Coon Hollow, about a mile distant. One man was reported to have taken out that day about fifteen hundred dollars. Before daylight next morning we started over the hill, intending to stake off a claim on the same ground; but even by the time we got there, the whole hillside was already pegged off into claims of thirty feet square, on each of which men were commencing to sink shafts, while hundreds of others were prowling about, too late to get a claim which would be thought worth taking up.

Those who had claims, immediately surrounding that of the lucky man who had caused all the excitement by letting his good fortune be known, were very sanguine. Two Cornish miners had got what was supposed to be the most likely claim, and declared they would not take ten thousand dollars for it. Of course, no one thought of offering such a sum; but so great was the excitement that they might have got eight hundred or a thousand dollars for their claim before ever they put a pick in the ground. As it turned out, however, they spent a month in sinking a shaft about a hundred feet deep ; and after drifting all round, they could not get a cent out of it, while many of the claims adjacent to theirs proved extremely rich.

Such diggings as these are called "coyote" diggings, receiving their name from an animal called the coyote, which abounds all over the plain lands of Mexico and California, and which lives in the cracks and crevices made in the plains by the extreme heat of summer. He is half dog, half fox, and, as an Irishman might say, half wolf also. They howl most dismally, just like a dog, on moonlight nights, and are seen in great numbers skulking about the plains.

Connected with them is a curious fact in natural history. They are intensely carnivorous – so are cannibals; but as cannibals object to the flavor of roasted sailor as being too salt, so coyotes turn up their noses at dead Mexicans as being too peppery. I have heard the fact mentioned over and over again, by Americans who had been in the Mexican war, that on going over the field after their battles, they found their own comrades with the flesh eaten off their bones by the coyotes, while never a Mexican corpse had been touched; and the only and most natural way to account for this phenomenon was in the fact that the Mexicans, by the constant and inordinate eating of the hot pepper-pod, the *Chili colorado,* had so impregnated their system with pepper as to render their flesh too savory a morsel for the natural and unvitiated taste of the coyotes.

These coyote diggings require to be very rich to pay, from the great amount of labor necessary before any pay-dirt can be obtained. They are generally worked by only two men. A shaft is sunk, over which is rigged a rude windlass, tended by one man, who draws up the dirt in a large bucket while his partner is digging down below. When the bed rock is reached on which the rich dirt is found, excavations are made all round, leaving only the necessary supporting pillars of earth, which are also ultimately removed, and replaced by logs of wood. Accidents frequently occur from the "caving-in" of these diggings, the result generally of the carelessness of the men themselves.

The Cornish miners, of whom numbers had come to California from the mines of Mexico and South America, generally devoted themselves to these deep diggings, as did also the lead-miners from Wisconsin. Such men were quite at home a hundred feet or so under ground, picking through hard rock by candlelight; at the same time, gold mining in any way was to almost every one a new occupation, and men who had passed their lives hitherto above ground, took quite as naturally to this subterranean style of digging as to any other.

We felt no particular fancy for it, however, especially as we could not get a claim; and having heard favorable accounts of the diggings on Weaver Creek, we concluded to migrate to that place. It was about fifteen miles off; and having hired a mule and cart from a man in Hangtown to carry our long tom, hoses, picks, shovels, blankets, and pot and pans, we started early the next morning, and arrived at our destination about noon. We passed through some beautiful scenery on the way. The ground was not yet parched and scorched by the sum-mer sun, but was still green, and on the hillsides were patches of wild-flowers growing so thick that they were quite soft and delightful to lie down upon. For some distance we followed a winding road between smooth rounded hills, thickly wooded with immense pines and cedars, gradually ascending till we came upon a comparatively level country, which had all the beauty of an En-glish park. The ground was quite smooth, though gently undulating, and the rich verdure was diversified with numbers of white, yellow, and purple flowers. The oaks of various kinds, which were here the only tree, were of an immense size, but not so numerous as to confine the view; and the only underwood was the mansanita, a very beautiful and graceful shrub, generally growing in single plants to the height of six or eight feet. There was no appearance of ruggedness or disorder; we might have imagined ourselves in a well-kept domain; and the solitude, and the vast unemployed wealth of nature, alone reminded us that we were among the wild mountains of California.

After traveling some miles over this sort of country, we got among the pine trees once more, and very soon came to the brink of the high mountains overhanging Weaver Creek. The descent was so steep that we had the greatest difficulty in getting the cart down without a capsize, having to make short tacks down the face of the hill, and generally steering for a tree to bring up upon in case of accidents. At the point where we reached the Creek was a store, and scattered along the rocky banks of the Creek were a few miners' tents and cabins. We had expected to have to camp out here, but seeing a small tent un-occupied near the store, we made inquiry of the storekeeper, and finding that it belonged to him, and that he had no objection to our using it, we took posses-sion accordingly, and proceeded to light a fire and cook our dinner.

Not knowing how far we might be from a store, we had brought along with us a supply of flour, ham, beans, and tea, with which we were quite indepen-dent. After prospecting a little, we soon found a spot on the bank of the stream which we judged would yield us pretty fair pay for our labor. We had some difficulty at first in bringing water to the long tom, having to lead our hose a considerable distance up the stream to obtain sufficient elevation; but we soon got everything in working order, and pitched in. The gold which we found here was of the finest kind, and required great care in washing. It was in exceedingly small thin scales – so thin, that in washing out in a pan at the end of the day, a scale of gold would occasionally float for an instant on the surface of the water. This is the most valuable kind of gold dust, and is worth one or two dollars an ounce more than the coarse chunky dust.

It was a wild rocky place where we were now located. The steep moun-tains, rising abruptly all round us, so confined the view that we seemed to be shut out from the rest of the world. The nearest village or settlement was about ten miles distant; and all the miners on the Creek within four or five miles living in isolated cabins, tents, and brush-houses, or camping out on the rocks, resorted for provisions to the small store already mentioned, which was sup-plied with a general assortment of provisions and clothing.

There had still been occasional heavy rains, from which our. tent was but poor protection, and we awoke sometimes in the morning, finding small pools of water in the folds of our blankets, and everything so soaking wet, inside the tent as well as outside, that it was hopeless to attempt to light a fire. On such occasions, raw ham, hard bread, and cold water was all the breakfast we could raise; eking it out however, with an extra pipe, and relieving our feelings by laying in fiercely with pick and shovel.

The weather very soon, however, became quite settled. The sky was al-ways bright and cloudless; all verdure was fast disappearing from the hills, and they began to look brown and scorched. The heat in the mines during summer is greater than in most tropical countries. I have in some parts seen the thermometer as high as 120 degrees in the shade during the greater part of the day for three weeks at a time; but the climate is not by any means so relaxing and oppressive as in countries where, though the range of the thermometer is much lower, the damp suffocating atmosphere makes the heat more severely felt. In the hottest weather in California, it is always agreeably cool at night – sufficiently so to make a blanket acceptable, and to enable one to enjoy a sound sleep, in which one recovers from all the evil effects of the previous day's baking; and even the extreme heat of the hottest hours of the day, though it crisps up one's hair like that of a nigger, is still light and exhilarating, and by no means disinclines one for bodily exertion.

We continued to work the claim we had first taken for two or three weeks with very good success, when the diggings gave out – that is to say, they ceased to yield sufficiently to suit our ideas: so we took up another claim about a mile further up the creek; and as this was rather an inconvenient distance from our tent, we abandoned it, and took possession of a log cabin near our claim which some men had just vacated. It was a very badly built cabin perched on a rocky platform overhanging the rugged pathway which led along the banks of the creek.

A cabin with a good shingle-roof is generally the coolest kind of abode in summer; but ours was only roofed with cotton cloth, offering scarcely any resistance to the fierce rays of the sun, which rendered the cabin during the day so intolerably hot that we cooked and ate our dinner under the shade of a tree.

A whole bevy of Chinamen had recently made their appearance on the creek. Their camp, consisting of a dozen or so of small tents and brush houses, was near our cabin on the side of the hill – too near to be pleasant, for they kept up a continual chattering all night, which was rather tiresome till we got used to it.

They are an industrious set of people, no doubt, but are certainly not calculated for gold-digging. They do not work with the same force or vigor as American or European miners, but handle their tools like so many women, as if they were afraid of hurting themselves. The Americans called it "scratching," which was a very expressive term for their style of digging. They did not venture to assert equal rights so far as to take up any claim which other miners would think it worth while to work; but in such places as yielded them a dollar or two a day they were allowed to scratch away unmolested. Had they happened to strike a rich lead, they would have been driven off their claim immediately. They were very averse to working in the water, and for four or five hours in the heat of the day they assembled under the shade of a tree, where they sat fanning themselves, drinking tea, and saying "too muchee hot."

On the whole, they seemed a harmless, inoffensive people; but one day, as we were going to dinner, we heard an unusual hullaballoo going on where the Chinamen were at work; and on reaching the place we found the whole tribe of Celestials divided into two equal parties, drawn up against each other in battle array, brandishing picks and shovels, lifting stones as if to hurl them at their adversaries' heads, and every man chattering and gesticulating in the most frantic manner. The miners collected on the ground to see the "muss," and cheered the Chinamen on to more active hostilities. But after taunting and threatening each other in this way for about an hour, during which time, although the excitement seemed to be continually increasing, not a blow was struck nor a stone thrown, the two parties suddenly, and without any apparent cause, fraternized, and moved off together to their tents. What all the row was about, or why peace was so suddenly proclaimed, was of course a mystery to us outside barbarians; and the tame and unsatisfactory termination of such warlike demonstrations was a great disappointment, as we had been every moment expecting that the ball would open, and hoped to see a general engagement.

It reminded me of the way in which a couple of French Canadians have a set-to. Shaking their fists within an inch of each other's faces, they call each other all the names imaginable, beginning with *sacré cochon*, and going through a long series of still less complimentary epithets, till finally *sacré astrologe* caps the climax. This is a regular smasher; it is supposed to be such a comprehensive term as to exhaust the whole vocabulary; both parties then give in for want of ammunition, and the fight is over. I presume it was by a similar process that the Chinamen arrived at a solution of their difficulty; at all events, discretion seemed to form a very large component part of Celestial valor.

Note

* Usually the tannin was extracted by placing the acorn flour in some sort of filter and letting water percolate through it. – ED.

CHAPTER VIII

MINERS' LAW

THE miners on the creek were nearly all Americans, and exhibited a great variety of mankind. Some, it was very evident, were men who had hitherto only worked with their heads; others one would have set down as having been mechanics of some sort, and as having lived in cities ; and there were numbers of unmistakable backwoodsmen and farmers from the Western States. Of these a large proportion were Missourians, who had emigrated across the plains. From the State of Missouri the people had flocked in thousands to the gold diggings, and particularly from a county in that state called Pike County.

The peculiarities of the Missourians are very strongly marked, and after being in the mines but a short time, one could distinguish a Missourian, or a "Pike," or "Pike County," as they are called, from the natives of any other western State. Their costume was always exceedingly old and greasy-looking ; they had none of the occasional foppery of the miner, which shows itself in brilliant red shirts, boots with flaming red tops, fancy-colored hats, silver-handled bowie-knives, and rich silk sashes. It always seemed to me that a Missourian wore the same clothes in which he had crossed the plains, and that he was keeping them to wear on his journey home again. Their hats were felt, of a dirty-brown color, and the shape of a short extinguisher. Their shirts had perhaps, in days gone by, been red, but were now a sort of purple ; their pantaloons were generally of a snuffy-brown color, and made of some woolly home-made fabric. Suspended at their back from a narrow strap buckled round the waist they carried a wooden-handled bowie-knife in an old leathern sheath, not stitched, but riveted with leaden nails; and over their shoulders they wore strips of cotton or cloth as suspenders – mechanical contrivances never thought of by any other men in the mines. As for their boots, there was no peculiarity about them, excepting that they were always old. Their coats, a garment not frequently seen in the mines for at least six months of the year, were very extraordinary things – exceedingly tight, short-waisted, long-skirted surtouts of homemade frieze of a greyish-blue color.

As for their persons, they were mostly long, gaunt, narrow-chested, round-shouldered men, with long, straight, light-colored, dried-up-looking hair, small thin sallow faces, with rather scanty beard and moustache, and small grey sunken eyes, which seemed to be keenly perceptive of everything around them. But in their movements the men were slow and awkward, and in the towns especially they betrayed a childish astonishment at the strange sights occasioned by the presence of the divers nations of the earth. The fact is, that till they came to California many of them had never in their lives before seen two houses together, and in any little village in the mines they witnessed more of the wonders of civilization than ever they had dreamed of.

In some respects, perhaps, the mines of California were as wild a place as any part of the Western States of America; but they were peopled by a community of men of all classes, and from different countries, who though living in a rough backwoods style, had nevertheless all the ideas and amenities of civilized life; while the Missourians, having come direct across the plains from their homes in the backwoods, had received no preparatory education to enable them to show off to advantage in such company.

And in this they labored under a great disadvantage, as compared with the lower classes of people of every country who came to San Francisco by way of Panama or Cape Horn. The men from the interior of the States learned something even on their journey to New York or New Orleans, having their eyes partially opened during the few days they spent in either of those cities en route; and on the passage to San Francisco they naturally received a certain degree of polish from being violently shaken up with a crowd of men of different habits and ideas from their own. They had to give way in many things to men whose motives of action were perhaps to them incomprehensible, while of course they gained a few new ideas from being brought into close contact with such sorts of men as they had hitherto only seen at a distance, or very likely had never heard of. A little experience of San Francisco did them no harm, and by the time they reached the mines they had become very superior men to the raw bumpkins they were before leaving their homes.

It may seem strange, but it is undoubtedly true, that the majority of men in whom such a change was most desirable became in California more humanized, and acquired a certain amount of urbanity; in fact, they came from civilized countries in the rough state, and in California got licked into shape, and polished.

I had subsequently, while residing on the Isthmus of Nicaragua, constant opportunities of witnessing the truth of this, in contrasting the outward-bound emigrants with the same class of men returning to the States after having received a California education. Every fortnight two crowds of passengers rushed across the Isthmus, one from New York, the other from San Francisco. The great majority in both cases were men of the lower ranks of life, and it is of course to them alone that my remarks apply. Those coming from New York – who were mostly Americans and Irish – seemed to think that each man could do just as he pleased, without regard to the comfort of his neighbors. They showed no accommodating spirit, but grumbled at everything, and were rude and surly in their manners; they were very raw and stupid, and had no genius for doing anything for themselves or each other to assist their progress, but perversely delighted in acting in opposition to the regulations and arrangements made for them by the Transit Company. The same men, however, on their return from California, were perfect gentlemen in comparison. They were orderly in their behavior; though rough, they were not rude, and showed great consideration for others, submitting cheerfully to any personal inconvenience necessary for the common good, and showing by their conduct that they had acquired some notion of their duties to balance the very enlarged idea of their rights which they had formerly entertained.

The Missourians, however, although they acquired no new accomplishments on their journey to California, lost none of those which they originally possessed. They could use an ax or a rifle with any man. Two of them would chop down a few trees and build a log cabin in a day and a half, and with their long five-foot-barrel rifle, which was their constant companion, they could "draw a bead" on a deer, a squirrel, or the white of an Indian's eye, with equal coolness and certainty of killing.

Though large-framed men, they were not remarkable for physical strength, nor were they robust in constitution; in fact, they were the most sickly set of men in the mines, fever and ague and diarrhoea being their favorite complaints.

We had many pleasant neighbors, and among them were some very amusing characters. One man, who went by the name of the "Philosopher," might possibly have earned a better right to the name, if he had had the resolution to abstain from whisky. He had been, I believe, a farmer in Kentucky, and was one of a class not uncommon in America, who, without much education, but with great ability and immense command of language, together with a very superficial knowledge of some science, hold forth on it most fluently, using such long words, and putting them so well together, that, were it not for the crooked ideas they enunciated, one might almost suppose they knew what they were talking about.

Phrenology was this man's hobby, and he had all the phrenological phraseology at his finger-ends. His great delight was to paw a man's head and to tell him his character. One Sunday morning he came into our cabin as he was going down to the store for provisions, and after a few minutes' conversation, of course he introduced phrenology; and as I knew I should not get rid of him till I did so, I gave him my permission to feel my head. He fingered it all over, and gave me a very elaborate synopsis of my character, explaining most minutely the consequences of the combination of the different bumps, and telling me how I would act in a variety of supposed contingencies. Having satisfied himself as to my character, he went off, and I was in hopes I was done with him, but an hour or so after dark, he came rolling into the cabin just as I was going to turn in. He was as drunk as he well could be; his nose was swelled and bloody, his eyes were both well blackened, and altogether he was very unlike a learned professor of phrenology. He begged to be allowed to stay all night; and as he would most likely have broken his neck over the rocks if he had tried to reach his own home that night, I made him welcome, thinking that he would immediately fall asleep without troubling me further. But I was very much mistaken; he had no sooner lain down, than he began to harangue me as if I were a public meeting or a debating society, addressing me as "gentlemen," and expatiating on a variety of topics, but chiefly on phrenology, the Democratic ticket, and the great mass of the people. He had a bottle of brandy with him, which I made him finish in hopes it might have the effect of silencing him ; but there was unfortunately not enough of it for that – it only made him worse, for he left the debating society and got into a bar-room, where, when I went to sleep, he was playing "poker" with some imaginary individual whom he called Jim.

In the morning he made most ample apologies, and was very earnest in expressing his gratitude for my hospitality. I took the liberty of asking him what bumps he called those in the neighborhood of his eyes. "Well, sir," he said, "you ask me a plain question, I'll give you a plain answer. I got into a 'muss' down at the store last night, and was whipped; and I deserved it too." As he was so penitent, I did not press him for further particulars; but I heard from another man the same day that when at the store he had taken the opportunity of an audience to lecture them on his favorite subject, and illustrated his theory by feeling several heads, and giving very full descriptions of the characters of the individuals. At last he got hold of a man who must have had something peculiar in the formation of his cranium, for he gave him a most dreadful character, calling him a liar, a cheat, and a thief, and winding up by saying that he was a man who would murder his father for five dollars.

The natural consequence was that the owner of this enviable character jumped up and pitched into the phrenologist, giving him the whipping which he had so candidly acknowledged, and would probably have murdered him without the consideration of the five dollars, if the bystanders had not interfered.

Very near where we were at work, a party of half-a-dozen men held a claim in the bed of the creek, and had as usual dug a race through which to turn the water, and so leave exposed the part they intended to work. This they were now anxious to do, as the creek had fallen sufficiently low to admit of it; but they were opposed by a number of miners whose claims lay so near the race that they would have been swamped had the water been turned into it.

They could not come to any settlement of the question among themselves; so, as was usual in such cases, they concluded to leave it to a jury of miners; and notice was accordingly sent to all the miners within two or three miles up and down the creek, requesting them to assemble on the claim in question the next afternoon. Although a miner calculates an hour lost as so much money out of his pocket, yet all were interested in supporting the laws of the diggings ; and about a hundred men presented themselves at the appointed time. The two opposing parties then, having tossed up for the first pick, chose six jurymen each from the assembled crowd.

When the jury had squatted themselves all together in an exalted position on a heap of stones and dirt, one of the plaintiffs, as spokesman for his party, made a. very pithy speech, calling several witnesses to prove his statements, and citing many of the laws of the diggings in support of his claims. The defendants followed in the same manner, making the most of their case; while the general public, sitting in groups on the different heaps of stones piled up between the holes with which the ground was honeycombed, smoked their pipes and watched the proceedings.

After the plaintiff and defendant had said all they had to say about it, the jury examined the state of the ground in dispute; they then called some more witnesses to give further information, and having laid their shaggy heads together for a few minutes, they pronounced their decision; which was, that the men working on the race should be allowed six days to work out their claims before the water should be turned in upon them.

Neither party was particularly well pleased with the verdict – a pretty good sign that it was an impartial one; but they had to abide by it, for had there been any resistance on either side, the rest of the miners would have enforced the decision of this august tribunal. From it there was no appeal; a jury of miners was the highest court known, and I must say I never saw a court of justice with so little humbug about it.

The laws of the creek, as was the case in all the various diggings in the mines, were made at meetings of miners held for the purpose. They were generally very few and simple. They defined how many feet of ground one man was entitled to hold in a ravine – how much in the bank, and in the bed of the creek; how many such claims he could hold at a time; and how long he could absent himself from his claim without forfeiting it. They declared what was necessary to be done in taking up and securing a claim which, for want of water, or from any other cause, could not be worked at the time; and they also provided for various contingencies incidental to the peculiar nature of the diggings.

Of course, like other laws they required constant revision and amendment, to suit the progress of the times ; and a few weeks after this trial, a meeting was held one Sunday afternoon for legislative purposes. The miners met in front of the store to the number of about two hundred; a very respectable-looking old chap was called to the chair; but for want of that article of furniture he mounted an empty pork-barrel, which gave him a commanding position; another man was appointed secretary, who placed his writing materials on some empty boxes piled up alongside of the chair. The chairman then, addressing the crowd, told them the object for which the meeting had been called, and said he would be happy to hear any gentleman who had any remarks to offer; whereupon some one proposed an amendment of the law relating to a certain description of claim, arguing the point in a very neat speech. He was duly seconded, and there was some slight opposition and discussion; but when the chairman declared it carried by the ayes, no one called for a division, so the secretary wrote it all down, and it became law.

Two or three other acts were passed, and when the business was concluded, a vote of thanks to the chairman was passed for his able conduct on the
top of the pork-barrel. The meeting was then declared to be dissolved, and accordingly dribbled into the store, where the legislators, in small detachments,
pledged each other in cocktails as fast as the storekeeper could mix them.
While the legislature was in session, however, everything was conducted
with the utmost formality, for Americans of all classes are particularly *au fait*
at the ordinary routine of public meetings.

After working our claim for a few weeks, my partner left me to go to
another part of the mines, and I joined two Americans in buying a claim five
or six miles up the creek. It was supposed to be very rich, and we had to pay a
long price for it accordingly, although the men who had taken it up, and from
whom we bought it, had not yet even prospected the ground. But the adjoining claims were being worked, and yielding largely, and from the position of
ours, it was looked on as an equally good one.

There was a great deal to be done, before it could be worked, in the way
of removing rocks and turning the water; and as three of us were not sufficient to work the place properly, we hired four men to assist us, at the usual
wages of five dollars a-day. It took about a fortnight to get the claim into
order before we could begin washing, but we then found that our labor had
not been expended in vain, for it paid uncommonly well.

When I bought this claim, I had to give up my cabin, as the distance
was so great, and I now camped with my partners close to our claim, where
we had erected a brush house. This is a very comfortable kind of abode in
summer, and does not cost an hour's labor to erect. Four uprights are stuck
in the ground, and connected with cross pieces, on which are laid heaps of
leafy brushwood, making a roof completely impervious to the rays of the sun.
Sometimes three sides are filled in with a basketwork of brush, which gives
the edifice a more compact and comfortable appearance. Very frequently a
brush shed of this sort was erected over a tent, for the thin material of which
tents were usually made offered but poor shelter from the burning sun.

When I left my cabin, I handed it over to a young man who had arrived
very lately in the country, and had just come up to the mines. On meeting him
a few days afterwards, and asking him how he liked his new abode, he told

me that the first night of his occupation he had not slept a wink, and had kept candles burning till daylight, being afraid to go to sleep on account of the rats.

Rats, indeed! poor fellow! I should think there were a few rats, but the cabin was not worse in that respect than any other in the mines. The rats were most active colonizers. Hardly was a cabin built in the most out-of-the-way part of the mountains, before a large family of rats made themselves at home in it, imparting a humanized and inhabited air to the place. They are not supposed to be indigenous to the country. They are a large black species, which I believe those who are learned in rats call the Hamburg breed. Occasionally a pure white one is seen, but more frequently in the cities than in the mines; they are probably the hoary old patriarchs, and not a distinct species.*

They are very destructive, and are such notorious thieves, carrying off letters, newspapers, handkerchiefs, and things of that sort, with which to make their nests, that I soon acquired a habit, which is common enough in the mines, of always ramming my stockings tightly into the toes of my boots, putting my neckerchief into my pocket, and otherwise securing all such matters before turning in at night. One took these precautions just as naturally, and as much as a matter of course, as when at sea one fixes things in such manner that they shall not fetch way with the motion of the ship. As in civilized life a man winds up his watch and puts it under his pillow before going to bed; so in the mines, when turning in, one just as instinctively sets to work to circumvent the rats in the manner described, and, taking off his revolver, lays it under his pillow, or at least under the coat or boots, or whatever he rests his head on.

I believe there are individuals who faint or go into hysterics if a cat happens to be in the same room with them. Any one having a like antipathy to rats had better keep as far away from California as possible, especially from the mines. The inhabitants generally, however, have no such prejudices; it is a free country – as free to rats as to Chinamen; they increase and multiply and settle on the land very much as they please, eating up your flour, and running over you when you are asleep, without ceremony.

No one thinks it worth while to kill individual rats – the abstract fact of their existence remains the same; you might as well wage war upon mosquitoes. I often shot rats, but it was for the sport, not for the mere object of killing them. Rat-shooting is capital sport, and is carried on in this wise : The most favorable place for it is a log cabin in which the chinks have not been filled up, so that there is a space of two or three inches between the logs; and the season is a moonlight night. Then when you lie down for the night (it would be absurd to call it "going to bed" in the mines), you have your revolver charged, and plenty of ammunition at hand. The lights are of course put out, and the cabin is in darkness; but the rats have a fashion of running along the tops of the logs, and occasionally standing still, showing clearly against the moonlight outside; then is your time to draw a bead upon them and knock them over – if you can. But it takes a good shot to do much at this sort of work, and a man who kills two or three brace before going to sleep has had a very splendid night's shooting.

Note

* Albino freaks. – ED.

CHAPTER IX

GOLD IS WHERE YOU FIND IT

WE worked our claim very successfully for about six weeks, when the creek at last became so dry that we had not water enough to run our long tom, and the claim was rendered for the present unavailable. It, of course, remained good to us for next season; but as I had no idea of being there to work it, I sold out my interest to my partners, and, throwing mining to the dogs, I broke out in a fresh place altogether.

I had always been in the habit of amusing myself by sketching in my leisure moments, especially in the middle of the day, for an hour or so after dinner, when all hands were taking a rest – "nooning," as the miners call it – lying in the shade, in the full enjoyment of their pipes, or taking a nap. My sketches were much sought after, and on Sundays I was beset by men begging me to do something for them. Every man wanted a sketch of his claim, or his cabin, or some spot with which he identified himself; and as they offered to pay very handsomely, I was satisfied that I could make paper and pencil much more profitable tools to work with than pick and shovel.

My new pursuit had the additional attraction of affording me an opportunity of gratifying the desire which I had long felt of wandering over the mines, and seeing all the various kinds of diggings, and the strange specimens of human nature to be found in them.

I sent to Sacramento for a fresh supply of drawing-paper, for which I had only to pay the moderate sum of two dollars and a half (ten shillings sterling) a sheet; and finding my old brother-miners very liberal patrons of the fine arts, I remained some time in the neighborhood actively engaged with my pencil.

I then had occasion to return to Hangtown. On my arrival there, I went as usual to the cabin of my friend the doctor, which I found in a pretty mess. The ground on which some of the houses were built had turned out exceedingly rich; and thinking that he might be as lucky as his neighbors, the doctor had got a party of six miners to work the inside of his cabin on half shares. He was to have half the gold taken out, as the rights of property in any sort of house or habitation in the mines extend to the mineral wealth below it. In his cabin were two large holes, six feet square and about seven deep; in each of these were three miners, picking and shoveling, or washing the dirt in rockers with the water pumped out of the holes. When one place had been worked out, the dirt was all shoveled back into the hole, and another one commenced alongside of it. They took about a fortnight in this way to work all the floor of the cabin, and found it very rich.

There was a young Southerner in Hangtown at this time, who had brought one of his slaves with him to California. They worked and lived together, master and man sharing equally the labors and hardships of the mines.

One night the slave dreamed that they had been working the inside of a certain cabin in the street, and had taken out a great pile of gold. He told his master in the morning, but neither of them thought much of it, as such golden dreams are by no means uncommon among the miners. A few nights afterwards, however, he had precisely the same dream, and was so convinced that their fortune lay waiting for them under this particular cabin, that he succeeded at last in persuading his master to believe it also. The master said nothing to any one about the dream, but made some pretext for wishing to become the owner of the cabin, and finally succeeded in buying it. He and his slave immediately moved in, and set to work digging up the earthen floor, and the dream proved to be so far true that before they had worked all the ground they had taken out twenty thousand dollars.

There were many slaves in various parts of the mines working with their masters, and I knew frequent instances of their receiving their freedom. Some slaves I have also seen left in the mines by their masters, working faithfully to make money enough wherewith to buy themselves. Of course, as California is a free State, a slave, when once taken there by his master, became free by law ; but no man would bring a slave to the country unless one on whose fidelity he could depend.

Niggers, in some parts of the mines, were pretty numerous, though by no means forming so large a proportion of the population as in the Atlantic States. As miners they were proverbially lucky, but they were also inveterate gamblers, and did not long remain burdened with their unwonted riches.

In the mines the Americans seemed to exhibit more tolerance of negro blood than is usual in the States – not that negroes were allowed to sit at table with white men, or considered to be at all on an equality, but, owing partly to the exigencies of the unsettled state of society, and partly, no doubt, to the important fact that a nigger's dollars were as good as any others, the Americans overcame their prejudices so far that negroes were permitted to lose their money in the gambling rooms; and in the less frequented drinking-shops they might be seen receiving drink at the hands of white bar-keepers. In a town or camp of any size there was always a "nigger boarding-house," kept, of course, by a darky, for the special accommodation of colored people; but in places where there was no such institution, or at wayside houses, when a negro wanted accommodation, he waited till the company had finished their meal and left the table before he ventured to sit down. I have often, on such occasions, seen the white waiter, or the landlord, when he filled that office himself, serving a nigger with what he wanted without apparently doing any violence to his feelings.

A very striking proof was seen, in this matter of waiting, of the revolution which California life caused in the feelings and occupations of the inhabitants. The Americans have an intense feeling of repugnance to any kind of menial service, and consider waiting at table as quite degrading to a free and enlightened citizen. In the United States there is hardly such a thing to be found as a native-born American waiting at table. Such service is always performed by negroes, Irishmen, or Germans; but in California, in the mines at least, it was very different. The almighty dollar exerted a still more powerful influence than in the old States, for it overcame all pre-existing false notions of dignity. The principle was universally admitted, and acted on, that no honest occupation was derogatory, and no questions of dignity interfered to prevent a man from employing himself in any way by which it suited his convenience to make his money. It was nothing uncommon to see men of refinement and education keeping restaurants or roadside houses, and waiting on any ragamuffin who chose to patronize them, with as much *empressement* as an English waiter who expects his customary coppers. But as no one considered himself demeaned by his occupation, neither was there any assumption of a superiority which was not allowed to exist; and whatever were their relative positions, men treated each other with an equal amount of deference.

After being detained a few days in Hangtown waiting for letters from San Francisco, I set out for Nevada City, about seventy miles north, intending from there to travel up the Yuba River, and see what was to be seen in that part of the mines.

My way lay through Middletown, the scene of my former mining exploits, and from that through a small village, called Cold Springs, to Caloma, the place where gold was first discovered. It lies at the base of high mountains, on the south fork of the American River. There were a few very neat well-painted houses in the village; but as the diggings in the neighborhood were not particularly good, there was little life or animation about the place; in fact, it was the dullest mining town in the whole country.

The first discovery of gold was accidentally made at this spot by some workmen in the employment of Colonel Sutter, while digging a race to convey water to a saw-mill. Colonel Sutter, a Swiss by birth, had, some years before, penetrated to California, and there established himself. The fort which he built for protection against the Indians, and in which he resided, is situated a few miles from where Sacramento City now stands.

I dined at Caloma, and proceeded on my way having a stiff hill to climb to gain the high land lying between me and the middle fork of the American River. Crossing the rivers is the most laborious part of California traveling; they flow so far below the average level of the country, which, though exceedingly rough and hilly, is comparatively easy to travel; but on coming to the brink of this high land, and looking down upon the river thousands of feet below one, the summit of the opposite side appears almost nearer than the river itself, and one longs for the loan of a pair of wings for a few moments to save the toil of descending so far, and having again to climb an equal height to gain such an apparently short distance.

Some miles from Caloma is a very pretty place called Greenwood Valley – a long, narrow, winding valley, with innumerable ravines running into it from the low hills on each side. For several miles I traveled down this valley: the bed of the creek which flowed through it, and all the ravines, had been dug up, and numbers of cabins stood on the hillsides; but at this season the creek was completely dry, and consequently no mining operations could be carried on. The cabins were all tenantless, and the place looked more desolate than if its solitude had never been disturbed by man.

At the lower end of Greenwood Valley was a small village of the same name, consisting of half-a-dozen cabins, two or three stores, and a hotel. While stopping here for the night, I enjoyed a great treat in the perusal of a number of late newspapers – among others the *Illustrated News*, containing accounts of the Great Exhibition. In the mines one was apt to get sadly behind in modern history. The express men in the towns made a business of selling editions of the leading papers of the United States, containing the news of the fortnight, and expressly got up for circulation in California. Of these the most popular with northern men was the *New York Herald*, and with the southern-ers the *New Orleans Delta*. The *Illustrated News* was also a great favorite, being usually sold at a dollar, while other papers only fetched half that price. But unless one happened to be in some town or village when the mail from the States arrived, there was little chance of ever seeing a paper, as they were all bought up immediately.

I struck the middle fork of the American River at a place called Span-ish Bar. The scenery was very grand. Looking down on the river from the summit of the range, it seemed a mere thread winding along the deep chasm formed by the mountains, which were so steep that the pine trees clinging to their sides looked as though they would slip down into the river. The face of the mountain by which I descended was covered with a perfect trellis-work of zigzag trails, so that I could work my way down by long or short tacks as I felt inclined. On the mountain on the opposite side I could see the faint line of the trail which I had to follow ; it did not look by any means inviting ; and I was thankful that, for the present at any rate, I was going downhill. Walking down a long hill, however, so steep that one dare not run, though not quite such hard work at the time as climbing up, is equally fatiguing in its results, as it shakes one's knees all to pieces.

I reached the river at last, and crossing over in a canoe, landed on the "Bar."

What they call a Bar in California is the flat which is usually found on the convex side of a bend in a river. Such places have nearly always proved very rich, that being the side on which any deposit carried down by the river will naturally lodge, while the opposite bank is generally steep and precipitous, and contains little or no gold. Indeed, there are not many exceptions to the rule that, in a spot where one bank of a river affords good diggings, the other side is not worth working.

The largest camps or villages on the rivers are on the bars, and take their name from them.

The nomenclature of the mines is not very choice or elegant. The rivers all retain the names given to them by the Spaniards, but every little creek, flat, and ravine, besides of course the towns and villages which have been called into existence, have received their names at the hands of the first one or two miners who have happened to strike the diggings. The individual pioneer has seldom shown much invention or originality in his choice of a name; in most cases he has either immortalized his own by tacking "ville" or "town" to the end of it, or has more modestly chosen the name of some place in his native State ; but a vast number of places have been absurdly named from some trifling incident connected with their first settlement; such as Shirt Tail Canon, Whisky Gulch, Port Wine Diggins, Humbug Flat, Murderer's Bar, Flapjack Canon, Yankee Jim's, Jackass Gulch, and hundreds of others with equally ridiculous names.

Spanish Bar was about half a mile in length, and three or four hundred yards wide. The whole place was honeycombed with the holes in which the miners were at work; all the trees had been cut down, and there was nothing but the red shirts of the miners to relieve the dazzling whiteness of the heaps of stones and gravel which reflected the fierce rays of the sun and made the extreme heat doubly severe.

At the foot of the mountain, as if they had been pushed back as far as possible off the diggings, stood a row of booths and tents, most of them of a very ragged and worn-out appearance. I made for the one which looked most imposing – a canvas edifice, which, from the huge sign all along the front, as-sumed to be the "United States" Hotel. It was not far from twelve o'clock, the universal dinner-hour in the mines; so I lighted my pipe, and lay down in the shade to compose myself for the great event.

The American system of using hotels as regular boarding-houses prevails also in California. The hotels in the mines are really boarding-houses, for it is on the number of their boarders they depend. The transient custom of travelers is merely incidental. The average rate of board per week at these institutions was twelve or fifteen dollars, and the charge for a single meal was a dollar, or a dollar and a half.

The "United States" seemed to have a pretty good run of business. As the hour of noon (feeding time) approached, the miners began to congregate in the bar-room; many of them took advantage of the few minutes before dinner to play cards, while the rest looked on, or took gin cocktails to whet their appetites. At last there could not have been less than sixty or seventy miners assembled in the bar-room, which was a small canvas enclosure about twenty feet square. On one side was a rough wooden door communicating with the *salle à manger;* to get as near to this as possible was the great object, and there was a press against it like that at the pit door of a theatre on a benefit night.

As twelve o'clock struck the door was drawn aside, displaying the banqueting hall, an apartment somewhat larger than the bar-room, and containing two long tables well supplied with fresh beef, potatoes, beans, pickles, and salt pork. As soon as the door was opened there was a shout, a rush, a scramble, and a loud clatter of knives and forks, and in the course of a very few minutes fifty or sixty men had finished their dinner. Of course many more rushed into the dining-room than could find seats, and the disappointed ones came out again looking rather foolish, but they "guessed there would be plenty to eat at the second table."

Having had some experience of such places, I had intended being one of the second detachment myself, and so I guessed likewise that there would be plenty to eat at the second table, and "cal'lated" also that I would have more time to eat it in than at the first.

We were not kept long waiting. In an incredibly short space of time the company began to return to the bar-room, some still masticating a mouthful of food, others picking their teeth with their fingers, or with sharp-pointed bowie-knives, and the rest, with a most provokingly complacent expression about their eyes, making horrible motions with their jaws, as if they were wiping out their mouths with their tongues, determined to enjoy the last lingering after-taste of the good things they had been eating – rather a disgusting process to a spectator at any time, but particularly aggravating to hungry men waiting for their dinner.

When they had all left the dining-room, the door was again closed while the table was being relaid. In the meantime there had been constant fresh arrivals, and there were now almost as many waiting for the second table as there had been for the first. A crowd very quickly began to collect round the door, and I saw that to dine at number two, as I had intended, I must enter into the spirit of the thing; so I elbowed my way into the crowd, and secured a pretty good position behind a tall Kentuckian, who I knew would clear the way before me. Very soon the door was opened, when in we rushed pell-mell. I labored under the disadvantage of not knowing the diggings; being a stranger, I did not know the lay of the tables, or whereabouts the joints were placed ; but immediately on entering I caught sight of a good-looking roast of beef at the far end of one of the tables, at which I made a desperate charge. I was not so green as to lose time in trying to get my legs over the bench and sit down, and in so doing perhaps be crowded out altogether; but I seized a knife and fork, with which I took firm hold of my prize, and occupying as much space as possible with my elbows, I gradually insinuated myself into my seat. Without letting go the beef, I then took a look round, and had the gratification of seeing about a dozen men leaving the room, with a most ludicrous expression of disappointment and hope long deferred. I have no doubt that when they got into the bar-room they guessed there would be lots to eat at table number three; I hope there was. I know there was plenty at number two; but it was a "grab game" – every man for himself. If I had depended on the waiter getting me a slice of roast beef, I should have had the hungry number threes down upon me before I had commenced my dinner.

Good-humor, however, was the order of the day; conversation, of course, was out of the question; but if you asked a man to pass you a dish, he did do so with pleasure, devoting one hand to your service, while with his knife or fork, as it might be, in the other, he continued to convey the contents of his plate to their ultimate destination. I must say that a knife was a favorite weapon with my *convives,* and in wielding it they displayed considerable dexterity, using it to feed themselves with such things as most people would eat with a spoon, if eating for a wager, or with a fork if only eating for ordinary purposes.

After dinner a smart-looking young gentleman opened a monte bank in the bar-room, laying out five or six hundred dollars on the table as his bank. For half an hour or so he did a good business, when the miners began to drop off to resume their work.

CHAPTER X

URSUS HORRIBILIS

I MADE inquiries as to my route, and found that the first habitation I should reach was a ranch called the Grizzly-Bear House, about fifteen miles off. The trail had been well traveled, and I had little difficulty in finding my way. After a few hours' walking, I was beginning to think that the fifteen miles must be nearly up; and as I heard an occasional crack of a rifle, I felt pretty sure I was getting near the end of my journey.

The ground undulated like the surface of the ocean after a heavy gale of wind, and as I rose over the top of one of the waves, I got a glimpse of a log cabin a few hundred yards ahead of me, which, seen through the lofty colonnade of stately pines, appeared no bigger than a rat-trap.

As I approached, I found it was the Grizzly-Bear House. There could be no mistake about it, for a strip of canvas, on which "The Grizzly-Bear House" was painted in letters a foot and a half high, was stretched along the front of the cabin over the door; and that there might be no doubt as to the meaning of this announcement, the idea was further impressed upon one by the skin of an enormous grizzly bear, which, spread out upon the wall, seemed to be taking the whole house into its embrace.

I found half-a-dozen men standing before the door, amusing themselves by shooting at a mark with their rifles. The distance was only about a hundred yards, but even at that distance, when it comes to hitting a card nailed to a pine-tree nine times out of ten, it is pretty good shooting.

Before dark, four or five other travelers arrived, and about a dozen of us sat down to supper together. The house was nothing more than a large log cabin. At one end was the bar, a narrow board three feet long, behind which were two or three decanters and some kegs of liquor, a few cigars in tumblers, some odd bottles of champagne, and a box of tobacco.

A couple of benches and a table occupied the center of the house, and sacks of flour and other provisions stood in the corners. Out in the forest, behind the cabin, was a cooking-stove, with a sort of awning over it. This was the kitchen ; and certainly the cook could not complain of want of room; but,

judging from our supper, he was not called upon to go through any very difficult maneuvers in the practice of his art. He knocked off his rifle practice about
half an hour before supper to go and light the kitchen fire, and the fruits of his
subsequent labors appeared in a large potful of tea and a lot of beefsteaks. The
bread was uncommonly stale, from which I presumed that, when he did bake,
he baked enough to last for about a week.

After supper, every man lighted his pipe, and though all were sufficiently
talkative, the attention of the whole party became very soon monopolized by
two individuals, who were decidedly the lions of the evening. One of them
was a man from Illinois, who had been in the Mexican war, and who no doubt
thought he might have been a General Scott, if he had only had the opportunity
of distinguishing himself. He commented on the tactics of the generals as if he
knew more of warfare than any of them ; and the awful yarns he told of how he
and the American army had whipped the Mexicans, and given them "particular
hell," as he called it, was enough to make a civilian's hair stand on end. Some
of his hearers swallowed every word he said, without even making a wry face
at it; but as he tried to make out that all the victories were gained by the Illinois
regiment, in which he served as full private, two or three of the party, who
knew something of the history of the war, and came from other States of the
Union, had no idea of letting Illinois have all the glory of the achievements,
and disputed the correctness of his statements. Illinois, however, was too many
for them; he was not to be stumped in that way; he had a stock of authentic
facts on hand for any emergency, with which he corroborated all his previous
assertions. The resistance he met with only stimulated him to greater efforts,
and the more one of his facts was doubted, the more incredible was the next;
till at last he detailed his confidential conversations with General Taylor, and
made himself out to be a sort of a fellow who swept Mexicans off the face of
the earth as a common man would kill mosquitoes.

He did not have all the talking to himself, however. One of the men who
kept the house was a bear-hunter by profession, and he had not hunted grizzlies for nothing. He had tales to tell of desperate encounters and hairbreadth
escapes, to which the adventures of Baron Munchausen were not a circumstance. He was a dry stringy-looking man, with light hair and keen gray eyes.
His features were rather handsome, and he had a pleasing expression; but he

was so dried up and tanned by exposure and the hard life he led, that his face conveyed no idea of flesh. One would rather have expected, on cutting into him, to find that he was composed of guttapercha, or something of that sort, and only colored on the outside. He and Illinois listened to each other's stories with silent contempt; in fact, they pretended not to listen at all, but at the same time each watched intently for the slightest halt in the other's narrative; and while the Illinois man was only taking breath during some desperate struggle with the Mexicans, the hunter in a moment plunged right into the middle of a bear-story, and was half eaten up by a grizzly before we knew what he was talking about; and as soon as ever that bear was disposed of, Illinois immediately went on with his story as if he had never been interrupted.

The hunter had rather the best of it; his yarns were uncommonly tough and hard of digestion, but there were no historical facts on record to bring against him. He had it all his own way, for the only witnesses of his exploits were the grizzlies, and he always managed to dispose of them very effectually by finishing their career along with his story. He showed several scars on different parts of his guttapercha person which he received from the paws of the grizzlies, and he was not the sort of customer whose veracity one would care to question, especially as implicit faith so much increased one's interest in his adventures. One man nearly got into a scrape by laughing at the most thrilling part of one of his best stories. After firing twice at a bear without effect, the bear, infuriated by the balls planted in his carcass, was rushing upon him. He took to flight, and, loading as he ran, he turned and put a ball into the bear's left eye. The bear winked a good deal, but did not seem to mind it much – he only increased his pace; so the hunter, loading again, turned round and put a ball into his right eye; whereupon the bear, now winking considerably with both eyes, put his nose to the ground, and began to run him down by scent. At this critical moment, a great stupid-looking lout, who had been sitting all night with his eyes and mouth wide open, sucking in and swallowing everything that was said, had the temerity to laugh incredulously. The hunter flared up in a moment. "What are you a-laafin' at?" he said. "D'ye mean to say I lie?"

"Oh," said the other, "if you say it was so, I suppose it's all right; you ought to know best. But I warn't laafin' at you ; I was laafin' at the bar."

"What do you know about bars?" said the hunter, "Did you ever kill a bar?"

The poor fellow had never killed a "bar," so the hunter snuffed him out with a look of utter contempt and pity, and went on triumphantly with his story, which ended in his getting up a tree, where he sat and peppered the bear as it went smelling round the stump, till it at last fell mortally wounded, with I don't know how many balls in its body.

The grizzlies are the commonest kind of bear found in California, and are very large animals, weighing sometimes sixteen or eighteen hundred pounds.*

Hunting them is rather dangerous sport, as they are extremely tenacious of life, and when wounded invariably show fight. But unless molested they do not often attack a man; in fact, they are hardly ever seen on the trails during the day. At night, however, they prowl about, and carry off whatever comes in their way. They had walked off with a young calf from this ranch the night before, and the hunter was going out the next day to wreak his vengeance upon them. A grizzly is well worth killing, as he fetches a hundred dollars or more, according to his weight. The meat is excellent, but it needs to be well spiced, for in process of cooking it becomes saturated with bear's grease. In the mines, however, pomatum is an article unknown, and so no unpleasantly greasy ideas occur to one while dining off a good piece of grizzly bear.

About ten o'clock, at the conclusion of a bear story, there was a general move towards one corner of the cabin where there were a lot of rifles, and where every man had thrown his roll of blankets. The floor was swept, and each one, choosing his own location, spread his blankets and lay down. Some slept in their boots, while others took them off, to put under their heads by way of pillows. I was one of the latter number, being rather partial to pillows; and selecting a spot for my head, where it would be as far from other heads as possible, I lay down, and stretching out my feet promiscuously, I was very soon in the land of dreams, where I went through the whole Mexican campaign, and killed more "bars" than ever the hunter had seen in his life.

People do not lie abed in the morning in California ; perhaps they would not anywhere, if they had no better beds than we had; so before daylight there was a general resurrection, and a very general ablution was performed in a tin basin which stood on a keg outside the cabin, alongside of which was a barrel of water. Over the basin hung a very small looking-glass, in which one could see one eye at a time; and attached to it by a long string was a comb for the use of those gentlemen who did not travel with their dressing-cases.

Some of the party, the warrior among the number, commenced the day by taking a gin cocktail, the hunter acting as bar-keeper, while his partner the cook, who had been up an hour before any of us, chopping wood and lighting a fire, was laying the table for breakfast.

Breakfast was an affair of but very few moments, and as soon as it was over, I set out in company with three or four of the party, who were going the same way.

We crossed the north fork of the American River at Kelly's Bar, a very rocky little place, covered with a number of dilapidated tents. We had the usual mountains to descend and ascend in crossing the river, but on gaining the summit we found ourselves again in a beautiful rolling country. Not far from the river was a very romantic little place called Illinois-town, consisting of three shanties and a saw-mill. The pine trees in the neighborhood were of an enormous size, and were being fast converted into lumber, which was in great demand for various mining operations, and sold at 120 dollars per thousand feet. We fared sumptuously on stewed squirrels at a solitary shanty in the forest a few miles farther on.

These little wayside inns, or "ranches," as they are usually called in the mines, are generally situated in a spot which offers some capabilities of cultivation, and where water, the great desideratum in the mountains, is to be had all the year. The owners employ themselves in fencing-in and clearing the land, and by degrees give the place an appearance of comfort and civilization. One finds such places in all the different stages of improvement, from a small tent or log cabin, with the wild forest around it as yet undisturbed, to good frame houses with two or three rooms, a boarded floor, and windows, and surrounded by several acres of cleared land under cultivation.

Oats and barley are the principal crops raised in the mountains. In some of the little valleys a species of wild oats, which makes excellent hay, grows very luxuriantly. In passing through one such place, where the grasshoppers were in clouds, we found a number of Indian squaws catching them with small nets attached to a short stick, in the style of an angler's landing-net. I believe they bruise them and knead them into a paste, somewhat of the consistency of potted shrimps; it may be as palatable also, but I cannot speak from experience on that point. My companions, as we traveled on, branched off one by one to their respective destinations, and I was again alone when I got to the ranch where

I intended to pass the night. It was somewhat the same style of thing as the Grizzly-Bear House, but the house was larger, and the accommodation more luxurious, inasmuch as we had canvas bunks or shelves to sleep upon.

I went on next day along with a young miner from Georgia, who was also bound for Nevada. We dined at a place where we crossed Bear River; and a villainous bad dinner it was – nothing but bad salt pork, bad pickled onions, and bad bread.

On resuming our journey, we were joined by a man who said he always liked to have company on that road. Several robberies and murders had been committed on it of late, and he very kindly pointed out to us, as we passed it, the exact spot where, a few days before, one man had been shot through the head, and another through the hat. One was robbed of seventy-five cents, the other of eight hundred dollars.

It was a very romantic place, and well calculated for the operations of the gentlemen of the road, being a little hollow darkened by the spreading branches of a grove of oak trees; the underwood was thick and very high, and as the trail twisted round trees and bushes, a traveler could not see more than a few feet before or behind him. We had our revolvers in readiness; but I was not very apprehensive, as three men, all showing pistols in their belts, are rather more than those ruffians generally care to tackle.

We arrived at Nevada City between five and six o'clock, when I took a look round to find the most likely place for a good supper, being particularly ravenous after the long walk and the salt-pork dinner. I found a house bearing the sign of "Hotel de Paris," and my choice was made at once. As I had half an hour to wait for supper, I strolled about the town to see what sort of a place it was. It is beautifully situated on the hills bordering a small creek, and had once been surrounded by a forest of magnificent pine trees, which, however, had been made to become useful instead of ornamental, and nothing now remained to show that they had existed but the numbers of stumps all over the hillsides. The bed of the creek, which had once flowed past the town, was now choked up with heaps of "tailings" – the washed dirt from which the gold has been extracted – the white color of the dirt rendering it still more unsightly. All the water of the creek was distributed among a number of small troughs, carried along the steep banks on either side at different elevations, for the purpose of supplying various quartz-mills and long toms.

The town itself – or, I should say, the "City," for from the moment of its birth it has been called Nevada City – is, like all mining towns, a mixture of staring white frame houses, dingy old canvas booths, and log cabins.

The only peculiarity about the miners was the white mud with which they were bespattered, especially those working in underground diggings, who were easily distinguished by the quantity of dry white mud on the tops of their hats.

The supper at the Hotel de Paris was the best-got-up thing of the kind I had sat down to for some months. We began with soup – rather flimsy stuff, but pretty good – then *bouilli,* followed by *filet-de-bœuf,* with cabbage, carrots, turnips, and onions ; after that came what the landlord called a "god-dam rosbif," with green peas, and the whole wound up with a salad of raw cabbage, a cup of good coffee, and cognac. I did impartial justice to every department, and rose from the table powerfully refreshed.

The company were nearly all French miners, among whom was a young Frenchman whom I had known in San Francisco, and whom I hardly recognized in his miner's costume.

We passed the evening together in some of the gambling-rooms, where we heard pretty good music; and as there were no sleeping quarters to be had at the house where I dined, I went to an American hotel close to it. It was in the usual style of a boarding-house in the mines, but it was a three-decker. All round the large sleeping apartment were three tiers of canvas shelves, partitioned into spaces six feet long, on one of which I laid myself out, choosing the top tier in case of accidents.

Next door was a large thin wooden building, in which a theatrical company were performing. They were playing Richard, and I could hear every word as distinctly as if I had been in the stage-box. I could even fancy I saw King Dick rolling his eyes about like a man in a fit, when he shouted for "A horse! a horse!" The fight between Richard and Richmond was a very tame affair ; they hit hard while they were at it, but it was too soon over. It was one-two, one-two, a thrust, and down went Dick. I heard him fall, and could hear him afterwards gasping for breath and scuffling about on the stage in his dying agonies.

After King Richard was disposed of, the orchestra, which seemed to consist of two fiddles, favored us with a very miscellaneous piece of music.

There was then an interlude performed by the audience, hooting, yelling, whistling, and stamping their feet; and that being over, the curtain rose, and we had Bombastes Furioso. It was very creditably performed, but, under the peculiar circumstances of the case, it did not sound to me nearly so absurd as the tragedy.

Some half-dozen men, the only occupants of the room besides myself, had been snoring comfortably all through the performances, and now about a dozen more came in and rolled themselves on to their respective shelves. They had been at the theater, but I am sure they had not enjoyed it so much as I did.

Note

* The grizzlies of early California were larger than those of the Rocky Mountains, but estimates of their weight were commonly exaggerated. The largest bear of any species of which there is record was one killed by J. C. Tolman, in October, 1889, at the head of English Bay, on Kadiak Island, Alaska. The skin, when moderately stretched on the ground, was 13 ft. 6 in. long by 11 ft. 6 in. wide; length of head, 20 in.; breadth, 12 in.; length of hind foot, 20 in. ; breadth, 12 in. ; weight of carcass with entrails and blood removed, 1,656 lbs.; estimated live weight, a little over a ton. – ED.

CHAPTER XI

ON THE TRAIL

IN this part of the country the pine trees are of an immense size, and of every variety. The most graceful is what is called the "sugar pine." It is perfectly straight and cylindrical, with a comparatively smooth bark, and, till about four-fifths of its height from the ground, without a branch or even a twig. The branches then spread straight out from the stem, drooping a good deal at the extremities from the weight of the immense cones which they bear. These are about a foot and a half long, and under each leaf is a seed the size of a cherrystone, which has a taste even sweeter than that of a filbert. The Indians are very fond of them, and make the squaws gather them for winter food.

A peculiarity of the pine trees in California is that the bark, from within eight or ten feet of the ground up to where the branches commence, is completely riddled with holes, such as might be made with musket-balls. They are, however, the work of the woodpeckers, who, like the Indians, are largely interested in the acorn crop. They are constantly making these holes, in each of which they stow away an acorn, leaving it as tightly wedged in as though it were driven in with a sledge-hammer.

There were several quartz veins in the neighborhood of Nevada, some of which were very rich, and yielded a large amount of gold; but, generally speaking, they were so unscientifically and unprofitably worked that they turned out complete failures.

Quartz mining is a scientific operation, of which many of those who undertook to work the veins had no knowledge whatever, nor had they sufficient capital to carry on such a business. The cost of erecting crushing-mills, and of getting the necessary iron castings from San Francisco, was very great. A vast deal of labor had to be gone through in opening the mine before any returns could be received ; and, moreover, the method then adopted of crushing the quartz and extracting the gold was so defective that not more than one half of it was saved.

There is a variety of diggings here, but the richest are deep diggings in the hills above the town, and are worked by means of shafts, or coyote holes, as they are called. In order to reach the gold-bearing dirt, these shafts have to be sunk to the depth of nearly a hundred feet, which requires the labor of at least two men for a month or six weeks; and when they have got down to the bottom, perhaps they may find nothing to repay them for their perseverance.

The miners always calculate their own labor at five dollars a day for every day they work, that being the usual wages for hired labor; and if a man, after working for a month in sinking a hole, finds no paydirt at the bottom of it, he sets himself down as a loser of a hundred and fifty dollars.

They make up heavy bills of losses against themselves in this way, but still there are plenty of men who prefer devoting themselves to this speculative style of digging, in hopes of eventually striking a rich lead, to working steadily at surface diggings, which would yield them, day by day, sure though moderate pay.

But mining of any description is more or less uncertain, and any man "hiring out," as it is termed, steadily throughout the year, and pocketing his five dollars a day, would find at the end of the year that he had done as well, perhaps, as the average of miners working on their own hook, who spend a considerable portion of their time in prospecting, and frequently, in order to work a claim which may afford them a month's actual washing, have to spend as long a time in stripping off top-dirt, digging ditches, or performing other necessary labor to get their claim into working order; so that the daily amount of gold which a man may happen to be taking out, is not to be taken in itself as the measure of his prosperity. He may take a large sum out of a claim, but may also have spent as much upon it before he began to wash, and half the days of the year he may get no gold at all.

There were plenty of men who, after two years' hard work, were not a bit better off than when they commenced, having lost in working one claim what they had made in another, and having frittered away their time in prospecting and wandering about the country from one place to another, always imagining that there were better diggings to be found than those they were in at the time.

Under any circumstances, when a man can make as much, or perhaps more, by working for himself, he has greater pleasure in doing so than in working for others; and among men engaged in such an exciting pursuit as gold-hunting, constantly stimulated by the success of some one of their neighbors, it was only natural that they should be loath to relinquish their chance of a prize in the lottery, by hiring themselves out for an amount of daily wages which was no more than any one, if he worked steadily, could make for himself.

Those who did hire out were of two classes – coldblooded philosophers, who calculated the chances, and stuck to their theory unmoved by the temptations around them; and men who had not sufficient inventive energy to direct their own labor and render it profitable.

The average amount of gold taken out daily at that time by men who really did work, was, I should think, not less than eight dollars; but the average daily yield of the mines to the actual population was probably not more than three or four dollars per head, owing to the great number of "loafers," who did not work more than perhaps one day in the week, and spent the rest of their time in bar-rooms, playing cards and drinking whisky. They led a listless life of mild dissipation, for they never had money enough to get very drunk. They were always in debt for their board and their whisky at the boarding-house where they lived; and when hard pressed to pay up, they would hire out for a day or two to make enough for their immediate wants, and then return to loaf away their existence in a bar-room, as long as the boarding-house keeper thought it advisable to give them credit. I never, in any part of the mines, was in a store or boarding-house that was not haunted by some men of this sort.

Other men, with more energy in their dissipation, and old sailors especially, would have periodical bursts, more intense but of shorter duration. After mining steadily for a month or two, and saving their money, they would set to work to get rid of it as fast as possible. An old sailor went about it most systematically. For the reason, as I supposed, that when going to have a "spree," he imagined himself to have come ashore off a voyage, he generally commenced by going to a Jew's slop-shop, where he rigged himself out in a new suit of clothes; he would then go the round of all the bar-rooms in the place, and insist on every one he found there drinking with him, informing them at the same time (though it was quite unnecessary, for the fact was very evident) that he was "on the spree." Of course, he soon made himself drunk, but before being very far gone he would lose the greater part of his money to the gamblers. Cursing his bad luck, he would then console himself with a rapid succession of "drinks," pick a quarrel with some one who was not interfering with him, get a licking, and be ultimately rolled into a comer to enjoy the more passive phase of his debauch. On waking in the morning he would not give himself time to get sober, but would go at it again, and keep at it for a week – most affectionately and confidentially drunk in the forenoon, fighting drunk in the afternoon, and dead-drunk at night. The next week he would get gradually sober, and, recovering his senses, would return to his work without a cent in his pocket, but quite contented and happy, with his mind relieved at having had what he considered a good spree. Four or five hundred dollars was by no means an unusual sum for such a man to spend on an occasion of this sort, even without losing much at the gaming-table. The greater part of it went to the bar-keepers for "drinks," for the height of his enjoyment was every few minutes to ask half-a-dozen men to drink with him.

The amount of money thus spent at the bars in the mines must have been enormous; the system of "drinks" was carried still further than in San Francisco; and there were numbers of men of this description who were fortunate in their diggings, and became possessed of an amount of gold of which they could not realize the value. They only knew the difference between having money and having none; a hundred dollars was to them as good as a thousand, and a thousand was in their ideas about the same as a hundred. It did not matter how much they had saved; when the time came for them to reward themselves with a spree after a month or so of hard work, they made a clean sweep of everything, and spent their last dollar as readily as the first.

I did not remain in Nevada, being anxious to get down to the Yuba before the rainy season should set in and put a stop to mining operations on the river.

Foster's Bar, about thirty miles off, was the nearest point on the Yuba, and for this place I started. I was joined on leaving the town by a German, carrying his gun and powder-horn: he was a hunter by profession, as he informed me, having followed that business for more than a year, finding ready sale for his game in Nevada.

The principal kinds of game in the mountains are deer, quail, hares, rabbits, and squirrels. The quails, which are very abundant, are beautiful birds, about the size of a pigeon, with a top-knot on their head; they are always in coveys, and rise with a whirr like partridges.

My hunting companion was at present going after deer, and, intending to stop out till he killed one, he carried his blanket and a couple of days' provisions.

I arrived about noon at a very pretty place called Hunt's Ranch. It was a large log house, with several well-cultivated fields around it, in which a number of men were at work. At dinner here there was the most extensive set-out of vegetables I ever saw in the country, consisting of green peas, French beans, cauliflower, tomatoes, onions, cucumbers, pumpkins, squash, and watermelons. It was a long time since I had seen such a display, and not knowing when I might have another opportunity, I pitched into them right and left.

I was lighting my pipe in the bar-room after dinner, when a man walked in whom I recognized at once as one of my fellow passengers from New York to Chagres. I was very glad to see him, as he was one of the most favorable specimens of that crowd; and according to the custom of the country, we immediately ratified our renewed acquaintance in a brandy cocktail. He was returning to his diggings about ten miles off, and our roads being the same, we set out together.

He gave me an account of his doings since he had been in the mines, from which he did not seem to have had much luck on his side, for most of the money he had made he had lost in buying claims which turned out valueless. He had owned a share in a company which was working a claim on the Yuba, but had sold it for a mere trifle before it was ascertained whether the claim was rich or not, and it was now yielding 150 dollars a day to the man.

We crossed the Middle Yuba, a small stream, at Emery's Bridge, where my friend left me, and I went on alone, having six or seven miles to go to reach my resting-place for the night.

I was now in a region of country so mountainous as to be perfectly impassable for wheeled vehicles. All supplies were brought to the various trading posts from Marysville on trains of pack-mules.

"Packing," as it is called, is a large business. A packer has in his train from thirty to fifty mules, and four or five Mexicans to tend them – mule-driving, or "packing," being one of the few occupations to which Mexicans devote themselves; and at this they certainly do excel. Though generally a lazy, indolent people, it is astonishing what activity and energy they display in an employment which suits their fancy. They drive the mules about twenty-five miles a day; and in camping for the night, they have to select a place where there is water, and where there is also some sort of picking for the mules, which, in the dry season, when every blade of vegetation is burned up, is rather hard to find.

I came across a train of about forty mules, under charge of four or five Mexicans, just as they were about to unpack, and make their camp. The spot they chose was a little grassy hollow in the middle of the woods, near which flowed a small stream of beautifully clear water. It was evidently a favorite camping ground, from the numbers of signs of old fires. The mules seemed to know it too, for they all stopped and commenced picking the grass. The Mexicans, who were riding tough little Californian horses, immediately dismounted and began to unpack, working with such vigor that one might have thought they were doing it for a wager.

Two men unpack a mule together. They first throw over his head a broad leathern belt, which hangs over his eyes to blind him and keep him quiet; then, one man standing on each side, they cast off the numerous hide ropes with which the cargo is secured ; and when all is cast loose, each man removes his half of the cargo and places it on the ground. Another mule is then led up to the same spot, and unpacked in like mariner; the cargo being all ranged along the ground in a row, and presenting a very miscellaneous assortment of sacks of flour, barrels of pork or brandy, bags of sugar, boxes of tobacco, and all sorts of groceries and other articles. When all the cargoes have been unpacked, they then take off the *aparejos,* or large Mexican pack-saddles, examining the back of each mule to see if it is galled. The pack-saddles are all set down in a row parallel with the cargo, the girth and saddle-cloth of each being neatly folded and laid on the top of it. The place where the mules have been unpacked, between the saddles and the cargo, is covered with quantities of rawhide ropes and other lashings, which are all coiled up and stowed away in a heap by themselves.

Every mule, as his saddle is taken off, refreshes himself by rolling about in the dust; and when all are unsaddled, the bell-horse is led away to water. The mules all follow him, and are left to their own devices till morning.

The bell-horse of a train of mules is a very curious institution. He is generally an old white horse, with a small bell hung round his neck. He carries no cargo, but leads the van in tow of a Mexican. The mules will follow him through thick and thin, but without him they will not move a step.

In the morning the mules are hunted up and driven into camp, when they are tied together in a row behind their pack-saddles, and brought round one by one to be saddled and packed. To pack a mule well, considerable art is necessary. His load must be so divided that there is an equal weight on each side, else the mule works at great disadvantage. If his load is not nicely balanced and tightly secured, he cannot so well pick his way along the steep mountain trails, and, as not unfrequently happens, topples over and rolls down to some place from which no mule returns.

CHAPTER XII

SITTERS FOR PORTRAITS

I ARRIVED about dusk at a ranch called the "Grass Valley House," situated in a forest of pines. It was a clapboard house, built round an old log cabin which formed one corner of the building, and was now the private apartment of the landlord and his wife. I was here only six miles from Foster's Bar, and set out for that place in the morning; but I made a mistake somewhere, and followed a wrong trail, which led me to a river, after walking six or seven miles without meeting any one of whom I could ascertain whether I was going right or not. The descent to the river was very steep, and as I went down I had misgivings that I was all wrong, and should have to come up again, but I expected at least to find some one there who could put me right. After scrambling down the best way I could, and reaching the river, I was disappointed to find nothing but the remains of an old tent; there was not even a sign of any work having been done there. The river flowed among huge masses of rock, from which the banks rose so steep and rugged that to follow the course of the stream seemed out of the question. I thought, however, that I could distinguish marks here and there on the rocks, as if caused by traveling over them, and these I followed with considerable difficulty for about half a mile, when they stopped at a place where the blackened rocks, the remains of burned wood, and a lot of old sardine-boxes, showed that some one had been camped. Here I fancied I could make out a trail going straight up the face of the hill, on the same side of the river by which I had come down. It looked a hard road to travel, but I preferred trying it to retracing my steps, especially as I judged it would be a shorter way back to the house I had started from.

I got on very well for a short distance, but very soon lost all sign of a trail. I was determined, however, to make my way up, which I did by dint of catching hold of branches of trees and bushes; and on my hands I had to place my greatest dependence, for the loose soil was covered with large stones, which gave way under my feet, and which I could hear rolling down far below me. Sometimes I came to a bare face of rock, up which I had to work my passage by means of the crevices and projecting ledges. It was useless to consider whether more formidable obstacles were still before me; my only chance was to go ahead, for if I had attempted to go down again, I should have found the descent rather too easy, and probably have broken my neck. It was dreadfully hot, and I was carrying my blankets slung over my shoulder, which, catching on trees and rocks, impeded my progress considerably; and though I was in pretty good condition for this sort of work, I had several times to get astride of a tree and take a spell.

At last, after a great deal of scrambling and climbing, my shins barked, my clothes nearly tom off my back, and my eyes half scratched out by the bushes, completely blown, and suffocated with the heat, I arrived at a place where I considered that I had got over the worst of it, as the ascent seemed to become a little more practicable. I was dying of thirst, and would have given a very long price for a drink of water; but the nearest water I expected to find was at a spring about five miles off, which I had passed in the morning. I could not help thinking what a delightful thing a quart pot of Bass's pale ale would be, with a lump of ice in it; then I thought I would prefer a sherry cobbler, but I could not drink that fast enough; and then it seemed that a quart pot of ale would not be enough, that I would like to drink it out of a bucket. I quaffed in imagination gigantic goblets, one after another, of all sorts of delicious fluids, but none of them did me any good; and so I concluded that I had better think of something else till I reached the spring.

The rest of the mountain was not very hard traveling, and when once on the top of the range, I struck off in a direction which I thought would hit my old trail. I very soon got on to it, and after half an hour's walking, I found the spring, where, as the Missourians say, "you may just bet *your* life," I did drink.

It was about three o'clock, and I thought my safest plan was to return to the house I had started from in the morning, about six miles off, where, on my arrival, I learned that I had been misled by an Indian trail, and had traveled far out of the right direction. It was too late to make a fresh start that day, so I was doomed to pass another night here, and in the evening amused myself by sketching a train of pack-mules which had camped near the house.

I was just setting off in the morning, when two or three men, who had seen me sketching the evening before, came and asked me to take their likenesses for them. As they were very anxious about it, I made them sit down, and very soon polished them all off, improving so much on their personal appearance, that they evidently had no idea before that they were such good-looking fellows, and expressed themselves highly satisfied. As I was finishing the last one, an old fellow came in, who, seeing what was up, was seized with a violent desire to have his sweet countenance "pictur'd off" likewise, to send to his wife. It struck me that his wife must be a woman of singular taste if she ever wished to see his face again. He was just about the ugliest man I ever saw in my life. He wanted to comb his hair, poor fellow, and make himself look as presentable as possible; but I had no mercy on him, and, making him sit down as he was, I did my best to represent him about fifty per cent. uglier than he really was. He was in great distress that he had not better clothes on for the occasion; so, to make up for caricaturing his features, I improved his costume, and gave him a very spicy black coat, black satin waistcoat, and very stiff stand-up collars. The fidelity of the likeness he never doubted, being so lost in admiration of his dress, that he seemed to think the face a matter of minor importance altogether.

I did not take many portraits in the mines; but from what little experience I had, I invariably found that men of a lower class wanted to be shown in the ordinary costume of the nineteenth century – that is to say, in a coat, waistcoat, white shirt and neckcloth; while gentlemen miners were anxious to appear in character, in the most ragged style of California dress.

I went to Foster's Bar after dinner with a man who was on his way there from Downieville, a town about thirty miles up the river. He told me that he and his partner had gone there a few months before, and had worked together for some time, when they separated, his partner joining a company which had averaged a hundred dollars a day to each man ever since, while my friend had bought a share in another company, and, after working hard for six weeks, had not, as he expressed it, made enough to pay for his grub. Such is mining.

Foster's Bar is a place about half a mile long, with the appearance of having slipped down off the face of the mountains, and thus formed a flat along the side of the river. The village or camp consisted of a few huts and cabins ; and all around on the rocks, wherever it suited their convenience, were parties of miners camping out.

I could only see one place which purported to be a hotel, and to it I went. It was a large canvas house, the front part of which was the bar-room, and behind it the dining-room. Alongside of the former an addition had been made as a sleeping apartment, and here, when I felt inclined to turn in about ten o'clock, I was accommodated with a cot.

A gambling-room in San Francisco is a tolerably quiet place, where little else is heard but good music or the chinking of dollars, and where, if it were necessary, one could sleep comfortably enough. But a gambling-room in a small camp in the mines is a very different affair. There not so much ceremony is observed, and the company are rather more apt to devote themselves to the social enjoyment of drinking, quarrelling, and kicking up a row generally. In this instance the uproar beat all my previous experience, and sleeping was out of the question. The bar-room, I found, was also the gambling-room of the diggings. Four or five monte tables were in full blast, and the room was crowded with all the rowdies of the place. As the night wore on and the brandy began to tell, they seemed to be having a general fight, and I half expected to see some of them pitched through the canvas into the sleeping apartment; or perhaps pistols might be used, in which case I should have had as good a chance of being shot as any one else.

I managed to drop off asleep during a lull in the storm; but when I awoke at daylight, it was only then finally subsiding. I found that some man had broken a monte bank, and, on the strength of his good fortune, had been treating the company to an unlimited supply of brandy all night, which fully accounted for the row ; but I did not fancy such sleeping quarters, and made up my mind to camp out while I remained in those diggings.

I selected a very pretty spot at the foot of a ravine, in which was a stream of water; and, buying a tin coffee-pot and some tea and sugar, I was completely set up. There was a baker and butcher in the camp, so I had very little trouble in my cooking arrangements, having merely to boil my pot, and then raking down the fire with my foot, lay a steak on the embers.

The weather was very hot and dry; but it was getting late in the season, and I generally awoke in the morning like the flowers the Irishman sings about to Molly Bawn, "with their rosy faces wet with dew." At least as far as the dew is concerned – for a rosy face is a thing not seen in the mines, the usual color of men's faces being a good standard leathery hue, a very little lighter than that of a penny-piece – all rosiness of cheek, where it ever existed, is driven out by the hot sun and dry atmosphere.

I found camping out a very pleasant way of living. With my blankets I made a first-rate awning during the day; and if I could not boast of a bed of roses, I at least had one of dahlias, for numbers of large flowers of that species grew in great profusion all round my camp, and these I was so luxurious as to pluck and strew thickly on the spot where I intended to sleep.

I remained here for about three weeks; and for two or three mornings before I left, I woke finding my blankets quite white with frost. On such occasions I was more active than usual in lighting my fire and getting my coffee-pot under a full head of steam ; but as soon as ever the sun was up, the frost was immediately dispelled, and half an hour after sunrise one was glad to get into the shade.

On leaving Foster's Bar, I went to a place a few miles up the river, where some miners were at work, who had asked me to visit their camp. The river here flowed through a narrow rocky gorge (a sort of place which, in California, is called by its Spanish name a "canon"), and was flumed for a distance of nearly half a mile; that is to say, it was carried past in an aqueduct supported on uprights, being raised from its natural bed, which was thus laid bare and rendered capable of being worked. It was late when I arrived, and the party of miners had just stopped work for the day. Some were taking off their wet boots, and washing their faces in the river; others were lighting their pipes or cutting up tobacco; and the rest were collected round the fire, making bets as to the quantity of gold which was being dried in an old frying-pan. This was the result of their day's work, and weighed four or five pounds. The banks of the river were so rough and precipitous that, for want of any level space on which to camp, they had been obliged to raise a platform of stone and gravel. On this stood a tent about twenty feet long, which was strewed inside with blankets, boots, hats, old newspapers, and such articles. In front of the tent was a long rough table, on each side of which a young pine tree, with two or three legs stuck into it here and there, did duty as a bench, some of the bark having been chipped off the top side, by way of making it an easy seat. At the foot of the rocks, close to the table, an immense fire was blazing, presided over by a darky, who was busy preparing supper; for where so many men messed together, it was economy to have a professional cook, though his wages were frequently higher than those paid to a miner. A quarter of beef hung from the limb of a tree ; and stowed away, in beautiful confusion, among the nooks and crannies of the rocks, were sacks, casks, and boxes containing various articles of provisions.

Within a few feet of us, and above the level of the camp, the river rushed past in its wooden bed, spinning round, as it went, a large water-wheel, by means of which a constant stream of water was pumped up from the diggings and carried off in the flume. The company consisted of eight members. They were all New Yorkers, and had been brought up to professional and mercantile pursuits. The rest of the party were their hired men, who, however, were upon a perfect social equality with their employers.

When it was time to turn in, I was shown a space on the gravelly floor of the tent, about six feet by one and a half, where I might stretch out and dream that I dwelt in marble halls. About a dozen men slept in the tent, the others lying outside on the rocks.

My intention was from this camp to go on to Downieville, about forty miles up the river; but I had first to return to Foster's Bar for some drawing-paper which I had ordered from Sacramento.

On my way I passed a most romantic little bridge, formed by two pine trees, which had been felled so as to span a deep and thickly wooded ravine. I sat down among the bushes a short distance off the trail, and was making a sketch of the place, when presently a man came along riding on a mule. I was quite aware that I should have a very suspicious appearance to a passer-by, and I was in hopes he might not observe me. I had no object in speaking to him, especially as, had I hailed him from my ambuscade, he might have been apt to reply with his revolver.

Just as he was passing, however, and when all I could see of him was his head and shoulders, his eyes wandered over the bank at the side of the trail, and he caught sight of my head looking down on him over the tops of the bushes. He gave a start, as I expected he would, and addressed me with "Good morning, Colonel." My promotion to the rank of colonel I most probably owed to the fact that he thought it advisable, under the circumstances, to be as conciliatory as possible until he knew my intentions. I saw a good deal of the same man afterwards, but he never again raised me above the rank of captain. I replied to his salutation, and he then asked the very natural question, "What are ye a-doin' of over there?" I gave an account of myself, which he did not seem to think altogether satisfactory, but, after making some remark on the weather, he passed on.

About an hour later, when I arrived at Foster's Bar, I found him sitting in a store with some half-dozen miners, to whom he had been recounting how he had seen a man concealed in the bushes off the trail. He expressed himself as having been "awful skeered," and said that he had his pistol out, and was thinking of shooting all the time he was speaking to me. I told him I had mine lying by my side, and would have returned the compliment, when, by way of showing me what sort of a chance I should have stood, he stuck up a card on a tree at about twenty paces, and put six balls into it one after another out of his heavy navy revolver. I confessed I could not beat such shooting as that, and was very well pleased that he had not taken it into his head to make a target of me.

It seemed that he was an express carrier, and as his partner had been robbed but a few days before, very near the place of our meeting, his suspicions of me were not at all unreasonable.

I was very desirous of seeing a friend of mine who was mining at a place about twenty miles off, so, having hired a mule for the journey, I set off early next morning, intending to return the same night. My way was through a part of the country very little traveled, and the trails were consequently very indistinct, but I got full directions how to find my way, where to leave the main trail, which side to take at a place where the trail forked, where I should cross another, and so on; also where I should pass an old cabin, a forked pine tree, and other objects, by which I might know that I was on the right road.

The man who gave me my directions said he hardly expected that I would be able to keep the right trail. I had some doubts about it myself, but I was determined to try at all events, and for seven or eight miles I got along very well, knowing I was right by the landmarks which I had passed.

The numbers of Indian trails, however, branching off to right and left were very confusing, being not a bit less indistinct than the trail I was endeavoring to follow. At last I felt certain that I had gone wrong, but as I fancied I was not going far out of the right direction, I kept on, and shortly afterwards came upon a small camp called Toole's Diggings. I was told here that I had only come five miles out of my way; and after dining and getting some fresh directions, I set out again. Having ridden for nearly an hour, I came to an Indian camp, situated by the side of a small stream in a very dense part of the forest. At first I could see no one but some children amusing themselves with a swing hung from a branch of an oak tree, but as I was going past, a number of Indians came running out from their brush huts. They were friendly Indians, and had picked up a few words of English from loafing about the camps of the miners. The usual style of salutation to them is, "How d'ye do?" to which they reply in the same words; but if you repeat the question, as if you really wanted to know the state of their health, they invariably answer "fuss-rate." Accordingly, having ascertained that they were all "fuss-rate," I mixed up a little broken English, some mongrel Spanish, and a word or two of Indian, and made inquiries as to my way. In much the same sort of language they directed me how to go; and though they seemed disposed to prolong the conversation, I very quickly bade them adieu and moved on, not being at all partial to such company.

I followed the dim trail up hill and down dale for several hours without seeing a human being, and I felt quite satisfied that I was again off my road, but I pushed on in hopes of reaching some sort of habitation before dark. At last, in traveling up the side of a small creek, just as the sun was taking leave of us, I caught sight of a log cabin among the pine trees. It seemed to have been quite recently built, so I was pretty sure it was inhabited, and on riding up I found two men in it, from whom I learned that I was still five miles from my destination. They recommended me to stop the night with them, as it was nearly dark, and the trail was hard enough to find by daylight.

I saw no help for it ; so, after staking out the mule where he could pick some green stuff, I joined my hosts, who were just sitting down to supper. It was not a very elaborate affair – nothing but tea and ham. They apologized for the meagerness of the turn-out, and especially for the want of bread, saying that they had been away for a couple of days, and on their return found that the Indians had taken the opportunity to steal all their flour.

We made the most of what we had, however, and putting a huge log on the fire, we lighted our pipes, and my entertainers, producing two violins, favored me with a selection of nigger melodies.

They had been mining lately at the place which I had been trying to reach all day, and in the course of conversation I found that I had had all my trouble for nothing, as the man whom I was in search of had a few days before left the diggings for San Francisco.

The next morning I returned to Foster's Bar, my friends putting me on a much shorter trail than the roundabout road I had traveled the day before.

CHAPTER XIII

ON THE WAY TO DOWNIEVILLE

FROM Foster's Bar I set out for Downieville. On leaving the river, I had as usual a long hill to climb, but once on the top, the trail followed the backbone of the ridge, and was comparatively easy to travel. It was the main "pack-trail" to Downieville, and, being traveled by all the trains of pack-mules, was nearly ankle-deep in dust. The soil of the California mountains is generally very red and sterile, and has the property of being easily converted into exceedingly fine dust, as red as brick-dust, or into equally fine mud, according to the season of the year. At the end of a day's journey in summer, the color of a man's face is hardly discernible through the thick coating of dust, which makes him look more like a red Indian than a white man.

The scenery was very beautiful. The pine trees were not too numerous to interrupt the view, and the ridge was occasionally so narrow that, on either hand, looking over the tops of the trees down below, there was a vast panorama of pine-clad mountains, on one side gradually diminishing, till, at a distance of forty or fifty miles, they merged imperceptibly into the plains, which, with the hazy heated atmosphere upon them, looked like a calm ocean; while, on the other side, one mountain ridge appeared above another, more barren as they became more lofty, till at last they faded away into a few hardly discernible snowy peaks. It was a pleasing change when sometimes a break occurred in the ridge, and the trail dipped into a dark shady hollow, and, winding its way through the dense mass of underwood, crossed a little stream of water, and, leading up the opposite bank, gained once more the open ground on the summit. I traveled about fifteen miles without meeting any one, and arrived at Slate Range House, a solitary cabin, so called from being situated at the spot where one begins to descend to Slate Range, a place where the banks of the river are composed of huge masses of slate. I dined here, and shortly afterwards overtook a little Englishman, whose English accent sounded very refreshing. He had been in the country since before the existence of gold was discovered ; but from his own account he did not seem to have profited much in his gold-hunting exploits from having had such a good start.

I stopped all night at Oak Valley, a small camp, consisting of three cabins and a hotel, and in the morning I resumed my journey in company with two miners, who had a pack-horse loaded with their mining tools, their pots and pans, their blankets, and all the rest of it. The horse, however, did not seem to approve of the arrangement, for, after having gone about a couple of miles, he wheeled round, and set off back again through the woods as hard as he could split, the pots and pans banging against his ribs, and making a fearful clatter. My companions started in chase of their goods and chattels ; but thinking the pair of them quite a match for the old horse, and not caring how the race turned out, I left them to settle it among themselves, and went on my way.

I met several trains of pack-mules, the jingling of the bell on the bell-horse, and the shouts of the Mexican muleteers, generally announcing their approach before they came in sight. They were returning to Marysville; and as they have no cargo to bring down from the mines, the mules were jogging along very cheerily; when loaded, they relieve their feelings by grunting and groaning at every step.

The next place I came to was a ranch called the "Nigger Tent." It was originally a small tent, kept by an enterprising nigger for the accommodation of travelers; but as his fortunes prospered, he had built a very comfortable cabin, which, however, retained the name of the old establishment.

In the afternoon I arrived at the place where the trail leaves the summit of the range, and commences to wind down the steep face of the mountain to Downieville. There was a ranch and a spring of deliciously cold water, which was very acceptable, as the last ten miles of my journey had been uphill nearly all the way, and the heat was intense, but not a drop of water was to be found on the road.

I overtook two or three miners on their way to Downieville, and went on in company with them. As we descended, we got an occasional view between the pine trees of the little town far down below us, so completely surrounded by mountains that it seemed to be at the bottom of an immense hole in the ground.

I had heard so much of Downieville, that on reaching the foot of the mountain I was rather disappointed at first to find it apparently so small a place, but I very soon discovered that there was a great deal compressed into a small compass. There was only one street in the town, which was three or four hundred yards long; indeed, the mountain at whose base it stood was so steep that there was not room for more than one street between it and the river.

This was the depot, however, for the supplies of a very large mining population. All the miners within eight or ten miles depended on Downieville for their provisions, and the street was consequently always a scene of bustle and activity, being crowded with trains of pack-mules and their Mexican drivers.

The houses were nearly all of wood, many of them well-finished two-story houses, with columns and verandas in front. The most prominent places in the town were of course the gambling saloons, fitted up in the usual style of showy extravagance, with the exception of the mirrors; for as everything had to be brought seventy or eighty miles over the mountains on the backs of mules, very large mirrors were a luxury hardly attainable; an extra number of smaller ones, however, made up for the deficiency. There were several very good hotels, and two or three French restaurants; the other houses in the town were nearly all stores, the mining population living in tents and cabins, all up and down the river.

I put up at a French house, which was kept in very good style by a pretty little Frenchwoman, and had quite the air of being a civilized place. I was accommodated with half of a bedroom, in which there was hardly room to turn round between the two beds; but I was so accustomed to rolling myself in my blankets and sleeping on the ground, or on the rocks, or at best being stowed away on a shelf with twenty or thirty other men in a large room, that it seemed to me most luxurious quarters. The *salle à manger* was underneath me, and as the floor was very thin, I had the full benefit of all the conversation of those who indulged in late suppers, whilst next-door was a ten-pin alley, in which they were banging away at the pins all night long; but such trifles did not much disturb my slumbers.

There was no lack of public amusements in the town. The same company which I had heard in Nevada were performing in a very comfortable little theater – not a very highly decorated house, but laid out in the orthodox fashion, with boxes, pit, and gallery – and a company of American glee-singers, who had been concertizing with great success in the various mining towns, were giving concerts in a large room devoted to such purposes. Their selection of songs was of a decidedly national character, and a lady, one of their party, had won the hearts of all the miners by singing very sweetly a number of old familiar ballads, which touched the feelings of the expatriated gold-hunters.

I was present at their concert one night, when, at the close of the performance, a rough old miner stood up on his seat in the middle of the room, and after a few preliminary coughs, delivered himself of a very elaborate speech, in which, on behalf of the miners of Downieville, he begged to express to the lady their great admiration of her vocal talents, and in token thereof begged her acceptance of a purse containing 500 dollars' worth of gold specimens. Compliments of this sort, which the Scotch would call "wiselike," and which the fair cantatrice no doubt valued as highly as showers of the most exquisite bouquets, had been paid to her in most of the towns she had visited in the mines. Some enthusiastic miners had even thrown specimens to her on the stage.

Downieville is situated at what is called the Forks of the Yuba River, and the town itself was frequently spoken of as "The Forks" in that part of the country. It may be necessary to explain that, in talking of the forks of a river in California, one is always supposed to be going up the river; the forks are its tributaries. The main rivers received their names, which they still retain, from the Spaniards and Indians; and the first gold-hunting pioneers, in exploring a fiver, when they came to a tributary, called one branch the north, and the other the south fork. When one of these again received a tributary, it either continued to be the north or south fork, or became the middle fork, as the case might be.

If a river was never to have more than two tributaries, this would do very well, hut the river above Downieville kept on forking about every half-a-mile, and the branches were all named on the same principle, so that there were half-a-dozen north, middle, and south forks.

The diggings at Downieville were very extensive; for many miles above it on each fork there were numbers of miners working in the bed and the banks of the river. The mountains are very precipitous, and the only communication was by a narrow trail which had been trodden into the hillside, and crossed from one side of the river to the other, as either happened to be more practicable; sometimes following the rocky bed of the river itself, and occasionally rising over high steep bluffs, where it required a steady head and a sure foot to get along in safety.

One spot in particular was enough to try the nerve of any one but a chamois hunter. It was a high bluff, almost perpendicular, round which the river made a sweep, and the only possible way of passing it was by a trail about eighty feet above the river. The trail hardly deserved the name – it was merely a succession of footsteps, sometimes a few inches of a projecting rock, or a root. Two men could pass each other with difficulty, and only at certain places, by holding on to each other; and from the trail to the river all was clear and smooth, not a tree or a bush to save one if he happened to miss his footing. At one spot there was an indentation in the precipice, where the rock was quite perpendicular: to get over this difficulty, a young pine tree was laid across by way of a bridge; it was only four or five inches in diameter, and lay nearly a couple of feet outside of the rock. In passing, one only rested one foot on the tree, and with the other took advantage of the inequalities in the face of the rock ; while looking down to see where to put one's feet, one saw far below, between his outstretched legs, the most uninviting jagged rocks, strongly suggestive of sudden death.

The miners had given this place the name of Cape Horn. Those who were camped on the river above it, were so used to it that they passed along with a hop, step, and a jump, though carrying a week's provisions on their backs, but a great many men had fallen over, and been instantly killed on the rocks below.

The last victim, at the time I was there, was a Frenchman, who very fool-ishly set out to return to his camp from Downieville after dark, having to pass this place on the way. He had taken the precaution to provide himself with a candle and some matches to light him round the Cape, but he was found dead on the rocks the next morning.

CHAPTER XIV

THE REASON FOR LYNCH LAW

A FEW weeks before my arrival there, Downieville had been the scene of great excitement on one of those occasions when the people took on themselves the administration and execution of justice.

A Mexican woman one forenoon had, without provocation, stabbed a miner to the heart, killing him on the spot. The news of the murder spread rapidly up and down the river, and a vast concourse of miners immediately began to collect in the town.

The woman, an hour or two after she committed the murder, was formally tried by a jury of twelve, found guilty, and condemned to be hung that afternoon. The case was so clear that it admitted of no doubt, several men having been witnesses of the whole occurrence; and the woman was hung accordingly, on the bridge in front of the town, in presence of many thousand people.

For those whose ideas of the proper mode of administering criminal law are only acquired from an acquaintance with the statistics of crime and its punishment in such countries as England, where a single murder excites horror throughout the kingdom, and is for days a matter of public interest, where judicial corruption is unknown, where the instruments of the law are ubiquitous, and its action all but infallible, – for such persons it may be difficult to realize a state of things which should render it necessary, or even excusable, that any number of irresponsible individuals should exercise a power of life and death over their fellow men.

And no doubt many sound theories may be brought forward against the propriety of administering Lynch law; but California, in the state of society which then existed, and in view of the total inefficiency, or worse than inefficiency, of the established courts of justice, was no place for theorizing upon abstract principles. Society had to protect itself by the most practical and unsophisticated system of retributive justice, quick in its action, and whose operation, being totally divested of all mystery and unnecessary ceremony, was perfectly comprehensible to the meanest understanding – a system inconsistent with public safety in old countries – unnecessary, in fact, where the machinery of the law is perfect in all its parts – but at the same time one which men most naturally adopt in the absence of all other protection ; and any one who lived in the mines of California at that time is bound gratefully to acknowledge that the feeling of security of life and person which he there enjoyed was due in a great measure to his knowledge of the fact that this admirable institution of Lynch law was in full and active operation.

There were in California the élite of the most desperate and consummate scoundrels from every part of the world; and the unsettled state of the country, the wandering habits of the mining population, scattered, as they were, all over the mountains, and frequently carrying an amount of gold on their persons inconvenient from its very weight, together with the isolated condition of many individuals, strangers to every one around them, and who, if put out of the way, would never have been missed – all these things tended apparently to render the country one where such ruffians would have ample room to practice their villainy. But, thanks to Lynch law, murders and robberies, numerous as they were, were by no means of such frequent occurrence as might have been expected, considering the opportunities and temptations afforded to such a large proportion of the population, who were only restrained from violence by a whole-some regard for the safety of their own necks.

And after all, the fear of punishment of death is the most effectual preventive of crime. To the class of men among whom murderers are found, it is probably the only feeling which deters them, and its influence is unconsciously felt even by those whose sense of right and wrong is not yet so dead as to allow them to contemplate the possibility of their committing a murder. In old States, however, fear of the punishment of death does not act with its full force on the mind of the intending criminal, for the idea of the expiation of his crime on the scaffold has to be preceded in his imagination by all the mysterious and tedious formalities of the law, in the uncertainty of which he is apt to flatter himself that he will by some means get an acquittal; and even if convicted, the length of time which must elapse before his ultimate punishment, together with the parade and circumstance with which it is attended, divests it in a great measure of the feelings of horror which it is intended to arouse.

But when Lynch law prevails, it strikes terror to the heart of the evil-doer. He has no hazy and undefined view of his ultimate fate in the distant future, but a vivid picture is before him of the sure and speedy consequence of crime. The formalities and delays of the law, which are instituted for the protection of the people, are for the same reason abolished, and the criminal knows that, instead of being tried by the elaborate and intricate process of law, his very ignorance of which leads him to over-estimate his chance of escape, he will have to stand before a tribunal of men who will try him, not by law, but by hard, straightforward common-sense, and from whom he can hope for no other verdict than that which his own conscience awards him; while execution follows so close upon sentence, that it forms, as it were, but part of the same ceremony: for Californians were eminently practical and earnest; what they meant to do they did "right off," with all their might, and as if they really meant to do it; and Lynch law was administered with characteristic promptness and decision. Sufficient time, however, or at least what was considered to be sufficient time, was always granted to the criminal to prepare for death. Very frequently he was not hanged till the day after his trial.

An execution, of course, attracted an immense crowd, but it was conducted with as little parade as possible. Men were hung in the readiest way which suggested itself – on a bough of the nearest tree, or on a tree close to the spot where the murder was committed. In some instances the criminal was run up by a number of men, all equally sharing the hangman's duty ; on other occasions, one man was appointed to the office of executioner, and a drop was extemporized by placing the culprit on his feet on the top of an empty box or barrel, under the bough of a tree, and at the given signal the box was knocked away from under him.

Not an uncommon mode was, to mount the criminal on a horse or mule, when, after the rope was adjusted, a cut of a whip was administered to the back of the animal, and the man was left suspended.

Petty thefts, which were of very rare occurrence, were punished by so many lashes with a cowhide, and the culprit was then banished from the camp. A man who would commit a petty theft was generally such a poor miserable devil as to excite compassion more than any other feeling, and not unfrequently, after his chastisement, a small subscription was raised for him, to help him along till he reached some other diggings.

Theft or robbery of any considerable amount, however, was a capital crime; and horse-stealing, to which the Mexicans more particularly devoted themselves, was invariably a hanging matter.

Lynch law had hitherto prevailed only in the mines; but about this time it had been found necessary to introduce it also in San Francisco. The number of murders and robberies committed there had of late increased to an alarming extent; and from the laxity and corruption of those intrusted with the punishment and prevention of crime, the criminal part of the population carried on their operations with such a degree of audacity, and so much apparent confidence in the immunity which they enjoyed, that society, in the total inefficiency of the system which it had instituted for its defense and preservation, threatened to become a helpless prey to the well-organized gang of ruffians who were every day becoming more insolent in their career.

At last human nature could stand it no longer, and the people saw the necessity of acting together in selfdefence. A Committee of Vigilance was accordingly formed, composed chiefly of the most prominent and influential citizens, which had the cordial approval, and the active support, of nearly the entire population of the city.

The first action of the Committee was to take two men out of jail who had already been convicted of murder and robbery, but for the execution of whose sentence the experience of the past afforded no guarantee. These two men, when taken out of the jail, were driven in a coach and four at full gallop through the town, and in half an hour they were swinging from the beams projecting over the windows of the store which was used as the committee rooms.

The Committee, during their reign, hanged four or five men, all of whom, by their own confessions, deserved hanging half-a-dozen times over. Their confessions disclosed a most extensive and wealthy organization of villainy, in which several men of comparatively respectable position were implicated. These were the projectors and designers of elaborate schemes of wholesale robbery, which the more practical members of the profession executed under their superintendence; and in the possession of some of these men there were found exact plans of the stores of many of the wealthiest merchants, along with programs of robberies to come off.

The operations of the Committee were not confined to hanging alone; their object was to purge the city of the whole herd of malefactors which infested it. Most of them, however, were panic-struck at the first alarm of Lynch law, and fled to the mines; but many of those who were denounced in the confessions of their brethren were seized by the Committee, and shipped out of the country. Several of the most distinguished scoundrels were graduates from our penal colonies; and to put a stop, if possible, to the further immigration of such characters, the Committee boarded every ship from New South Wales as she arrived, and satisfied themselves of the respectability of each passenger before allowing him to land.

The authorities, of course, were greatly incensed at the action of the Vigilance Committee in taking from them the power they had so badly used, but they could do nothing against the unanimous voice of the people, and had to submit with the best grace they could.

The Committee, after a very short but very active reign, had so far accomplished their object of suppressing crime, and driving the scum of the population out of the city, that they resigned their functions in favor of the constituted authorities; at the same time, however, intimating that they remained alert, and only inactive so long as the ordinary course of law was found effectual.

From that time till the month of May, 1856, the Vigilance Committee did not interfere; and to any one familiar with the history of San Francisco during this period, it will appear extraordinary that the people should have remained so long inactive under the frightful mal-administration of criminal law to which they were subjected.

The crime which at last roused the people from their apathy, but which was not more foul than hundreds which had preceded it, and only more aggravated, inasmuch as the victim was one of the most universally respected citizens of the State, was the assassination, in open day and in the public street, of Mr. James King, of William, by a man named Casey.

The causes which had gradually been driving the people to assert their own power, as they did on this occasion, differed very materially from those which gave birth to the Vigilance Committee of '51, when their object was merely to root out a gang of housebreakers.

To explain the necessity of the revolution which took place in San Francisco in May, '56, would require a dissertation on San Francisco politics, which might not be very interesting; suffice it to say, that the power of controlling the elections had gradually got into the hands of men who "stuffed" the ballot-boxes, and sold the elections to whom they pleased; and the natural consequences of such a state of things led to the revolution.

In the *Alta California* of San Francisco of the 1st of June [1857] is a short article, which gives such a complete idea of the state of affairs that I take the liberty to transcribe it. It was written when the Vigilance Committee, having, a day or two before, hanged two men, were still actively engaged making numerous arrests; and it is remarkable that just at this time the authorities actually hung a man too.

The *Alta* announces the fact in the following article : –

"A man was executed yesterday for murder, after a due compliance with all forms of law.

"That he had been guilty of the crime for which he suffered there can be no doubt ; and yet it is entirely probable that, but for the circumstances which have occurred in San Francisco within the past three weeks, he never would have paid to the offended law the penalty affixed to his crime.

"It is a very remarkable fact in the history of this execution, that the condemned man, at the time of the murder of Mr. King, was living only under the respite of the Governor, and that that respite was obtained through the active interposition of Casey, who little dreamed that he would suffer the death-penalty before the man whom he had labored to save.

"This is the third execution only, under the forms of law, which has ever been had in San Francisco since it became an American city. Murder after murder has been committed, and murderer after murderer has been arrested and tried. Those who were blessed with friends and money have usually succeeded in escaping through the forms of law before a conviction was reached. Those who failed in this respect have, with the exceptions we have stated, been saved from punishment through the unwarranted interference of the executive officer of the State. So murder has enjoyed in San Francisco almost a certain immunity from punishment ; and the consequence has been that it has stalked abroad high-handed and bold. Over a year ago, we understood the district attorney to state, in an argument before a jury in a murder case, that, since the settlement of San Francisco by the American people, there had been twelve hundred murders committed here. We thought at the time the number stated was unduly large, and think so still; but it has been large enough, beyond doubt, to give us the unenviable reputation we have obtained abroad.

"And yet, in spite of these facts, but three criminals have suffered the death-penalty awarded to the crimes of which they have been guilty. These were all friendless, moneyless men. A sad commentary this on that motto, 'Equal and exact justice to all,' which we delight to blazon over our constitution and laws.

"Was it not time for a change – time, if need be, for a revolution which should inaugurate a new state of things – which should give an assurance that human life should be protected from the hand of the gentlemanly and moneyed assassin, as well as from the miserable, the poor, and the friendless? Such a revolution has been made by the people, and it has been the inauguration of a new and bright era in our history, in which an assurance has been given that neither the technicalities of a badly administered law, nor the interference of the Executive, can save the murderer from the punishment he justly merits. It has been brought about by the very evils it is intended to remedy. Had crime been punished here as it should have been – had the law done its duty, Casey would never have dared to shoot down the lamented King in broad daylight, with the hope that through the forms of law he would escape punishment. There would have been no necessity for a Vigilance Committee, no need of a revolution. Let us hope that in future the law will be no longer a mockery, but become, what it was intended by its founders to be, 'a terror to evil-doers.' "

The number of murders here given is no doubt appalling, but it is apt to give an idea of an infinitely more dreadful state of society, and of much greater insecurity of life to peaceable citizens than was actually the case.

If these murders were classified, it would be found that the frequency of fatal duels had greatly swelled the list, while, in the majority of cases, the murders would turn out to be the results of rencontres between desperadoes and ruffians, who, by having their little difficulties among themselves, and shooting and stabbing each other, and thus diminishing their own numbers, were rather entitled to the thanks of the respectable portion of the community.

It is very certain that in San Francisco crime was fostered by the laxity of the law, but it is equally reasonable to believe that in the mines, where Lynch law had full swing, the amount of crime actually committed by the large criminally disposed portion of the community, consisting of lazy Mexican *ladrones* and cutthroats, well-trained professional burglars from populous countries, and outcast desperadoes from all the corners of the earth, was not so great as would have resulted from the presence of the same men in any old country, where the law, clothed in all its majesty, is more mysterious and slow, however irresistible, in its action.

CHAPTER XV

GROWING OVER NIGHT

W ITHOUT having visited some distant place in the mountains, such as Downieville, it was impossible to realize fully the extraordinary extent to which the country had, in so short a time, been overrun and settled by a population whose energy and adaptive genius had immediately seized and improved every natural advantage which presented itself, and whose quickly acquired wealth enabled them to introduce so much luxury, and to afford employment to so many of those branches of industry which usually flourish only in old communities, that in some respects California can hardly be said to have ever been a new country, as compared with other parts of the world to which that term is applied.

The men who settled the country imparted to it a good deal of their own nature, which knows no period of boyhood. The Americans spring at once from childhood, or almost from infancy, to manhood; and California, no less rapid in its growth, became a full-grown State, while one-half the world still doubted its existence.

The amount of labor which had already been performed in the mines was almost incredible. Every river and creek from one end to the other presented a busy scene; on the "bars," of course, the miners were congregated in the greatest numbers; but there was scarcely any part of their course where some work was not going on, and the flumes were so numerous, that for about one-third of their length the rivers were carried past in those wooden aqueducts.

The most populous part of the mines, however, was in the high mountain-land between the rivers, and here the whole country had been ransacked, every flat and ravine had been prospected; and wherever extensive diggings had been found, towns and villages had sprung up.

Young as California was, it was in one respect older than its parent country, for life was so fast that already it could show ruins and deserted villages. In out-of-the-way places one met with cabins fallen into disrepair, which the proprietors had abandoned to locate themselves elsewhere; and even villages of thirty or forty shanties were to be seen deserted and deso-

late, where the diggings had not proved so productive as the original founders had anticipated.

Labor, however, was not exclusively devoted to mining operations. Roads
had in many parts been cut in the sides of the mountains, bridges had been
built, and innumerable saw-mills, most of them driven by steam power, were
in full operation, many of them having been erected in anticipation of a demand
for lumber, and before any population existed around them. Every little valley
in the mountains where the soil was at all fit for cultivation was already fenced
in, and producing crops of barley or oats; and canals, in some cases forty or
fifty miles long, were in course of construction, to bring the waters of the rivers
to the mountain-tops, to diggings which were otherwise unavailable.

Life for the most part was hard enough certainly, but every village was a
little city of itself, where one could live in comparative luxury. Even Downieville had its theater and concerts, its billiard-rooms and saloons of all sorts, a
daily paper, warm baths, and restaurants where men in red flannel shirts, with
bare arms, spread a napkin over their muddy knees, and studied the bill of fare
for half an hour before they could make up their minds what to order for dinner.

I was sitting on a rock by the side of the river one day sketching, when
I became aware that a most ragamuffinish individual was looking over my
shoulder. He was certainly, without exception, the most tattered and torn man
I ever saw in my life ; even his hair and beard gave the idea of rags, which was
fully realized by his costume. He was a complete caricature of an old miner,
and quite a picture by himself, seen from any point of view.

The rim of his old brown hat seemed ready to drop down on his shoulders
at a moment's notice, and the sides, having dissolved all connection with the
crown, presented at the top a jagged circumference, festooned here and there
with locks of light brown hair, while, to keep the whole fabric from falling
to pieces of its own weight, it was bound round with a piece of string in lieu
of a hat-band. His hair hung all over his shoulders in large straight flat locks,
just as if a handkerchief had been nailed to the top of his head and then torn
into shreds, and a long beard of the same pattern fringed a face as brown as a
mahogany table. His shirt had once been red flannel – of course it was flannel
yet, what remained of it – but it was in a most dilapidated condition. Half-way
down to his elbows hung some shreds, which led to the belief that at one time
he had possessed a pair of sleeves; but they seemed to have been removed by

the action of time and the elements, which had also been busy with other parts of the garment, and had, moreover, changed its original scarlet to different shades of crimson and purple. There was enough of his shirt left almost to meet a pair of – not trousers, but still less mentionable articles, of the same material as the shirt, and in the same stage of decomposition. He must have had trousers once on a time, but I suppose he had worn them out ; and I could not help thinking what extraordinary things they must have been on the morning when he came to the conclusion that they were not good enough to wear. I daresay he would have put them on if he could, but perhaps they were so full of holes that he did not know which to get into. His boots at least had reached this point, and to acknowledge that they had been boots was as much as a conscientious man could say for them. They were more holes than leather, and had no longer any title to the name of boots.

He was a man between thirty and forty, and, notwithstanding his rags, there was nothing in his appearance at all dirty or repulsive; on the contrary, he had a very handsome, prepossessing face, with an air about him which at once gave the idea that he had been used to polite society. I was, consequently, not surprised at the style of his address. He talked with me for some time, and I found him a most amusing and gentlemanly fellow. He was a German doctor, but it was hard to detect any foreign accent in his pronunciation.

The claim he was working was a mile or two up the river, and his company, he told me, was one of the greatest curiosities in the country. It consisted of two Americans, two Frenchmen, two Italians, two Mexicans, and my ragged friend, who was the only man in the company who spoke any language but his mother tongue. He was captain of the company, and interpreter-general for the crowd. I quite believed him when he said it was hard work to keep them all in order, and that when he was away no work could be done at all, and for that reason he was now hurrying back to his claim. But before leaving me he said, "I saw you sketching from the trail, and I came down to ask a favor of you."

There is as much vanity sometimes in rags as in gorgeous apparel; and what he wanted of me was to make a sketch of him, rags and all, just as he was. To study such a splendid figure was exactly what I wanted to do myself, so I made an appointment with him for the next day, and begged of him in the meantime not to think of combing his hair, which, indeed, to judge from its appearance, he had not done for some time.

I found afterwards that he was a well-known character, and went by the name of the Flying Dutchman.

I passed by his claim one day, and such a scene it was! The Tower of Babel was not a circumstance to it. The whole of the party were up to their waists in water, in the middle of the river, trying to build a wing-dam. The Americans, the Frenchmen, the Italians, and the Mexicans, were all pulling in different directions at an immense unwieldy log, and bestowing on each other most frightful oaths, though happily in unknown tongues; while the directing genius, the Flying Dutchman, was rushing about among them, and gesticulating wildly in his endeavors to pacify them, and to explain what was to be done. He spoke all the modern languages at once, occasionally talking Spanish to a Frenchman, and English to the Italians, then cursing his own stupidity in German, and blowing them all up collectively in a promiscuous jumble of national oaths, when they all came to a stand-still, the Flying Dutchman even seeming to give it up in despair. But after addressing a few explanatory remarks to each nation separately, in their respective languages, he persuaded them to try once more, when they got along well enough for a few minutes, till something went wrong, and then the Tower-of-Babel scene was enacted over again.

What induced the Flying Dutchman to form a company of such incongruous materials, and to take so much trouble in trying to work it, I can't say, unless it was a little of the same innocent vanity which was apparent in his exaggerated style of dress.

There was a considerable number of Frenchmen in the neighborhood of Downieville, but they kept very much to themselves. So very few of them, even of the better class, could speak English, and so few American miners knew anything of French, that scarcely ever were they found working together.

In common intercourse of buying and selling, or asking and giving any requisite information, neither party was ever very much at a loss; a few words of broken English, a word or two of French, and a large share of pantomime, carried them through any conference.

When any one capable of acting as interpreter happened to be present, the Frenchman, in his impatience, was constantly asking him *"Qu'est ce qu'il dit?"* *"Qu'est ce qu'il dit?"* This caught the ear of the Americans more than anything else, and a "Keskydee" came at last to be a synonym for a "Parleyvoo."

The "Dutchmen" in the mines, under which denomination are included all manner of Germans, showed much greater aptitude to amalgamate with the people around them. Frenchmen were always found in gangs, but "Dutchmen" were usually met with as individuals, and more frequently associated with Americans than with their own countrymen. For the most part they spoke English very well, and there were none who could not make themselves perfectly intelligible.

But in making such a comparison between the Germans and the French, it would not be fair to leave unmentioned the fact that the great majority of the former were men who had the advantage of having lived for a greater or less time in the United States, while the Frenchmen had nearly all immigrated in shiploads direct from their native country.

About thirty miles above Downieville is one of the highest mountains in the mines. The view from the summit, which is composed of several rocky peaks in line with each other, like the teeth of a saw, was said to be one of the finest in California, and I was desirous of seeing it; but the mountain was on the verge of settlement, and there was no camp or house of accommodation nearer to it than Downieville. However, the Frenchman in whose house I was staying told me that a friend of his, who was mining there, would be down in a day or two, and that he would introduce me to him. He came down the next day for a supply of provisions, and I gladly took the opportunity of returning with him.

The trail followed the river all the way, and was very rough, many parts of it being nearly as bad as "Cape Horn." The Frenchman had a pack-mule loaded with his stock of provisions, which gave him an infinity of trouble. He was such a bad packer that the cargo was constantly shifting, and requiring to be re-packed and secured. At one spot, where there was a steep descent from the trail to the river of about a hundred feet, the whole cargo broke loose, and fell to the ground. The only article, however, which rolled off the narrow trail was a keg of butter, which went bounding down the hill till it reached the bottom, where at one smash it buttered the whole surface of a large flat rock in the middle of the river. The Frenchman climbed down by a circuitous route to recover what he could of it, while I remained to repack the cargo. Without further accident we arrived about dark at my companion's cabin, where we found his partners just preparing supper; – and a very good supper it was; for, with only the ordinary materials of flour, ham, and beef, it was astonishing what a very superior, mess a Frenchman could get up.

After smoking an infinite number of pipes, I stretched out on the floor, with my feet to the fire, and slept like a top till morning, when, having got directions from the Frenchman as to my route, I set out to climb the mountain. The cabin was situated at the base of one of the spurs into which the mountain branched off, and was about eight miles distant from the summit.

When I had got about half-way up, I came in sight of a quartz-grinding establishment, situated on an exceedingly steep place, where a small stream of water came dashing over the rocks. In the face of the hill a step had been cut out, on which a cabin was built, and immediately below it were two "rasters"* in full operation.

These are the most primitive kind of contrivances for grinding quartz. They are circular places, ten or twelve feet in diameter, flagged with flat stones, and in these the quartz is crushed by two large heavy stones dragged round and round by a mule harnessed to a horizontal beam, to which they are also attached.

The quartz is already broken up into small pieces before being put into the "raster," and a constant supply of water is necessary to facilitate the operation, the stuff, while being ground, having the appearance of a rich white mud. The Mexicans, who use this machine a great deal, have a way of ascertaining when the quartz is sufficiently ground, by feeling it between the finger and thumb of one hand, while with the other they feel the lower part of their ear; and when the quartz has the same soft velvety feel, it is considered fine enough, and the gold is then extracted By amalgamation with quicksilver.

A considerable amount of work had been done at this place. The quartz vein was several hundred yards above the "rasters," and from it there was laid a double line of railway on the face of the mountain, for the purpose of bringing down the quartz. The loaded car was intended to bring up the empty one; but the railway was so steep that it looked as if a car, once started, would never stop till it reached the river, two or three miles below.

The vein was not being worked just now; and I only found one man at the place, who was employed in keeping the two mules at work in the "rasters." He told me that the ascent from that point was so difficult that it would be dark before I could return, and persuaded me to pass the night with him, and start early the next morning.

The nights had been getting pretty chilly lately, and up here it was particularly so; but with the aid of a blazing fire we managed to make ourselves comfortable. I lay down before the fire, with the prospect of having a good sleep, but woke in the middle of the night, feeling it most bitterly cold. The fact is, the log cabin was merely a log cage, the chinks between the logs having never been filled up, and it had come on to blow a perfect hurricane. The spot where the cabin stood was very much exposed, and the gusts of wind blew against it and through it as if it would carry us all away.

This pleasant state of things lasted two days, during which time I remained a prisoner in the cabin, as the force of the wind was so great that one could scarcely stand outside, and the cold was so intense that the pools in the stream which ran past were covered with ice. The cabin was but poor protection, the wind having full play through it, even blowing the tin plates off the table while we were at dinner; and heavy gusts coming down the chimney filled the cabin with smoke, ashes, and burning wood. Two days of this was rather miserable work, but with the aid of my pencil and two or three old novels I managed to weather it out.

The third day the gale was over, and though still cold, the weather was beautifully bright and clear. On setting out on my expedition to the summit of the mountain, I had first to climb up the railway, which went as far as the top of the ridge, where the quartz cropped out in large masses. From this there was a gradual ascent to the summit, about four miles distant, over ground which was stony, like a newly macadamized road, and covered with wiry brushwood waist-high. This was rendered a still more pleasant place to travel over by being infested by grizzly bears, whose tracks I could see on every spot of ground capable of receiving the impression of their feet. At last I arrived at the foot of the immense masses of rock which formed the summit of the mountain, and the only means of continuing the ascent was by climbing up long slides of loose sharp-cornered stones of all sizes. Every step I took forward, I went about half a step backward, the stones giving way under my feet, and causing a general commotion from top to bottom. On reaching the top of this place, after suffering a good deal in my shins and shoe-leather, I found myself on a ledge of rock, with a similar one forty or fifty feet above me, to be gained by climbing another slide of loose stones; and having spent about an hour in working my passage up a succession of places of this sort, I arrived at the foot of the immense wall of solid rock which crowned the summit of the mountain. To reach the lowest point of the top of the perpendicular wall above me, I had some fifteen or twenty feet to climb the best way I could, and the prospect of any failure in the attempt was by no means encouraging, as, had I happened to fall, I should have been carried down to the regions below with an avalanche of loose rocks and stones. Even as I stood studying how I should make the ascent by means of the projecting ledges, and tracking out my course before I made the attempt, I felt the stones beginning to give way under my feet; and seeing there was no time to lose, I went at it, and after a pretty hard struggle I reached the top. This, however, was not the summit – I was only between the teeth of the saw; but I was enabled to gain the top of one of the peaks by means of a ledge, about a foot and a half wide, which slanted up the face of the rock. Here I sat down to enjoy the view, and certainly I felt amply repaid for all the labor of the ascent, by the vastness and grandeur of the panorama around me. I looked back for more than a hundred miles over the mountainous pine-clad region of the "Mines," where, from the shapes of some of the mountains, I could distinguish many places which I had visited. Beyond this lay the wide plains of the Sacramento Valley, in which the course of the rivers could be traced by the trees which grew along their banks; and beyond the plains the coast range was distinctly seen.

On the other side, from which I had made the ascent, there was a sheer precipice of about two hundred feet, at the foot of which, in eternal shade, lay heaps of snow. The mountains in this direction were more rugged and barren, and beyond them appeared the white peaks of the Sierra Nevada. The atmosphere was intensely clear; it was as if there were no atmosphere at all, and the view of the most remote objects was so vivid and distinct that any one not used to such a clime would have been slow to believe that their distance was so great as it actually was. Monte Diablo, a peculiarly shaped mountain within a few miles of San Francisco, and upwards of three hundred miles* from where I stood, was plainly discernible, and with as much distinctness as on a clear day in England a mountain is seen at a distance of fifty or sixty miles.

The beauty of the view, which consisted chiefly in its vastness, was greatly enhanced by being seen from such a lofty pinnacle. It gave one the idea of being suspended in the air, and cut off from all communication with the world below. The perfect solitude of the place was quite oppressive, and was rendered still more awful by the occasional loud report of some piece of rock, which, becoming detached from the mass, went bounding down to seek a more humble resting-place. The gradual disruption seemed to be incessant, for no sooner had one fragment got out of hearing down below, than another started after it. There was a keen wind blowing, and it was so miserably cold, that when I had been up here for about an hour, I became quite benumbed and chilled. It was rather ticklish work coming down from my exalted position, and more perilous a good deal than it had been to climb up to it; but I managed it without accident, and reached the cabin of my quartz-grinding friend before dark.

Here I found there had arrived in the meantime three men from a ranch which they had taken up in a small valley, about thirty miles farther up in the mountains. There were no other white men in that direction, and this cabin was the nearest habitation to them. They had come in with six or seven mule-loads of hay for the use of the unfortunate animals who were kept in a state of constant revolution in the "rasters."

Note

* Arrastres. – ED.

* Under two hundred miles in an air line. – ED.

CHAPTER XVI

A BAND OF WANDERERS

I RETURNED to Downieville the next day, and as the weather was now getting rather cold and disagreeable, and I did not wish to be caught quite so far up in the mountains by the rainy season, I began to make my way down the river again to more accessible diggings.

On leaving, I took a trail which kept along the bank of the river for some miles, before striking up to the mountain ridge. Immediately below the town the mountain was very steep and smooth, and round this wound the trail, at the height of three or four hundred feet above the river. It was a mere beaten path – so narrow that two men could not walk abreast, while there was hardly a bush or a tree to interrupt one's progress in rolling down from the trail to the river.

When trains of pack-mules met at this place, they had the greatest difficulty in passing. The "down train," being of course unloaded, had to give way to the other. The mules understood their own rights perfectly well. Those loaded with cargo kept sturdily to the trail, while the empty mules scrambled up the bank, where they stood still till the others had passed. It not unfrequently happened, however, that a loaded mule got crowded off the trail, and rolled down the hill. This was always the last journey the poor mule ever performed. The cargo was recovered more or less damaged, but the remnants of deceased mules on the rocks down below remained as a warning to all future travelers. It was only a few days before that a man was riding along here, when, from some cause, his mule stumbled and fell off the trail. The mule, of course, went as a small contribution to the collection of skeletons of mules which had gone before him; and his rider would have shared the same fate, had he not fortunately been arrested in his progress by a bush, the only object in his course which could possibly have saved him.

The trail, after passing this spot, kept more among the rocks on the river side; and though it was rough traveling, the difficulties of the way were beguiled by the numbers of miners' camps through which one passed, and in observing the different varieties of mining operations being carried on. For miles the river was borne along in a succession of flumes, in which were set innumerable water-wheels, for working all sorts of pumps, and other contrivances for economizing labor. The bed of the river was alive with miners; and here and there, in the steep banks, were rows of twenty or thirty tunnels, out of which came constant streams of men, wheeling the dirt down to the riverside, to be washed in their long toms.

At Goodyear's Bar, which is a place of some size, the trail leaves the river, and ascends a mountain which is said to be the worst in that part of the country, and for my part I was quite willing to believe it was. I met several men coming down, who were all anxious to know if they were near the bottom. I was equally desirous to know if I was near the top, for the forest of pines was so thick, that, looking up, one could only get a glimpse between the trees of the zigzag trail far above.

About half-way up the mountain, at a break in the ascent, I found a very new log cabin by the side of a little stream of water. It bore a sign about as large as itself, on which was painted the "Florida House"; and as it was getting dark, and the next house was five miles farther on, I thought I would take up my quarters here for the night. The house was kept by an Italian, or an "Eyetalian," as he is called across the Atlantic. He had a Yankee wife, with a lot of children, and the style of accommodation was as good as one usually found in such places.

I was the only guest that night; and as we sat by the fire, smoking our pipes after supper, my host, who was a cheerful sort of fellow, became very communicative. He gave me an interesting account of his California experiences, and also of his farming operations in the States, where he had spent the last few years of his life. Then, going backwards in his career, he told me that he had lived for some years in England and Scotland, and spoke of many places there as if he knew them well. I was rather curious to know in what capacity such an exceedingly dingy-looking individual had visited all the cities of the kingdom, but he seemed to wish to avoid cross examination on the subject, so I did not press him. He became intimately connected in my mind, however, with sundry plaster-of-Paris busts of Napoleon, the Duke of Wellington, Sir Walter Scott, and other distinguished characters. I could fancy I saw the whole collection of statuary on the top of his head, and felt very much inclined to shout out "Images!" to see what effect it would have upon him.

In the course of the evening he asked me if I would like to hear some music, saying that he played a little on the Italian fiddle. I said I would be delighted, particularly as I did not know the instrument. The only national fiddle I had ever heard of was the Caledonian, and I trusted this instrument of his was a different sort of thing; but I was very much amused when it turned out to be nothing more or less than a genuine orthodox hurdy-gurdy. It put me more in mind of home than anything I had heard for a long time. At the first note, of course, the statuary vanished, and was replaced by a vision of an unfortunate monkey in a red coat, while my friend's extensive travels in the United Kingdom became very satisfactorily accounted for, and I thought it by no means unlikely that this was not the first time I had heard the sweet strains of his Italian fiddle. He played several of the standard old tunes; but hurdy-gurdy music is of such a character that a little of it goes a great way; and I was not sorry when a couple of strings snapped – to the great disgust, however, of my friend, for he had no more with which to replace them.

Hurdy-gurdy player or not, he was a very entertaining, agreeable fellow. I only hope all the fraternity are like him (perhaps they are, if one only knew them), and attain ultimately to such a respectable position in life, dignifying their instruments with the name of Italian fiddles, and reserving them for the entertainment of their particular friends.

I was on my way to Slate Range, a place some distance down the river, but the next day I only went as far as Oak Valley, traveling the last few miles with a young fellow from one of the Southern States, whom I overtook on the way. He had been mining, he told me, at Downieville, and was now going to join some friends of his at a place some thirty miles off.

At supper he did not make his appearance, which I did not observe, as there were a number of men at table, till the landlord asked me if that young fellow who arrived with me was not going to have any supper, and suggested that perhaps he was "strapped," "dead-broke" – *Anglicé,* without a cent in his pocket. I had not inferred anything of the sort from his conversation, but on going out and asking him why he did not come to supper, he reluctantly admitted that the state of his finances would not admit of it. I told him, in the language of Mr. Toots, that it was of no consequence, and made him come in, when he was most unceremoniously lectured by the rest of the party, and by the landlord particularly, on the absurdity of his intention of going supperless to bed merely because he happened to be "dead-broke," getting at the same time some useful hints how to act under such circumstances in future from several of the men present, who related how, when they had found themselves in such a predicament, they had, on frankly stating the fact, been made welcome to everything.

To be "dead-broke" was really, as far as a man's immediate comfort was concerned, a matter of less importance in the mines than in almost any other place. There was no such thing as being out of employment, where every man employed himself, and could always be sure of ample remuneration for his day's work. But notwithstanding the want of excuse for being "strapped," it was very common to find men in that condition. There were everywhere numbers of lazy, idle men, who were always without a dollar; and others reduced themselves to that state by spending their time and money on claims which, after all, yielded them no return, or else gradually exhausted their funds in traveling about the country, and prospecting, never satisfied with fair average diggings, but always having the idea that better were to be found elsewhere. Few miners located themselves permanently in any place, and there was a large proportion of the population continually on the move. In almost every place I visited in the mines, I met men whom I had seen in other diggings. Some men I came across frequently, who seemed to do nothing but wander about the country, satisfied with asking the miners in the different diggings how they were "making out," but without ever taking the trouble to prospect for themselves.

Coin was very scarce, what there was being nearly all absorbed by the gamblers, who required it for convenience in carrying on their business. Ordinary payments were made in gold dust, every store being provided with a pair of gold scales, in which the miner weighed out sufficient dust from his buckskin purse to pay for his purchases.

In general trading, gold dust was taken at sixteen dollars the ounce; but in the towns and villages, at the agencies of the various San Francisco bankers and express companies, it was bought at a higher price, according to the quality of the dust, and as it was more or less in demand for remittance to New York.

The express business of the United States is one which has not been many years established, and which was originally limited to the transmission of small parcels of value. On the discovery of gold in California, the express houses of New York immediately established agencies in San Francisco, and at once became largely engaged in transmitting gold dust to the mint in Philadelphia, and to various parts of the United States, on account of the owners in California. As a natural result of doing such a business, they very soon began to sell their own drafts on New York, and to purchase and remit gold dust on their own account.

They had agencies also in every little town in the mines, where they enjoyed the utmost confidence of the community, receiving deposits from miners and others, and selling drafts on the Atlantic States. In fact, besides carrying on the original express business of forwarding goods and parcels, and keeping up an independent post-office of their own, they became also, to all intents and purposes, bankers, and did as large an exchange business as any legitimate banking firm in the country.

The want of coin was equally felt in San Francisco, and coins of all countries were taken into circulation to make up the deficiency. As yet a mint had not been granted to California, but there was a Government Assay Office, which issued a large octagonal gold piece of the value of fifty dollars – a roughly executed coin, about twice the bulk of a crown-piece; while the greater part of the five, ten, and twenty dollar pieces were not from the United States Mint, but were coined and issued by private firms in San Francisco

Silver was still more scarce, and many pieces were consequently current at much more than their value. A quarter of a dollar was the lowest appreciable sum represented by coin, and any piece approaching it in size was equally current at the same rate. A franc passed for a quarter of a dollar while a five-franc piece only passed for a dollar, which is about its actual worth. As a natural consequence of francs being thus taken at 25 per cent. more than their real value, large quantities of them were imported and put into circulation. In 1854, however, the bankers refused to receive them, and they gradually disappeared.

There was wonderfully little precaution taken in conveying the gold down from the mountains, and yet, although nothing deserving the name of an escort ever accompanied it, I never knew an instance of an attack upon it being attempted. On several occasions I saw the express messenger taking down a quantity of gold from Downieville. He and another man, both well mounted, were driving a mule loaded with leathern sacks, containing probably two or three hundred pounds' weight of gold. They were well armed, of course; but a couple of robbers, had they felt so inclined, might easily have knocked them both over with their rifles in the solitude of the forest, without much fear of detection. Bad as California was, it appeared a proof that it was not altogether such a country as was generally supposed, when large quantities of gold were thus regularly brought over the lonely mountain-trails, with even less protection than would have been thought necessary in many parts of the Old World.

From Oak Valley I went down to Slate Range with an American who was anxious I should visit his camp there. After climbing down the mountain side, we at last reached the river, which here was confined between huge masses of slate rock, turning in its course, and disappearing behind bold rocky points so abruptly, that seldom could more of the length than the breadth of the river be seen at a time.

An hour's scrambling over the sharp-edged slate rocks on the side of the river brought us to his camp, or at least the place where he and his partners camped out, which was on the bare rocks, in a corner so overshadowed by the steep mountain that the sun never shone upon it. It was certainly the least luxurious habitation, and in the most wild and rugged locality, I had yet seen in the mines. On a rough board which rested on two stones were a number of tin plates, pannikins, and such articles of table furniture, while a few flat stones alongside answered the purpose of chairs. Scattered about, as was usual in all miners' camps, were quantities of empty tins of preserved meats, sardines, and oysters, empty bottles of all shapes and sizes, innumerable ham-bones, old clothes, and other rubbish. Round the blackened spot which was evidently the kitchen were pots and frying-pans, sacks of flour and beans, and other provisions, together with a variety of cans and bottles, of which no one could tell the contents without inspection; for in the mines everything is perverted from its original purpose, butter being perhaps stowed away in a tin labeled "fresh lobsters," tea in a powder canister, and salt in a sardine-box.

There was nothing in the shape of a tent or shanty of any sort; it was not required as a shelter from the heat of the sun, as the place was in the perpetual shade of the mountain, and at night each man rolled himself up in his blankets, and made a bed of the smoothest and softest piece of rock he could find.

This part of the river was very rich, the gold being found in the soft slate rock between the layers and in the crevices.

My friend and his partners were working in a "wing dam" in front of their camp, and the river, being pushed back off one half of its bed, rushed past in a roaring torrent, white with foam. A large water-wheel was set in it, which worked several pumps, and a couple of feet above it lay a pine tree, which had been felled there so as to serve as a bridge. The river was above thirty feet wide, and the tree, not more than a foot and a half in diameter, was in its original condition, perfectly round and smooth, and was, moreover, kept constantly wet with the spray from the wheel, which was so close that one could almost touch it in passing. If one had happened to slip and fall into the water, he would have had about as much chance of coming out alive as if he had fallen before the paddles of a steamer; and any gentleman with shaky legs and unsteady nerves, had he been compelled to pass such a bridge, would most probably have got astride of it, and so worked his passage across. In the mines, however, these "pine-log crossings" were such a very common style of bridge, that every one was used to them, and walked them like a rope-dancer: in fact, there was a degree of pleasant excitement in passing a very slippery and difficult one such as this.

CHAPTER XVII

CHINESE IN THE EARLY DAYS

W HILE at this camp, I went down the river two or three miles to see a place called Mississippi Bar, where a company of Chinamen were at work. After an hour's climbing along the rocky banks, and having crossed and recrossed the river some half-dozen times on pine logs, I at last got down among the Celestials.

There were about a hundred and fifty of them here, living in a perfect village of small tents, all clustered together on the rocks. They had a claim in the bed of the river, which they were working by means of a wing dam. A "wing dam," I may here mention, is one which first runs half-way across the river, then down the river, and back again to the same side, thus damming off a portion of its bed without the necessity of the more expensive operation of lifting up the whole river bodily in a "flume."

The Chinamen's dam was two or three hundred yards in length, and was built of large pine trees laid one on the top of the other. They must have had great difficulty in handling such immense logs in such a place; but they are exceedingly ingenious in applying mechanical power, particularly in concentrating the force of a large number of men upon one point.

There were Chinamen of the better class among them, who no doubt directed the work, and paid the common men very poor wages – poor at least for California. A Chinaman could be hired for two, or at most three dollars a day by any one who thought their labor worth so much; but those at work here were most likely paid at a still lower rate, for it was well known that whole shiploads of Chinamen came to the country under a species of bondage to some of their wealthy countrymen in San Francisco, who, immediately on their arrival, shipped them off to the mines under charge of an agent, keeping them completely under control by some mysterious celestial influence, quite independent of the accepted laws of the country.

They sent up to the mines for their use supplies of Chinese provisions and clothing, and thus all the gold taken out by them remained in Chinese hands, and benefited the rest of the community but little by passing through the ordinary channels of trade.

In fact, the Chinese formed a distinct class, which enriched itself at the expense of the country, abstracting a large portion of its latent wealth without contributing, in a degree commensurate with their numbers, to the prosperity of the community of which they formed a part.

The individuals of any community must exist by supplying the wants of others; and when a man neither does this, nor has any wants of his own but those which he provides for himself, he is of no use to his neighbors; but when, in addition to this, he also diminishes the productiveness of the country, he is a positive disadvantage in proportion to the amount of public wealth which he engrosses, and becomes a public nuisance.

What is true of an individual is true also of a class; and the Chinese, though they were no doubt, as far as China was concerned, both productive and consumptive, were considered by a very large party in California to be merely destructive as far as that country was interested.

They were, of course, not altogether so, for such a numerous body as they were could not possibly be so isolated as to be entirely independent of others; but any advantage which the country derived from their presence was too dearly paid for by the quantity of gold which they took from it; and the propriety of expelling all the Chinese from the State was long discussed, both by the press and in the Legislature; but the principles of the American constitution prevailed; the country was open to all the world, and the Chinese enjoyed equal rights with the most favored nation. In some parts of the mines, however, the miners had their own ideas on the subject, and would not allow the Chinamen to come among them; but generally they were not interfered with, for they contented themselves with working such poor diggings as it was not thought worth while to take from them.

This claim on the Yuba was the greatest undertaking I ever saw attempted by them.

They expended a vast deal of unnecessary labor in their method of working, and their individual labor, in effect, was as nothing compared with that of other miners. A company of fifteen or twenty white men would have wing-dammed this claim, and worked it out in two or three months, while here were about a hundred and fifty Chinamen humbugging round it all the season, and still had not worked one half the ground.

Their mechanical contrivances were not in the usual rough straightforward style of the mines; they were curious, and very elaborately got up, but extremely wasteful of labor, and, moreover, very ineffective.

The pumps which they had at work here were an instance of this. They were on the principle of a chain-pump, the chain being formed of pieces of wood about six inches long, hinging on each other, with cross-pieces in the middle for buckets, having about six square inches of surface. The hinges fitted exactly to the spokes of a small wheel, which was turned by a Chinaman at each side of it working a miniature treadmill of four spokes on the same axle. As specimens of joiner-work they were very pretty, but as pumps they were ridiculous; they threw a mere driblet of water: the chain was not even encased in a box – it merely lay in a slanting trough, so that more than one half the capacity of the buckets was lost. An American miner, at the expenditure of one-tenth part of the labor of making such toys, would have set a water-wheel in the river to work an elevating pump, which would have thrown more water in half an hour than four-and-twenty Chinamen could throw in a day with a dozen of these gim-crack contrivances. Their camp was wonderfully clean: when I passed through it, I found a great many of them at their toilet, getting their heads shaved, or plaiting each other's pigtails; but most of them were at dinner, squatted on the rocks in groups of eight or ten round a number of curious little black pots and dishes, from which they helped themselves with their chopsticks. In the center was a large bowl of rice. This is their staple article, and they devour it most voraciously. Throwing back their heads, they hold a large cupful to their wide-open mouths, and, with a quick motion of the chopsticks in the other hand, they cause the rice to flow down their throats in a continuous stream.

I received several invitations to dinner, but declined the pleasure, preferring to be a spectator. The rice looked well enough, and the rest of their dishes were no doubt very clean, but they had a very dubious appearance, and were far from suggesting the idea of being good to eat. In the store I found the storekeeper lying asleep on a mat. He was a sleek dirty-looking object, like a fat pig with the hair scalded off, his head being all close shaved excepting the pigtail. His opium-pipe lay in his hand, and the lamp still burned beside him, so I supposed he was already in the seventh heaven. The store was like other stores in the mines, inasmuch as it contained a higgledy-piggledy collection of provisions and clothing, but everything was Chinese excepting the boots. These are the only articles of barbarian costume which the Chinaman adopts, and he always wears them of an enormous size, on a scale commensurate with the ample capacity of his other garments.

The next place I visited was Wamba's Bar, some miles lower down the river; and from here I intended returning to Nevada, as the season was far advanced, and fine weather could no longer be depended upon.

The very day, however, on which I was to start, the rain commenced, and came down in such torrents that I postponed my departure. It continued to rain heavily for several days, and I had no choice but to remain where I was, as the river rose rapidly to such a height as to be perfectly impassable. It was now about eighty yards wide, and rushed past in a raging torrent, the waves rolling several feet high. Some of the miners up above, trusting to a longer continuance of the dry season, had not removed their flumes from the river, and these it was now carrying down, all broken up into fragments, along with logs and whole pine trees, which occasionally, as they got foul of other objects, reared straight up out of the water. It was a grand sight; the river seemed as if it had suddenly arisen to assert its independence, and take vengeance for all the restraints which had been placed upon it, by demolishing flumes, dams, and bridges, and carrying off everything within its reach.

The house I was staying in was the only one in the neighborhood, and was a sort of half store, half boarding-house. Several miners lived in it, and there were, besides, two or three storm-stayed travelers like myself. It was a small clapboard house, built on a rock immediately over the river, but still so far above it that we anticipated no danger from the flood. We were close to the mouth of a creek, however, which we one night fully expected would send the house on a voyage of discovery down the river. Some drift-logs up above had got jammed, and so altered the course of the stream as to bring it sweeping past the corner of the house, which merely rested on a number of posts. The waters rose to within an inch or two of the floor; and as they carried logs and rocks along with them, we feared that the posts would be carried away, when the whole fabric would immediately slip off the rocks into the angry river a few feet below. There was a small window at one end through which we might have escaped, and this was taken out that no time might be lost when the moment for clearing out should arrive, while axes also were kept in readiness, to smash through the back of the house, which rested on *terra firma*. It was an exceedingly dark night, very cold, and raining cats and dogs, so that the prospect of having to jump out of the window and sit on the rocks till morning was by no means pleasant to contemplate; but the idea of being washed into the river was still less agreeable, and no one ventured to sleep, as the water was already almost up to the floor, and a very slight rise would have smashed up the whole concern so quickly, that it was best to be on the alert. The house fortunately stood it out bravely till daylight, when some of the party put an end to the danger by going up the creek, and removing the accumulation of logs which had turned the water from its proper channel.

After the rain ceased, we had to wait for two days till the river fell sufficiently to allow of its being crossed with any degree of safety; but on the third day, along with another man who was going to Nevada, I made the passage in a small skiff – not without considerable difficulty, however, for the river was still much swollen, and covered with logs and driftwood. On landing on the other side, we struck straight up the face of the mountain, and soon gained the high land, where we found a few inches of snow fast disappearing before the still powerful rays of the sun.

We arrived at Nevada after a day and a half of very muddy traveling, but the weather was bright and clear, and seemed to be a renewal of the dry season. It did not last long, however, for a heavy snowstorm soon set in, and it continued snowing, raining, and freezing for about three weeks, – the snow lying on the ground all the time, to the depth of three or four feet. The continuance of such weather rendered the roads so impracticable as to cut off all supplies from Marysville or Sacramento, and accordingly prices of provisions of all kinds rose enormously. The miners could not work with so much snow on the ground, and altogether there was a prospect of hard times. Flour was exceedingly high even in San Francisco, several capitalists having entered into a flour-monopoly speculation, buying up every cargo as it arrived, and so keeping up the price. In Nevada it was sold at a dollar a pound, and in other places farther up in the mountains it was doled out, as long as the stock lasted, at three or four times that price. In many parts the people were reduced to the utmost distress from the scarcity of food, and the impossibility of obtaining any fresh supplies. At Downieville, the few men who had remained there were living on barley, a small stock of which was fortunately kept there as mule-feed. Several men perished in the snow in trying to make their escape from distant camps in the mountains; two or three lost their lives near the ranch of my friend the Italian hurdy-gurdy player, while carrying flour down to their camps on the river; and in some places people saved themselves from starvation by eating dogs and mules.

Men kept pouring into Nevada from all quarters, starved out of their own camps, and all bearing the same tale of starvation and distress, and glad to get to a place where food was to be had. The town, being a sort of harbor of refuge for miners in remote diggings, became very full; and as no work could be done in such weather, the population had nothing to do but to amuse themselves the best way they could. A theatrical company was performing nightly to crowded houses; the gambling saloons were kept in full blast; and in fact, every day was like a Sunday, from the number of men one saw idling about, playing cards, and gambling.

Although the severity of the weather interrupted mining operations for the time, it was nevertheless a subject of rejoicing to the miners generally, for many localities could only be worked when plenty of water was running in the ravines, and it was not unusual for men to employ themselves in the dry season in "throwing up" heaps of dirt, in anticipation of having plenty of water in winter to wash it. This was commonly done in flats and ravines where water could only be had immediately after heavy rains. It was easy to distinguish a heap of thrown-up dirt from a pile of "tailings," or dirt already washed, and property of this sort was quite sacred, the gold being not less safe there – perhaps safer – than if already in the pocket of the owner. In whatever place a man threw up a pile of dirt, he might leave it without any concern for its safety, and remove to another part of the country, being sure to find it intact when he returned to wash it, no matter how long he might be absent.

CHAPTER XVIII

DOWN WITH THE FLOOD

I HAD occasion to return to San Francisco at this time, and the journey was about the most unpleasant I ever performed. The roads had been getting worse all the time, and were quite impassable for stages or wagons. The mail was brought up by express messengers, but other communication there was none. The nearest route to San Francisco – that by Sacramento – was perfectly impracticable, and the only way to get down there was by Marysville, situated about fifty miles off, at the junction of the Yuba and Feather rivers.

I set out one afternoon with a friend who was also going down, and who knew the way, which was rather an advantage, as the trails were hidden under three or four feet of snow. We occasionally, however, got the benefit of a narrow path, trodden down by other travelers; and though we only made twelve miles that day, we in that distance gradually emerged from the snow, and got down into the regions of mud and slush and rain. We stayed the night at a road-side house, where we found twenty or thirty miners starved out of their own camps, and in the morning we resumed our journey in a steady pour of rain. The mud was more than ankle-deep, but was so well diluted with water that it did not cause much inconvenience in walking, while at the foot of every little hollow was a stream to be waded waist-high; for we were now out of the mining regions, and crossing the rolling country between the mountains and the plains, where the water did not run off so quickly.

When we reached the only large stream on our route, we found that the bridge, which had been the usual means of crossing, had been carried away, and the banks on either side were overflowed to a considerable distance. A pine tree had been felled across when the waters were lower, but they now flowed two or three feet over the top of it – the only sign that it was there being the branches sticking up, and marking its course across the river.

It was not very pleasant to have to cross such a swollen stream on such a very visionary bridge, but there was no help for it; so cutting sticks wherewith to feel for a footing under water, we waded out till we reached the original bank of the stream, where we had to take to the pine log, and travel it as best we could with the assistance of the branches, the water rushing past nearly up to our waists. We had fifty or sixty feet to go in this way, but the farther end of the log rose nearly to the surface of the water, and landed us on an island, from which we had to pass to dry land through a thicket of bushes under four feet of water.

Towards evening we arrived at a ranch, about twenty miles from Marysville, which we made the end of our day's journey. We were saturated with rain and mud, but dry clothes were not to be had; so we were obliged to pass another night under hydropathic treatment, the natural consequence of which was that in the morning we were stiff and sore all over. However, after walking a short distance, we got rid of this sensation – receiving a fresh ducking from the rain, which continued to fall as heavily as ever.

The plains, which we had now reached, were almost entirely under water, and at every depression in the surface of the ground a slough had to be waded of corresponding depth – sometimes over the waist. The road was only in some places discernible, and we kept to it chiefly by steering for the houses, to be seen at intervals of a few miles.

About six miles from Marysville we crossed the Yuba, which was here a large rapid river a hundred yards wide. We were ferried over in a little skiff, and had to pull up the river nearly half a mile, so as to fetch the landing on the other side. I was not sorry to reach *terra firma* again, such as it was, for the boat was a flat-bottomed, straight-sided little thing, about the size and shape of a coffin, and was quite unsuitable for such work. The waves were running so high that it was with the utmost difficulty we escaped being swamped, and all the swimming that could have been done in such a current would not have done any one much good.

From this point to Marysville the country was still more flooded. We passed several teams, which, in a vain endeavor to get up to the mountains with supplies, were hopelessly stuck in the mud at the bottom of the hollows, with only the rim of the wheels appearing above water.

Marysville is a city of some importance: being situated at the head of navigation, it is the depot and starting-point for the extensive district of mining country lying north and east of it. It is well laid out in wide streets, containing numbers of large brick and wooden buildings, and the ground it stands upon is ten or twelve feet above the usual level of the river. But when we waded up to it, we found the portion of the town nearest the river completely flooded, the water being nearly up to the first floor of the houses, while the people were going about in boats. In the streets farther back, however, it was not so bad; one could get along without having to go much over the ankles. The appearance of the place, as seen through the heavy rain, was far from cheering. The first idea which occurred to me on beholding it was that of rheumatism, and the second fever and ague; but I was glad to find myself here, nevertheless, if only to experience once more the sensation of having on dry clothes.

I learned that several men had been drowned on different parts of the plains in attempting to cross some of the immense pools or sloughs such as we had passed on our way; while cattle and horses were drowned in numbers, and were dying of starvation on insulated spots, from which there was no escape.

I saw plenty of this, however, the next day in going down by the steamboat to Sacramento. The distance is fifty or sixty miles through the plains all the way, but they had now more the appearance of a vast inland sea.

It would have been difficult to keep to the channel of the river, had it not been for the trees appearing on each side, and the numbers of squatters' shanties generally built on a spot where the bank was high and showed itself above water, though in many cases nothing but the roof of the cabin could be seen.

On the tops of the cabins and sheds, on piles of firewood, or up in the trees, were fowls calmly waiting their doom; while pigs, cows, and horses were all huddled up together, knee-deep in water, on any little rising ground which offered standing-room, dying by inches from inanition. The squatters themselves were busy removing in boats whatever property they could, and at those cabins whose occupants were not yet completely drowned out, a boat was made fast alongside as a means of escape for the poor devils, who, as the steamer went past, looked out of the door the very pictures of woe and dismay. We saw two men sitting resolutely on the top of their cabin, the water almost up to their feet ; a boat was made fast to the chimney, to be used when the worst came to the worst, but they were apparently determined to see it out if possible. They looked intensely miserable, though they would not own it, for they gave us a very feigned and uncheery hurrah as we steamed past.

The loss sustained by these settlers was very great. The inconvenience of being for a time floated off the face of the earth in a small boat was bad enough of itself; but to have the greater part of their worldly possessions floating around them, in the shape of the corpses of what had been their live stock, must have rather tended to damp their spirits. However, Californians are proof against all such reverses, – they are like India-rubber, the more severely they are cast down, the higher they rise afterwards.

It was hardly possible to conceive what an amount of rain and snow must have fallen to lay such a vast extent of country under water ; and though the weather was now improving, the rain being not so constant, or so heavy, it would still be some time before the waters could subside, as the snow which had fallen in the mountains had yet to find its way down, am would serve to keep up the flood.

Sacramento City was in as wretched a plight as a city can well be in.

The only dry land to be seen was the top of the levee built along the bank of the river in front of the town; all the rest was water, out of which rose the houses, or at least the upper parts of them. The streets were all so many canals crowded with boats and barges carrying on the customary traffic; watermen plied for hire in the streets instead of cabs, and independent gentlemen poled themselves about on rafts, or On extemporized boats made of empty boxes. In one part of the town, where the water was not deep enough for general navigation, a very curious style of conveyance was in use. Pairs of horses were harnessed to large flat-bottomed boats, and numbers of these vehicles, carrying passengers or goods, were to be seen cruising about, now dashing through a foot or two of mud which the horses made to fly in all directions as they floundered through it, now grounding and bumping over some very dry spot, and again sailing gracefully along the top of the water, so deep as nearly to cover the horses' backs.

The water in the river was some feet higher than that in the town, and it was fortunate that the levee did not give way, or the loss of life would have been very great. As it was, some few men had been drowned in the streets. The destruction of property, and the pecuniary loss to the inhabitants, were of course enormous, but they had been flooded once or twice before, besides having several times had their city burned down, and were consequently quite used to such disasters; in fact, Sacramento suffered more from fire and flood together than any city in the State, without, however, apparently retarding the growing prosperity of the people.

I arrived in Sacramento too late for the steamer for San Francisco, and so had the pleasure of passing a night there, but I cannot say I experienced any personal inconvenience from the watery condition of the town.

It seemed to cause very little interruption to the usual order of things in hotels, theaters, and other public places; there was a good deal of anxiety as to the security of the levee, in which was the only safety of the city; but in the meantime the ordinary course of pleasure and business was unchanged, except in the substitution of boats for wheeled vehicles; and the great source of consolation and congratulation to the sufferers from the flood, and to the population generally, was in endeavoring to compute how many millions of rats would be drowned.

On arriving in San Francisco the change was very great – it was like entering a totally different country. In place of cold and rain and snow, flooded towns, and no dry land, or snowed-up towns in the mountains with no food, here was a clear bright sky, and a warm sun shining down upon a city where everything looked bright and gay. It was nearly a year since I had left San Francisco, and in the meantime the greater part of it had been burned down and rebuilt. The appearance of most of the principal streets was completely altered ; large brick stores had taken the place of wooden buildings; and so rapidly had the city extended itself into the bay that the principal business was now conducted on wide streets of solid brick and stone warehouses, where a year before had been fifteen or twenty feet of water. All, excepting the more unfrequented streets, were planked, and had good stone or plank sidewalks, so that there was but little mud notwithstanding the heavy rains which had fallen. In the upper part of the town, however, where the streets were still in their original condition, the amount of mud was quite inconceivable. Some places were almost impassable, and carts might be seen almost submerged, which half-a-dozen horses were vainly trying to extricate.

The climate of San Francisco has the peculiarity of being milder in winter than in summer. Winter is by far the most pleasant season of the year. It is certainly the rainy season, but it only rains occasionally, and when it does it is not cold. The ordinary winter weather is soft, mild, subdued sunshine, not unlike the Indian summer of North America. The San Francisco summer, however, is the most disagreeable and trying season one can be subjected to. In the morning and forenoon it is generally beautifully bright and warm: one feels inclined to dress as one would in the tropics; but this cannot be done with safety, for one has to be prepared for the sudden change in temperature which occurs nearly every day towards the afternoon, when there blows in off the sea a cold biting wind, chilling the very marrow in one's bones. The cold is doubly felt after the heat of the fore part of the day, and to some constitutions such extreme variations of temperature within the twenty-four hours are no doubt very injurious, especially as the wind not unfrequently brings a damp fog along with it.

The climate is nevertheless generally considered salubrious, and is thought by some people to be one of the finest in the world. For my own part, I much prefer the summer weather of the mines, where the sky is always bright, and the warm temperature of the day becomes only comparatively cool at night, while the atmosphere is so dry, that the heat, however intense, is never oppressive, and so clear that everything within the range of vision is as clearly and distinctly seen as if one were looking upon a flat surface, and could equally examine each separate part of it, so satisfactory and so minute in detail is the view of the most distant objects.

Considering the very frequent use of pistols in San Francisco, it is a most providential circumstance that the climate is in a high degree favorable for the cure of gunshot wounds. These in general heal very rapidly, and many miraculous recoveries have taken place, effected by nature and the climate, after the surgeons, experienced as they are in that branch of practice, had exhausted their skill upon the patient.

CHAPTER XIX

A BULL AND BEAR FIGHT

THE long tract of mountainous country lying north and south, which comprises the mining districts, is divided into the northern and southern mines – the former having communication with San Francisco through Sacramento and Marysville, while the latter are more accessible by way of Stockton, a city situated at the head of navigation of the San Joaquin, which joins the Sacramento about fifty miles above San Francisco.

My wanderings had hitherto been confined to the northern mines, and when, after a short stay in San Francisco, business again led me to Placerville, I determined from that point to travel down through the southern mines, and visit the various places of interest *en route*.

It was about the end of March when I started. The winter was quite over; all that remained of it was an occasional heavy shower of rain; the air was mild and soft, and the mountains, covered with fresh verdure, were blooming brightly in the warm sunshine with many-colored flowers. In every ravine, and through each little hollow in the high lands, flowed a stream of water; and wherever water was to be found, there also were miners at work. From the towns and camps, where the supply of water was constant, and where the diggings could consequently be worked at any time of the year, they had expanded themselves over the whole face of the country; and in traveling through the depths of the forests, just as the solitude seemed to be perfect, one got a glimpse in the distance, through the dark columns of the pine trees, of the red shirts of two or three straggling miners, taking advantage of the short period of running water to reap a golden harvest in some spot of fancied richness. This was the season of all others to see to the best advantage the grandeur and beauty of the scenery, and at the same time to realize how widely diffused and inexhaustible is the wealth of the country. Inexhaustible is, of course, only a comparative term; for the amount of gold still remaining in California is a definite quantity becoming less and less every day, and already vastly reduced from what it was when the mines lay intact seven years ago; but still the date at which the yield of the California mines is to cease, or even to begin to fall off, seems to be as far distant as ever. In fact, the continued labor of constantly increasing numbers of miners, instead of exhausting the resources of the mines, as some persons at first supposed would be the case, has, on the contrary, only served to establish confidence in the permanence of their wealth.

It is true that such diggings are now rarely to be met with as were found in the early days, when the pioneers, pitching, as if by instinct, on those spots where the superabundant richness of the country had broken out, dug up gold as they would potatoes; nor is the average yield to the individual miner so great as it was in those times. Subsequent research, however, has shown that the gold is not confined to a few localities, but that the whole country is saturated with it. The mineral produce of the mines increases with the population, though not in the same ratio; for only a certain proportion of the immigrants betake themselves to mining, the rest finding equally profitable occupation in the various branches of mechanical and agricultural industry which have of late years sprung up; while the miner, though perhaps not actually taking out as much gold as in 1849, is nevertheless equally prosperous, for he lives amid the comforts of civilized life, which he obtains at a reasonable rate, instead of being reduced to a half-savage state, and having to pay fabulous prices for every article of consumption.

The first large camp on my way south from Hangtown was Moquelumne Hill, about sixty miles distant, and as there were no very interesting localities in the intermediate country, I traveled direct to that place. After passing through a number of small camps, I arrived about noon of the second day at Jacksonville, a small village called after General Jackson, of immortal memory. I had noticed a great many French miners at work at I came along, and so I was prepared to find it rather a French-looking place. Half the signs over the stores and hotels were French, and numbers of Frenchmen were sitting at small tables in front of the houses playing at cards.

As I walked up the town I nearly stumbled over a young grizzly bear, about the size of two Newfoundland dogs rolled into one, which was chained to a stump in the middle of the street. I very quickly got out of his way; but I found afterwards that he was more playful than vicious. He was the pet of the village, and was delighted when he could get any one to play with, though he was rather beyond the age at which such a playmate is at all desirable. I don't think he was likely to enjoy long even the small amount of freedom he possessed ; he would probably be caged up and shipped to New York; for a live grizzly is there a valuable piece of property, worth a good deal more than the same weight of bear's meat in California, even at two dollars a pound.

From this place there was a steep descent of two or three miles to the Moquelumne River, which I crossed by means of a good bridge, and, after ascending again to the upper world by a long winding road, I reached the town of Moquelumne Hill, which is situated on the very brink of the high land overhanging the river.

It lies in a sort of semicircular amphitheater of about a mile in diameter, surrounded by a chain of small eminences, in which gold was found in great quantities. The diggings were chiefly deep diggings, worked by means of "coyote holes," a hundred feet deep, and all the ground round the town was accordingly covered with windlasses and heaps of dirt. The heights at each end of the amphitheater had proved the richest spots, and were supposed to have been volcanoes. But many hills in the mines got the credit of having been volcanoes, for no other reason than that they were full of gold; and this was probably the only claim to such a distinction which could be made in this case.

The population was a mixture of equal proportions of French, Mexicans, and Americans, with a few stray Chinamen, Chilians, and suchlike.

The town itself, with the exception of two or three wooden stores and gambling-saloons, was all of canvas. Many of the houses were merely skeletons clothed in dirty rags of canvas, and it was not difficult to tell what part of the population they belonged to, even had there not been crowds of lazy Mexicans vegetating about the doors.

The Indians, who were pretty numerous about here, seemed to be a slightly superior race to those farther north. I judged so from the fact that they apparently had more money, and consequently must have had more energy to dig for it. They were also great gamblers, and particularly fond of monte, at which the Mexicans fleeced them of all their cash, excepting what they spent in making themselves ridiculous with stray articles of clothing.

But perhaps their appreciation of monte, and their desire to copy the costume of white men, are signs of a greater capability of civilization than they generally get credit for. Still their presence is not compatible with that of a civilized community, and, as the country becomes more thickly settled, there will be no longer room for them. Their country can be made subservient to man, but as they themselves cannot be turned to account, they must move off, and make way for their betters.

This may not be very good morality, but it is the way of the world, and the aborigines of California are not likely to share a better fate than those of many another country. And though the people who drive them out may make the process as gradual as possible by the system of Indian grants and reservations, yet, as with wild cattle, so it is with Indians, so many head, and no more, can live on a given quantity of land, and, if crowded into too small a compass, the result is certain though gradual extirpation, for by their numbers they prevent the reproduction of their means of subsistence.

At the time of my arrival in Moquelumne Hill, the town was posted all over with placards, which I had also observed stuck upon trees and rocks by the roadside as I traveled over the mountains. They were to this effect: –

"WAR! WAR!! WAR!!!

The celebrated Bull-killing Bear,

GENERAL SCOTT,

will fight a Bull on Sunday the 15th inst.,
at 2 p.m., at Moquelumne Hill.

"The Bear will be chained with a twenty-foot chain in the middle of the arena. The Bull will be perfectly wild, young, of the Spanish breed, and the best that can be found in the country. The Bull's horns will be of their natural length, and '*not sawed off to prevent accidents.*' The Bull will be quite free in the arena, and not hampered in any way whatever."

The proprietors then went on to state that they had nothing to do with the humbugging which characterized the last fight, and begged confidently to assure the public that this would be the most splendid exhibition ever seen in the country.

I had often heard of these bull-and-bear fights as popular amusements in some parts of the State, but had never yet had an opportunity of witnessing them; so, on Sunday the 15th, I found myself walking up towards the arena, among a crowd of miners and others of all nations, to witness the performances of the redoubted General Scott.

The amphitheater was a roughly but strongly built wooden structure, un-covered of course; and the outer enclosure, which was of boards about ten feet high, was a hundred feet in diameter. The arena in the center was forty feet in diameter, and enclosed by a very strong five-barred fence. From the top of this rose tiers of seats, occupying the space between the arena and the outside enclosure.

As the appointed hour drew near, the company continued to arrive till the whole place was crowded ; while, to beguile the time till the business of the day should commence, two fiddlers – a white man and a gentleman of color – performed a variety of appropriate airs.

The scene was gay and brilliant, and was one which would have made a crowded opera-house appear gloomy and dull in comparison. The shelving bank of human beings which encircled the place was like a mass of bright flow-ers. The most conspicuous objects were the shirts of the miners, red, white, and blue being the fashionable colors, among which appeared bronzed and beard-ed faces under hats of every hue; revolvers and silver-handled bowie-knives glanced in the bright sunshine, and among the crowd were numbers of gay Mexican blankets, and red and blue French bonnets, while here and there the fair sex was represented by a few Mexican women in snowy-white dresses, puffing their cigaritas in delightful anticipation of the exciting scene which was to be enacted. Over the heads of the highest circle of spectators was seen mountain beyond mountain fading away in the distance, and on the green turf of the arena lay the great center of attraction, the hero of the day, General Scott.

He was, however, not yet exposed to public gaze, but was confined in his cage, a heavy wooden box lined with iron, with open iron bars on one side, which for the present was boarded over. From the center of the arena a chain led into the cage, and at the end of it no doubt the bear was to be found. Beneath the scaffolding on which sat the spectators were two pens, each con-taining a very handsome bull, showing evident signs of indignation at his con-finement. Here also was the bar, without which no place of public amusement would be complete.

There was much excitement among the crowd as to the result of the battle, as the bear had already killed several bulls; but an idea prevailed that in former fights the bulls had not had fair play, being tied by a rope to the bear, and having the tips of their horns sawed off. But on this occasion the bull was to have every advantage which could be given him; and he certainly had the good wishes of the spectators, though the bear was considered such a successful and experienced bull-fighter that the betting was all in his favor. Some of my neighbors gave it as their opinion, that there was "nary bull in Calaforny as could whip that bar."

At last, after a final tattoo had been beaten on a gong to make the stragglers hurry up the hill, preparations were made for beginning the fight.

The bear made his appearance before the public in a very bearish manner. His cage ran upon very small wheels, and some bolts having been slipped connected with the face of it, it was dragged out of the ring, when, as his chain only allowed him to come within a foot or two of the fence, the General was rolled out upon the ground all of a heap, and very much against his inclination apparently, for he made violent efforts to regain his cage as it disappeared. When he saw that was hopeless, he floundered halfway round the ring at the length of his chain, and commenced to tear up the earth with his fore-paws. He was a grizzly bear of pretty large size, weighing about twelve hundred pounds.

The next thing to be done was to introduce the bull. The bars between his pen and the arena were removed, while two or three men stood ready to put them up again as soon as he should come out. But he did not seem to like the prospect, and was not disposed to move till pretty sharply poked up from behind, when, making a furious dash at the red flag which was being waved in front of the gate, he found himself in the ring face to face with General Scott.

The General, in the meantime, had scraped a hole for himself two or three inches deep, in which he was lying down. This, I was told by those who had seen his performances before, was his usual fighting attitude.

The bull was a very beautiful animal, of a dark purple color marked with white. His horns were regular and sharp, and his coat was as smooth and glossy as a racer's. He stood for a moment taking a survey of the bear, the ring, and the crowds of people; but not liking the appearance of things in general, he wheeled round, and made a splendid dash at the bars, which had already been put up between him and his pen, smashing through them with as much ease as the man in the circus leaps through a hoop of brown paper. This was only losing time, however, for he had to go in and fight, and might as well have done so at once. He was accordingly again persuaded to enter the arena, and a perfect barricade of bars and boards was erected to prevent his making another retreat. But this time he had made up his mind to fight; and after looking steadily at the bear for a few minutes as if taking aim at him, he put down his head and charged furiously at him across the arena. The bear received him crouching down as low as he could, and though one could hear the bump of the bull's head and horns upon his ribs, he was quick enough to seize the bull by the nose before he could retreat. This spirited commencement of the battle on the part of the bull was hailed with uproarious applause; and by having shown such pluck, he had gained more than ever the sympathy of the people.

In the meantime, the bear, lying on his back, held the bull's nose firmly between his teeth, and embraced him round the neck with his fore-paws, while the bull made the most of his opportunities in stamping on the bear with his hind-feet. At last the General became exasperated at such treatment, and shook the bull savagely by the nose, when a promiscuous scuffle ensued, which resulted in the bear throwing his antagonist to the ground with his fore-paws.

For this feat the bear was cheered immensely, and it was thought that, having the bull down, he would make short work of him; but apparently wild beasts do not tear each other to pieces quite so easily as is generally supposed, for neither the bear's teeth nor his long claws seemed to have much effect on the hide of the bull, who soon regained his feet, and, disengaging himself, retired to the other side of the ring, while the bear again crouched down in his hole.

Neither of them seemed to be very much the worse of the encounter, excepting that the bull's nose had rather a ragged and bloody appearance; but after standing a few minutes, steadily eyeing the General, he made another rush at him. Again poor bruin's ribs resounded, but again he took the bull's nose into chancery, having seized him just as before. The bull, however, quickly disengaged himself, and was making off, when the General, not wishing to part with him so soon, seized his hind-foot between his teeth, and, holding on by his paws as well, was thus dragged round the ring before he quitted his hold.

This round terminated with shouts of delight from the excited spectators, and it was thought that the bull might have a chance after all. He had been severely punished, however; his nose and lips were a mass of bloody shreds, and he lay down to recover himself. But he was not allowed to rest very long, being poked up with sticks by men outside, which made him very savage. He made several feints to charge them through the bars, which, fortunately, he did not attempt, for he could certainly have gone through them as easily as he had before broken into his pen. He showed no inclination to renew the combat; but by goading him, and waving a red flag over the bear, he was eventually worked up to such a state of fury as to make another charge. The result was exactly the same as before, only that when the bull managed to get up after being thrown, the bear still had hold of the skin of his back.

In the next round both parties fought more savagely than ever, and the advantage was rather in favor of the bear: the bull seemed to be quite used up, and to have lost all chance of victory.

The conductor of the performances then mounted the barrier, and, addressing the crowd, asked them if the bull had not had fair play, which was unanimously allowed. He then stated that he knew there was not a bull in California which the General could not whip, and that for two hundred dollars he would let in the other bull, and the three should fight it out till one or all were killed.

This proposal was received with loud cheers, and two or three men going round with hats soon collected, in voluntary contributions, the required amount. The people were intensely excited and delighted with the sport, and double the sum would have been just as quickly raised to insure a continuance of the scene. A man sitting next to me, who was a connoisseur in bear-fights, and passionately fond of the amusement, informed me that this was "the finest fight ever fit in the country."

The second bull was equally handsome as the first, and in as good condition. On entering the arena, and looking around him, he seemed to understand the state of affairs at once. Glancing from the bear lying on the ground to the other bull standing at the opposite side of the ring, with drooping head and bloody nose, he seemed to divine at once that the bear was their common enemy, and rushed at him full tilt. The bear, as usual, pinned him by the nose; but this bull did not take such treatment so quietly as the other: struggling violently, he soon freed himself, and, wheeling round as he did so, he caught the bear on the hind-quarters and knocked him over; while the other bull, who had been quietly watching the proceedings, thought this a good opportunity to pitch in also, and rushing up, he gave the bear a dig in the ribs on the other side before he had time to recover himself. The poor General between the two did not know what to do, but struck out. blindly with his fore-paws with such a suppliant pitiable look that I thought this the most disgusting part of the whole exhibition.

After another round or two with the fresh bull, it was evident that he was no match for the bear, and it was agreed to conclude the performances. The bulls were then shot to put them out of pain, and the company dispersed, all apparently satisfied that it had been a very splendid fight.

The reader can form his own opinion as to the character of an exhibition such as I have endeavored to describe. For my own part, I did not at first find the actual spectacle so disgusting as I had expected I should; for as long as the animals fought with spirit, they might have been supposed to be following their natural instincts; but when the bull had to be urged and goaded on to return to the charge, the cruelty of the whole proceeding was too apparent; and when the two bulls at once were let in upon the bear, all idea of sport or fair play was at an end, and it became a scene which one would rather have prevented than witnessed.

In these bull-and-bear fights the bull sometimes kills the bear at the first charge, by plunging his horns between the ribs, and striking a vital part. Such was the fate of General Scott in the next battle he fought, a few weeks afterwards; but it is seldom that the bear kills the bull outright, his misery being in most cases ended by a rifle-ball when he can no longer maintain the combat.

I took a sketch of the General the day after the battle. He was in the middle of the now deserted arena, and was in a particularly savage humor. He seemed to consider my intrusion on his solitude as a personal insult, for he growled most savagely, and stormed about in his cage, even pulling at the iron bars in his efforts to get out. I could not help thinking what a pretty mess he would have made of me if he had succeeded in doing so; but I regarded with peculiar satisfaction the massive architecture of his abode; and, taking a seat a few feet from him, I lighted my pipe, and waited till he should quiet down into an attitude, which he soon did, though very sulkily, when he saw that he could not help himself.

He did not seem to be much the worse for the battle, having but one wound, and that appeared to be only skin deep.

Such a bear as this, alive, was worth about fifteen hundred dollars. The method of capturing them is a service of considerable danger, and requires a great deal of labor and constant watching.

A spot is chosen in some remote part of the mountains, where it has been ascertained that bears are pretty numerous. Here a species of cage is built, about twelve feet square and six feet high, constructed of pine logs, and fastened after the manner of a log cabin. This is suspended between two trees, six or seven feet from the ground, and inside is hung a huge piece of beef, communicating by a string with a trigger, so contrived that the slightest tug at the beef draws the trigger, and down comes the trap, which has more the appearance of a log cabin suspended in the air than anything else. A regular locomotive cage, lined with iron, has also to be taken to the spot, to be kept in readiness for bruin's accommodation, for the pine log trap would not hold him long; he would soon eat and tear his way out of it. The enterprising bear-catchers have therefore to remain in the neighborhood, and keep a sharp lookout.

Removing the bear from the trap to the cage is the most dangerous part of the business. One side of the trap is so contrived as to admit of being opened or removed, and the cage is drawn up alongside, with the door also open, when the bear has to be persuaded to step into his new abode, in which he travels down to the more populous parts of the country, to fight bulls for the amusement of the public.

CHAPTER XX

A MOUNTAIN OF GOLD

THE want of water was the great obstacle in the way of mining at Moquelumne Hill. As it stood so much higher than the surrounding country, there were no streams which could be introduced, and the only means of getting a constant supply was to bring the water from the Moquelumne River, which flowed past, three or four thousand feet below the diggings. In order to get the requisite elevation to raise the waters so far above their natural channel, it was found necessary to commence the canal some fifty or sixty miles up the river. The idea had been projected, but the execution of such a piece of work required more capital than could be raised at the moment; but the diggings at Moquelumne Hill were known to be so rich, as was also the tract of country through which the canal would pass, that the speculation was considered sure to be successful; and a company was not long after formed for the purpose of carrying out the undertaking, which amply repaid those embarked in it, and opened up a vast extent of new field for mining operations, by supplying water in places which otherwise could only have been worked for two or three months of the year.

This was only one of many such undertakings in California, some of which were even on a larger scale. The engineering difficulties were very great, from the rocky and mountainous nature of the country through which the canals were brought. Hollows and valleys were spanned at a great height by aqueducts, supported on graceful scaffoldings of pine logs, and precipitous mountains were girded by wooden flumes projecting from their rocky sides. Throughout the course of a canal, wherever water was wanted by miners, it was supplied to them at so much an inch, a sufficient quantity for a party of five or six men costing about seven dollars a day.

I remained a few days at Moquelumne Hill in a holey old canvas hotel, which freely admitted both wind and water; but in this respect it was not much worse than its neighbors. A French physician resided on the opposite side of the street in a tent not much larger than a sentry-box, on the front of which appeared the following promiscuous announcement, in letters as large as the space admitted –

"PHARMACIEN DE PARIS.

DRUGS AND MEDICINES.

BOTICA.

DOCTOR – DENTISTE.

COLD CREAM.

DESTRUCTION TO RATS.

MORT AUX SOURIS."

From Moquelumne I went to Volcano Diggings, a distance of eighteen miles, but which I lengthened to nearly thirty by losing my way in crossing an unfrequented part of the country where the trails were very indistinct.

The principal diggings at Volcano are in the banks of a gulch, called Soldiers' Gulch, from its having been first worked by United States' soldiers, and were of a peculiar nature, differing from any other diggings I had seen, inasmuch as, though they had been worked to a depth of forty or fifty feet from the surface, they had been equally rich from top to bottom, and as yet no bed-rock had been reached. It was seldom such a depth of pay-dirt was found. The gold was usually only found within a few feet of the bottom, but in this case the stiff clay soil may have retained the gold, and prevented its settling down so readily as through sand or gravel. The clay was so stiff that it was with difficulty it could be washed, and lately the miners had taken to boiling it in large boilers, which was found to dissolve it very quickly.

To mineralogists I should think that this is the most interesting spot in the mines, from the great variety of curious stones found in large quantities in the diggings. One kind is found, about the size of a man's head, which when broken appears veined with successive brightly-colored layers round a beautifully-crystallized cavity in the center, the whole being enveloped in a rough outside crust an inch in thickness. The colors are more various and the veins closer together than those of a Scotch pebble, and the stone itself is more flinty and opaque. Quantities of lava were also found here, and masses of limestone rock appeared above the surface of the ground.

This place lay north of Moquelumne Hill, and might be called the most southern point of the northern mines.

Between the scenery of the northern mines and that of the south there is a very marked difference, both in the exterior formation of the country, and in the kind of trees with which it is wooded. In both the surface of the country is smooth – that is to say, there is an absence of ruggedness of detail – the mountains appear to have been smoothed down by the action of water; but, both north and south, the country as a whole is rough in the extreme, the mountain sides, as well as the table-lands, being covered with swellings, and deeply indented by ravines. An acre of level land is hardly to be found. The difference, however, exists in this, that in the north the mountains themselves, and every little swelling upon them, are of a conical form, while in the south they are all more circular. The mountains spread themselves out in hemispherical projections one beyond another; and in many parts of the country are found groups of eminences of the same form, and as symmetrical as if they had been shaped by artificial means.

There is just as much symmetry in the conical forms of the northern mines, but they appear more natural, and the pyramidal tops of the pine trees are quite in keeping with the outlines of the country which they cover; and it is remarkable that where the conical formation ceases, there also the pine ceases to be the principal tree of the country. There are pines, and plenty of them, in the southern mines, but the country is chiefly wooded with various kinds of oaks, and other trees of still more rounded shape, with only here and there a solitary pine towering above them to break the monotony of the curvilinear outline.

As might be expected from this circular formation, the rivers in the south do not follow such a sharp zigzag course as in the north ; they take wider sweeps : the mountains are not so steep, and the country generally is not so rough. In fact, there is scarcely any camp in the southern mines which is not accessible by wheeled vehicles.

Besides this great change in the appearance of the country, one could not fail to observe also, in traveling south, the equally marked difference in the inhabitants. In the north, one saw occasionally some straggling Frenchmen and other European foreigners, here and there a party of Chinamen, and a few Mexicans engaged in driving mules, but the total number of foreigners was very small: the population was almost entirely composed of Americans, and of these the Missourians and other western men formed a large proportion.

The southern mines, however, were full of all sorts of people. There were many villages peopled nearly altogether by Mexicans, others by Frenchmen; in some places there were parties of two or three hundred Chilians forming a community of their own. The Chinese camps were very numerous; and besides all such distinct colonies of foreigners, every town of the southern mines contained a very large foreign population. The Americans, however, were of course greatly the majority, but even among them one remarked the comparatively small number of Missourians and such men, who are so conspicuous in the north.

There was still another difference in a very important feature – in fact, the most important of all – the gold. The gold of the northern mines is generally flaky, in exceedingly small thin scales; that of the south is coarse gold, round and "chunky." The rivers of the north afford very rich diggings, while in the south they are comparatively poor, and the richest deposits are found in the flats and other surface-diggings on the highlands.

In the north there were no such canvas towns as Moquelumne Hill. Log cabins and frame houses were the rule, and canvas the exception; while in the southern mines the reverse was the case, excepting in some of the larger towns.

It is singular that the State should be thus divided by nature into two sections of country so unlike in many important points; and that the people inhabiting them should help to heighten the contrast is equally curious, though it may possibly be accounted for by supposing that Frenchmen, Mexicans, and other foreigners, preferred the less wild-looking country and more temperate winters of the southern mines, while the absence of the Western backwoodsmen in the south was owing to the fact that they came to the country across the plains by a route which entered the State near Placerville. Their natural instinct would have led them to continue on a westward course, but this would have brought them down on the plains of the Sacramento Valley, where there is no gold; so, thinking that sunset was more north than south, and knowing also there was more western land in that direction, they spread all over the northern part of the State, till they connected themselves with the settlements in Oregon.

In the neighborhood of Volcano there is a curious cave, which I went to visit with two or three miners. The entrance to it is among some large rocks on the bank of the creek, and is a hole in the ground just large enough to admit of a man's dropping himself into it lengthways. The descent is perpendicular between masses of rock for about twenty feet, and is accomplished by means of a rope; the passage then takes a slanting direction for the same distance, and lands one in a chamber thirty or forty feet wide, the roof and sides of which are composed of groups of immense stalactites. The height varies very much, some of the stalactites reaching within four or five feet of the ground; and there are several small openings in the walls, just large enough to creep through, which lead into similar chambers. We brought a number of pieces of candle with us, with which we lighted up the whole place. The effect was very fine; the stalactites, being tinged with pale blue, pink, and green, were grouped in all manner of grotesque forms, in one corner giving an exact representation of a small petrified waterfall.

Coming down into the cave was easy enough, the force of gravity being the only motive power, but to get out again we found rather a difficult operation. The sides of the passage were smooth, offering no resting-place for the foot; and the only means of progression was to haul oneself up by the rope hand over hand – rather hard work in the inclined part of the passage, which was so confined that one could hardly use one's arms.

At the hotel I stayed at here I found very agreeable company; most of the party were Texans, and were doctors and lawyers by profession, though miners by practice. For the first time since I had been in the mines I here saw whist played, the more favorite games being poker, euchre, and all-fours, or "seven up," as it is there called. There were also some enthusiastic chess-players among the party, who had manufactured a set of men with their bowie-knives; so what with whist and chess every night, I fancied I had got into a civilized country.

The day before I had intended leaving this village, some Mexicans came into the camp with a lot of mules, which they sold so cheap as to excite suspicions that they had not come by them honestly. In the evening it was discovered that they were stolen animals, and several men started in pursuit of the Mexicans; but they had already been gone some hours, and there was little chance of their being overtaken. I waited a day, in hopes of seeing them brought back and hung by process of Lynch law, which would certainly have been their fate had they been caught; but, fortunately for them, they succeeded in making good their escape. The men who had gone in chase returned empty-handed, so I set out again for Moquelumne Hill on my way south.

I was put upon a shorter trail than the one by which I had come from there; and though it was very dim and little traveled, I managed to keep it: and passing on my way through a small camp called Clinton, inhabited principally by Chilians and Frenchmen, I struck the Moquelumne River at a point several miles above the bridge where I had crossed it before.

The river was still much swollen with the rains and snow of winter, and the mode of crossing was not by any means inviting. Two very small canoes lashed together served as a ferry-boat, in which the passenger hauled himself across the river by means of a rope made fast to a tree on either bank, the force of the current keeping the canoes bow on. When I arrived here, this contrivance happened to be on the opposite side, where I saw a solitary tent which seemed to be inhabited, but I hallooed in vain for some one to make his appearance and act as ferryman. There seemed to be a trail from the tent leading up the river ; so, following that direction for about half a mile, I found a party of miners at work on the other side – one of whom, in the obliging spirit universally met with in the mines, immediately left his work and came down to ferry me across.

On the side I was on was an old race about eighteen feet wide, through which the waters rushed rapidly past. A pile of rocks prevented the boat from crossing this, so there was nothing for it but to wade. Some stones had been thrown in, forming a sort of submarine stepping-stones, and lessening the depth to about three feet; but they were smooth and slippery, and the water was so intensely cold, and the current so strong, that I found the long pole which the man told me to take a very necessary assistance in making the passage. On reaching the canoes, and being duly enjoined to be careful in getting in and to keep perfectly still, we crossed the main body of the river ; and very ticklish work it was, for the waves ran high, and the utmost care was required to avoid being swamped. We got across safe enough, when my friend put me under additional obligations by producing a bottle of brandy from his tent and asking me to "liquor," which I did with a great deal of pleasure, as the water was still gurgling and squeaking in my boots, and was so cold that I felt as if I were half immersed in ice-cream.

After climbing the steep mountain side and walking a few miles farther, I arrived at Moquelumne Hill, having, in the course of my day's journey, gradually passed from the pine-tree country into such scenery as I have already described as characterizing the southern mines.

I went on the next morning to San Andres by a road which wound through beautiful little valleys, still fresh and green, and covered with large patches of flowers. In one long gulch through which I passed, about two hundred Chilians were at work washing the dirt, panful by panful, in their large flat wooden dishes. This is a very tedious process, and a most unprofitable expenditure of labor; but Mexicans, Chilians, and other Spanish Americans, most obstinately adhered to their old-fashioned primitive style, although they had the example before them of all the rest of the world continually making improvements in the method of abstracting the gold, whereby time was saved and labor rendered tenfold more effective.

I soon after met a troop of forty or fifty Indians galloping along the road, most of them riding double – the gentlemen having their squaws seated behind them. They were dressed in the most grotesque style, and the clothing seemed to be pretty generally diffused throughout the crowd. One man wore a coat, another had the remains of a shirt and one boot, while another was fully equipped in an old hat and a waistcoat: but the most conspicuous and generally worn articles of costume were the colored cotton handkerchiefs with which they bandaged up their heads. As they passed they looked down upon me with an air of patronizing condescension, saluting me with the usual "wally wally," in just such a tone that I could imagine them saying to themselves at the same time, "Poor devil! he's only a white man."

They all had their bows and arrows, and some were armed besides with old guns and rifles, but they were doubtless only going to pay a friendly visit to some neighboring tribe. They were evidently anticipating a pleasant time, for I never before saw Indians exhibiting such boisterous good humor.

A few miles in from San Andres I crossed the Calaveras, which is here a wide river, though not very deep. There was neither bridge nor ferry, but fortunately some Mexicans had camped with a train of pack-mules not far from the place, and from them I got an animal to take me across.

CHAPTER XXI

IN LIGHTER MOOD

IF one can imagine the booths and penny theaters on a race-course left for a year or two till they are tattered and torn, and blackened with the weather, he will have some idea of the appearance of San Andres. It was certainly the most out-at-elbows and disorderly looking camp I had yet seen in the country.

The only wooden house was the San Andres Hotel, and here I took up my quarters. It was kept by a Missourian doctor, and being the only establishment of the kind in the place, was quite full. We sat down forty or fifty at the table-d'hôte.

The Mexicans formed by far the most numerous part of the population. The streets – for there were two streets at right angles to each other – and the gambling-rooms were crowded with them, loafing about in their blankets doing nothing. There were three gambling-rooms in the village, all within a few steps of each other, and in each of them was a Mexican band playing guitars, harps and flutes. Of course, one heard them all three at once, and as each played a different tune, the effect, as may be supposed, was very pleasing.

The sleeping apartments in the hotel itself were all full, and I had to take a cot in a tent on the other side of the street, which was a sort of colony of the parent establishment. It was situated between two gambling-houses, one of which was kept by a Frenchman, who, whenever his musicians stopped to take breath or brandy, began a series of doleful airs on an old barrel-organ. Till how late in the morning they kept it up I cannot say, but whenever I happened to awake in the middle of the night, my ears were still greeted by these sweet sounds.

There was one canvas structure, differing but little in appearance from the rest, excepting that a small wooden cross surmounted the roof over the door. This was a Roman Catholic church. The only fitting up of any kind in the interior was the altar, which occupied the farther end from the door, and was decorated with as much display as circumstances admitted, being draped with the commonest kind of colored cotton cloths, and covered with candlesticks, some brass, some of wood, but most of them regular California candlesticks – old claret and champagne bottles, arranged with due regard to the numbers and grouping of those bearing the different ornamental labels of St. Julien, Medoc, and other favorite brands.

I went in on Sunday morning while service was going on, and found a number of Mexican women occupying the space nearest the altar, the rest of the church being filled with Mexicans, who all maintained an appearance of respectful devotion. Two or three Americans, who were present out of curiosity, naturally kept in the background near the door, excepting two great hulking fellows who came swaggering in, and jostled their way through the crowd of Mexicans, making it evident, from their demeanor, that their only object was to show their supreme contempt for the congregation, and for the whole proceedings. Presently, however, the entire congregation went down on their knees, leaving these two awkward louts standing in the middle of the church as sheepish-looking a pair of asses as one could wish to see. They were hemmed in by the crowd of kneeling Mexicans – there was no retreat for them, and it was extremely gratifying to see how quickly their bullying impudence was taken out of them, and that it brought upon them a punishment which they evidently felt so acutely. The officiating priest, who was a Frenchman, afterwards gave a short sermon in Spanish, which was listened to attentively, and the people then dispersed to spend the remainder of the day in the gambling-rooms.

The same afternoon a drove of wild California cattle passed through the camp, and as several head were being drafted out, I had an opportunity of witnessing a specimen of the extraordinary skill of the Mexican in throwing the lasso. Galloping in among the herd, and swinging the *riata* round his head, he singles out the animal he wishes to secure, and, seldom missing his aim, he throws his lasso so as to encircle its horns. As soon as he sees that he has accomplished this, he immediately wheels round his horse, who equally well understands his part of the business, and stands prepared to receive the shock when the bull shall have reached the length of the rope. In his endeavors to escape, the bull then gallops round in a circle, of which the center is the horse, moving slowly round, and leaning over with one of his fore-feet planted well out, so as to enable him to hold his own in the struggle. An animal, if he is not very wild, may be taken along in this way, but generally another man rides up behind him, and throws his lasso so as to catch him by the hind-leg. This requires great dexterity and precision, as the lasso has to be thrown in such a way that the bull shall put his foot into the noose before it reaches the ground. Having an animal secured by the horns and a hind-foot, they have him completely under command; one man drags him along by the horns, while the other steers him by the hind-leg. If he gets at all obstreperous, however, they throw him, and drag him along the ground.

The lasso is about twenty yards long, made of strips of rawhide plaited, and the end is made fast to the high horn which sticks up in front of the Mexican saddle ; the strain is all upon the saddle, and the girth, which is consequently immensely strong, and lashed up very tight. The Mexican saddles are well adapted for this sort of work, and the Mexicans are unquestionably splendid horsemen, though they ride too long for English ideas, the knee being hardly bent at all.

Two of the Vigilance Committee rode over from Moquelumne Hill next morning, to get the Padre to return with them to confess a Mexican whom they were going to hang that afternoon, for having cut into a tent and stolen several hundred dollars. I unfortunately did not know anything about it till it was so late that had I gone there I should not have been in time to see the execution: not that I cared for the mere spectacle of a poor wretch hanging by the neck, but I was extremely desirous of witnessing the ceremonies of an execution by Judge Lynch; and though I was two or three years cruising about in the mines, I never had the luck to be present on such an occasion. I particularly regretted having missed this one, as, from the accounts I afterwards heard of it, it must have been well worth seeing.

The Mexican was at first suspected of the robbery, from his own folly in going the very next morning to several stores, and spending an unusual amount of money on clothes, revolvers, and so on. When once suspected, he was seized without ceremony, and on his person was found a quantity of gold specimens and coin, along with the purse itself, all of which were identified by the man who had been robbed. With such evidence, of course, he was very soon convicted, and was sentenced to be hung. On being told of the decision of the jury, and that he was to be hung the next day, he received the information as a piece of news which no way concerned him, merely shrugging his shoulders and saying, *"'stá bueno,"* in the tone of utter indifference in which the Mexicans generally use the expression, requesting at the same time that the priest might be sent for.

When he was led out to be hanged, he walked along with as much nonchalance as any of the crowd, and when told at the place of execution that he might say whatever he had to say, he gracefully took off his hat, and blowing a farewell whiff of smoke through his nostrils, he threw away the cigarita he had been smoking, and, addressing the crowd, he asked forgiveness for the numerous acts of villainy to which he had already confessed, and politely took leave of the world with *"Adios, caballeros."* He was then run up to a butcher's derrick by the Vigilance Committee, all the members having hold of the rope, and thus sharing the responsibility of the act.

A very few days after I left San Andres, a man was lynched for a robbery committed very much in the same manner. But if stringent measures were wanted in one part of the country more than another, it was in such flimsy canvas towns as these two places, where there was such a population of worthless Mexican *canaille,* who were too lazy to work for an honest livelihood.

I went on in a few days to Angel's Camp, a village some miles farther south, composed of well-built wooden houses, and altogether a more respectable and civilized-looking place than San Andres. The inhabitants were nearly all Americans, which no doubt accounted for the circumstance.

While walking round the diggings in the afternoon, I came upon a Chinese camp in a gulch near the village. About a hundred Chinamen had here pitched their tents on a rocky eminence by the side of their diggings. When I passed they were at dinner or supper, and had all the curious little pots and pans and other "fixins" which I had seen in every Chinese camp, and were eating the same dubious-looking articles which excite in the mind of an outside barbarian a certain degree of curiosity to know what they are composed of, but not the slightest desire to gratify it by the sense of taste. I was very hospitably asked to partake of the good things, which I declined; but as I would not eat, they insisted on my drinking, and poured me out a pannikin full of brandy, which they seemed rather surprised I did not empty. They also gave me some of their cigaritas, the tobacco of which is aromatic, and very pleasant to smoke, though wrapped up in too much paper.

- 199 -

The Chinese invariably treated in the same hospitable manner any one who visited their camps, and seemed rather pleased than otherwise at the interest and curiosity excited by their domestic arrangements.

In the evening, a ball took place at the hotel I was staying at, where, though none of the fair sex were present, dancing was kept up with great spirit for several hours. For music the company were indebted to two amateurs, one of whom played the fiddle and the other the flute. It is customary in the mines for the fiddler to take the responsibility of keeping the dancers all right. He goes through the dance orally, and at the proper intervals his voice is heard above the music and the conversation, shouting loudly his directions to the dancers, "Lady's chain," "Set to your partner," with other dancing-school words of command ; and after all the legitimate figures of the dance had been performed, out of consideration for the thirsty appetites of the dancers, and for the good of the house, he always announced, in a louder voice than usual, the supplementary finale of "Promenade to the bar, and treat your partners." This injunction, as may be supposed, was most rigorously obeyed, and the "ladies," after their fatigues, tossed off their cocktails and lighted their pipes just as in more polished circles they eat ice-creams and sip lemonade.

It was a strange sight to see a party of long-bearded men, in heavy boots and flannel shirts, going through all the steps and figures of the dance with so much spirit, and often with a great deal of grace, hearty enjoyment depicted on their dried-up sunburned faces, and revolvers and bowie-knives glancing in their belts; while a crowd of the same rough-looking customers stood around, cheering them on to greater efforts, and occasionally dancing a step or two quietly on their own account. Dancing parties such as these were very common, especially in small camps where there was no such general resort as the gambling-saloons of the larger towns. Wherever a fiddler could be found to play, a dance was got up. Waltzes and polkas were not so much in fashion as the lancers which appeared to be very generally known, and, besides, gave plenty of exercise to the light fantastic toes of the dancers ; for here men danced, as they did everything else, with all their might; and to go through the lancers in such company was a very severe gymnastic exercise. The absence of ladies was a difficulty which was very easily overcome, by a simple arrangement whereby it was understood that every gentleman who had a patch on a certain part of his inexpressibles should be considered a lady for the time being. These patches were rather fashionable, and were usually large squares of canvas, showing brightly on a dark ground, so that the "ladies" of the party were as conspicuous as if they had been surrounded by the usual quantity of white muslin.

A *pas seul* sometimes varied the entertainment. I was present on one occasion at a dance at Foster's Bar, when, after several sets of the lancers had been danced, a young Scotch boy, who was probably a runaway apprentice from a Scotch ship – for the sailor-boy air was easily seen through the thick coating of flour which he had acquired in his present occupation in the employment of a French baker – was requested to dance the Highland fling for the amusement of the company. The music was good, and he certainly did justice to it; dancing most vigorously for about a quarter of an hour, shouting and yelling as he was cheered by the crowd, and going into it with all the fury of a wild savage in a war-dance. The spectators were uproarious in their applause. I daresay many of them never saw such an exhibition before. The youngster was looked upon as a perfect prodigy, and if he had drunk with all the men who then sought the honor of "treating" him, he would never have lived to tread another measure.

CHAPTER XXII

SONORA AND THE MXICANS

FROM Angel's Camp I went on a few miles to Carson's Creek, on which there was a small camp, lying at the foot of a hill, which was named after the same man. On its summit a quartz vein cropped out in large masses to the height of thirty or forty feet, looking at a distance like the remains of a solid wall of fortification. It had only been worked a few feet from the surface, but already an incredible amount of gold had been taken out of it.

Every place in the mines had its traditions of wonderful events which had occurred in the olden times; that is to say, as far back as "'49" – for three years in such a fast country were equal to a century; and at this place the tradition was, that, when the quartz vein was first worked, the method adopted was to put in a blast, and, after the explosion, to go round with handbaskets and pick up the pieces. I believe this was only a slight exaggeration of the truth, for at this particular part of the vein there had been found what is there called a "pocket," a spot not more than a few feet in extent, where lumps of gold in unusual quantities lie imbedded in the rock. No systematic plan had been followed in opening the mine with a view to the proper working of it; but several irregular excavations had been made in the rock wherever the miners had found the gold most plentiful. For nearly a year it had not been worked at all, in consequence of several disputes as to the ownership of the claims; and in the meantime the lawyers were the only parties who were making anything out of it.

On the other side of the hill, however, was a claim on the same vein, which was in undisputed possession of a company of Americans, who employed a number of Mexicans to work it, under the direction of an experienced old Mexican miner. They had three shafts sunk in the solid rock, in a line with each other, to the depth of two hundred feet, from which galleries extended at different points, where the gold-bearing quartz was found in the greatest abundance. No ropes or windlasses were used for descending the shafts; but at every thirty feet or so there was a sort of step or platform, resting on which was a pole with a number of notches cut all down one side of it; and the rock excavated in the various parts of the mine was brought up in leathern sacks on the shoulders of men who had to make the ascent by climbing a succession of these poles. The quartz was then conveyed on pack-mules down to the river by a circuitous trail, which had been cut on the steep side of the mountain, and was there ground in the primitive Mexican style in "rasters." The whole operation seemed to be conducted at a most unnecessary expenditure of labor; but the mine was rich, and, even worked in this way, it yielded largely to the owners.

Numerous small wooden crosses were placed throughout the mine, in niches cut in the rock for their reception, and each separate part of the mine was named after a saint who was supposed to take those working in it under his immediate protection. The day before I visited the place had been some saint's day, and the Mexicans, who of course had made a holiday of it, had employed themselves in erecting, on the side of the hill over the mine, a large cross, about ten feet high, and had completely clothed it with the beautiful wild-flowers which grew around in the greatest profusion. In fact, it was a gigantic cruciform nosegay, the various colors of which were arranged with a great deal of taste.

This mine is on the great quartz vein which traverses the whole State of California. It has a direction northeast and southwest, perfectly true by compass; and from many points where an extensive view of the country is obtained, it can be distinctly traced for a great distance as it "crops out" here and there, running up a hillside like a colossal stone wall, and then disappearing for many miles, till, true to its course, it again shows itself crowning the summit of some conical-shaped mountain, and appearing in the distant view like so many short white strokes, all forming parts of the same straight line.

The general belief was that at one time all the gold in the country had been imbedded in quartz, which, being decomposed by the action of the elements, had set the gold at liberty, to be washed away with other debris, and to find a resting-place for itself. Rich diggings were frequently found in the neighborhood of quartz veins, but not invariably so, for different local causes must have operated to assist the gold in traveling from its original starting-point.

As a general rule, the richest diggings seemed to be in the rivers at those points where the eddies gave the gold an opportunity of settling down instead of being borne further along by the current, or in those places on the highlands where, owing to the flatness of the surface or the want of egress, the debris had been retained while the water ran off; for the first idea one formed from the appearance of the mountains was, that they had been very severely washed down, but that there had been sufficient earth and debris to cover their nakedness, and to modify the sharp angularity of their formation.

I crossed the Stanislaus – a large river, which does not at any part of its course afford very rich diggings – by a ferry which was the property of two or three Englishmen, who had lived for many years in the Sandwich Islands. The force of the current was here very strong, and by an ingenious contrivance was made available for working the ferry. A stout cable was stretched across the river, and traversing on this were two blocks, to which were made fast the head and stern of a large scow. By lengthening the stem line, the scow assumed a diagonal position, and, under the influence of the current and of the opposing force of the cable, she traveled rapidly across the river, very much on the same principle on which a ship holds her course with the wind abeam.

Ferries or bridges, on much-traveled roads, were very valuable property. They were erected at those points on the rivers where the mountain on each side offered a tolerably easy ascent, and where, in consequence, a line of travel had commenced. But very frequently more easy routes were found than the one first adopted; opposition ferries were then started, and the public got the full benefit of the competition between the rival proprietors, who sought to secure the traveling custom by improving the roads which led to their respective ferries.

In opposition to this ferry on the Stanislaus, another had been started a few miles down the river; so the Englishmen, in order to keep up the value of their property and maintain the superiority of their route, had made a good wagon-road, more than a mile in length, from the river to the summit of the mountain.

After ascending by this road and traveling five or six miles over a rolling country covered with magnificent oak trees, and in many places fenced in and under cultivation, I arrived at Sonora, the largest town of the southern mines. It consisted of a single street, extending for upwards of a mile along a sort of hollow between gently sloping hills. Most of the houses were of wood, a few were of canvas, and one or two were solid buildings of sun-dried bricks. The lower end of the town was very peculiar in appearance as compared with the prevailing style of California architecture. Ornament seemed to have been as much consulted as utility, and the different tastes of the French and Mexican builders were very plainly seen in the high-peaked overhanging roofs, the staircases outside the houses, the corridors round each story, and other peculiarities; giving the houses – which were painted, moreover, buff and pale blue – quite an old-fashioned air alongside of the staring white rectangular fronts of the American houses. There was less pretence and more honesty about them than about the American houses, for many of the latter were all front, and gave the idea of a much better house than the small rickety clapboard or canvas concern which was concealed behind it. But these façades were useful as well as ornamental, and were intended to support the large signs, which conveyed an immense deal of useful information. Some small stores, in fact, seemed bursting with intelligence, and were broken out all over with short spasmodic sentences in English, French, Spanish, and German, covering all the available space save the door, and presenting to the passer-by a large amount of desultory reading as to the nature of the property within and the price at which it could be bought. This, however, was not by any means peculiar to Sonora – it was the general style of thing throughout the country.

The Mexicans and the French also were very numerous, and there was an extensive assortment of other Europeans from all quarters, all of whom, save French, English, and "Eyetalians," are in California classed under the general denomination of Dutchmen, or more frequently "d – d Dutchmen," merely for the sake of euphony.

Sonora is situated in the center of an extremely rich mining country, more densely populated than any other part of the mines. In the neighborhood are a number of large villages, one of which, Columbia, only two or three miles distant, was not much inferior in size to Sonora itself. The place took its name from the men who first struck the diggings and camped on the spot – a party of miners from the state of Sonora in Mexico. The Mexicans discovered many of the richest diggings in the country – not altogether, perhaps, through good luck, for they had been gold-hunters all their lives, and may be supposed to have derived some benefit from their experience. They seldom, however, remained long in possession of rich diggings; never working with any vigor, they spent most of their time in the passive enjoyment of their cigaritas, or in playing monte, and were consequently very soon run over and driven off the field by the rush of more industrious and resolute men.

There were a considerable number of Mexicans to be seen at work round Sonora, but the most of those living in the town seemed to do nothing but bask in the sun and loaf about the gambling-rooms. How they managed to live was not very apparent, but they can live where another man would starve. I have no doubt they could subsist on cigaritas alone for several days at a time.

I got very comfortable quarters in one of the French hotels, of which there were several in the town, besides a number of good American houses; German restaurants, where lager beer was drunk by the gallon ; Mexican fondas, which had an exceedingly greasy look about them; and also a Chinese house, where everything was most scrupulously clean. In this latter place a Chinese woman, dressed in European style, sat behind the bar and served out drinkables to thirsty outside barbarians, while three Chinamen entertained them with celestial music from a drum something like the top of a skull covered with parchment and stuck upon three sticks, a guitar like a long stick with a knob at the end of it, and a sort of fiddle with two strings. I asked the Chinese landlord, who spoke a little English, if the woman was his wife. "Oh, no," he said, very indignantly, "only hired woman – China woman; hired her for show – that's all." Some of these Chinamen are pretty smart fellows, and this was one of them. The novelty of the "show," however, wore off in a few days, and the Chinawoman disappeared – probably went to show herself in other diggings.

One could live here in a way which seemed perfectly luxurious after cruising about the mountains among the small out-of-the-way camps; for, besides having a choice of good hotels, one could enjoy most of the comforts and conveniences of ordinary life; even ice-creams and sherry-cobblers were to be had, for snow was packed in on mules thirty or forty miles from the Sierra Nevada, and no one took even a cocktail without its being iced. But what struck me most as a sign of civilization, was seeing a drunken man, who was kicking up a row in the street, deliberately collared and walked off to the lock-up by a policeman. I never saw such a thing before in the mines, where the spectacle of drunken men rolling about the streets unmolested had become so familiar to me that I was almost inclined to think it an infringement of the individual liberty of the subject – or of the citizen, I should say – not to allow this hog of a fellow to sober himself in the gutter, or to drink himself into a state of quiescence if he felt so inclined. This policeman represented the whole police force in his own proper person, and truly he had no sinecure. He was not exactly like one of our own blue-bottles ; he was not such a stoical observer of passing events, nor so shut out from all social intercourse with his fellow-men. There was nothing to distinguish him from other citizens, except perhaps the unusual size of his revolver and bowie-knife; and his official dignity did not prevent him from mixing with the crowd and taking part in whatever amusement was going on.

The people here dressed better than was usual in other parts of the mines. On Sundays especially, when the town was thronged with miners, it was quite gay with the bright colors of the various costumes. There were numerous spec-imens of the genuine old miner to be met with – the miner of '49, whose pride it was to be clothed in rags and patches; but the prevailing fashion was to dress well; indeed there was a degree of foppery about many of the swells, who were got up in a most gorgeous manner. The weather was much too hot for any one to think of wearing a coat, but the usual style of dress was such as to appear quite complete without it; in fact, a coat would have concealed the most showy article of dress, which was a rich silk handkerchief, scarlet, crimson, orange, or some bright hue, tied loosely across the breast, and hanging over one shoulder like a shoulder belt. Some men wore flowers, feathers, or squirrel's tails in their hats; occasionally the beard was worn plaited and coiled up like a twist of tobacco, or was divided into three tails hanging down to the waist. One man, of original ideas, who had very long hair, brought it down on each side of the face, and tied it in a large bow-knot under his chin ; and many other eccentricities of this sort were indulged in. The numbers of Mexican women with their white dresses and sparkling black eyes were by no means an unpleasing addition to the crowd, of which the Mexicans themselves formed a conspicuous part in their variegated blankets and broad-brimmed hats. There were men in *bonnets rouges* and *bonnets bleus*, the cut of whose mustache and beard was of itself sufficient to distinguish them as Frenchmen; while here and there some forlorn individual exhibited himself in a black coat and a stove-pipe hat, looking like a bird of evil omen among a flock of such gay plumage.

CHAPTER XXIII

BULL FIGHTING

A COMPANY of Mexican bull-fighters were at this time performing in Sonora every Sunday afternoon. The amphitheater was a large well-built place, erected for the purpose on a small hill behind the street. The arena was about thirty yards in diameter, and enclosed in a very strong six-barred fence, gradually rising from which, all round, were several tiers of seats, shaded from the sun by an awning.

I took the first opportunity of witnessing the spectacle, and found a very large company assembled, among whom the Mexicans and Mexican women in their gay dresses figured conspicuously. A good band of music enlivened the scene till the appointed hour arrived, when the bull-fighters entered the arena. The procession was headed by a clown in a fantastic dress, who acted his part throughout the performances uncommonly well, cracking jokes with his friends among the audience, and singing comic songs. Next came four men on foot, all beautifully dressed in satin jackets and knee-breeches, slashed and embroidered with bright colors. Two horsemen, armed with lances, brought up the rear. After marching round the arena, they stationed themselves in their various places, one of the horsemen being at the side of the door by which the bull was to enter. The door was then opened, and the bull rushed in, the horseman giving him a poke with his lance as he passed, just to waken him up. The footmen were all waving their red flags to attract his attention, and he immediately charged at one of them; but, the man stepping gracefully aside at the proper moment, the bull passed on and found another red flag waiting for him, which he charged with as little success. For some time they played with the bull in this manner, hopping and skipping about before his horns with so much confidence, and such apparent ease, as to give one the idea that there was neither danger nor difficulty in dodging a wild bull. The bull did not charge so much as he butted, for, almost without changing his ground, he butted quickly several times in succession at the same man. The man, however, was always too quick for him, sometimes just drawing the flag across his face as he stepped aside, or vaulting over his horns and catching hold of his tail before he could turn round.

After this exhibition one of the horsemen endeavored to engage the attention of the bull, and when he charged, received him with the point of his lance on the back of the neck. In this position they struggled against each other, the horse pushing against the bull with all his force, probably knowing that that was his only chance. On one occasion the lance broke, when horse and rider seemed to be at the mercy of the bull, but as quick as lightning the footmen were fluttering their flags in his face and diverting his fury, while the horseman got another lance and returned to the charge.

Shortly afterwards the footmen laid aside their flags and proceeded to what is considered a more dangerous, and consequently more interesting, part of the performances. They lighted cigars, and were handed small pieces of wood, with a barbed point at one end and a squib at the other. Having lighted his squibs at his cigar, one of their number rushes up in front of the bull, shouting and stamping before him, as if challenging him to come on. The bull is not slow of putting down his head and making at him, when the man vaults nimbly over his horns, leaving a squib fizzing and cracking on each side of his neck. This makes the bull still more furious, but another man is ready for him, who plays him the same trick, and so they go on till his neck is covered with squibs. One of them then takes a large rosette, furnished in like manner with a sharp barbed point, and this, as the bull butts at him, he sticks in his forehead right between the eyes. Another man then engages the bull, and, while eluding his horns, removes the rosette from his forehead. This is considered a still more difficult feat, and was greeted with immense applause, the Mexican part of the audience screaming with delight.

The performers were all uncommonly well made, handsome men ; their tight dresses greatly assisted their appearance, and they moved with so much grace, and with such an expression on their countenance of pleasure and confidence, even while making their greatest efforts, that they might have been supposed to be going through the figures of a ballet on the stage, instead of risking death from the horns of a wild bull at every step they executed. During the latter part of the performance, being without their red flags, they were of course in greater danger; but it seemed to make no difference to them; they put a squib in each side of the bull's neck, while evading his attack, with as much apparent ease as they had dodged him from behind their red flags. Sometimes, indeed, when they were hard pressed, or when attacked by the bull so close to the barrier that they had no room to maneuver round him, they sprang over it in among the spectators.

The next thing in the program was riding the bull, and this was the most amusing scene of all. One of the horsemen lassoes him over the horns, and the other, securing him in his lasso by the hind-leg, trips him up, and throws him without the least difficulty. By keeping the lassoes taut, he is quite helpless. He is then girthed with a rope, and one of the performers, holding on by this gets astride of the prostrate bull in such a way as to secure his seat, when the animal rises. The lassoes are then cast off, when the bull immediately gets up, and, furious at finding a man on his back, plunges and kicks most desperately, jumping from side to side, and jerking himself violently in every way, as he vainly endeavors to bring his horns round so as to reach his rider. I never saw such horsemanship, if horsemanship it could be called; nor did I ever see a horse go through such contortions, or make such spasmodic bounds and leaps: but the fellow never lost his seat, he stuck to the bull as firm as a rock, though thrown about so violently that it seemed enough to jerk the head off his body. During this singular exhibition the spectators cheered and shouted most uproariously, and the bull was maddened to greater fury than ever by the footmen shaking their flags in his face, and putting more squibs on his neck. It seemed to be the grand climax; they had exhausted all means to infuriate the bull to the very utmost, and they were now braving him more audaciously than ever. Had any of them made a slip of the foot, or misjudged his distance but a hairbreadth, there would have been a speedy end of him; but fortunately no such mishap occurred, for the blind rage of the bull was impotent against their coolness and precision.

When the man riding the bull thought he had enough of it, he took an opportunity when the bull came near the outside of the arena, and hopped off his back on to the top of the barrier. A door was then opened, and the bull was allowed to depart in peace. Three or four more bulls in succession were fought in the same manner. The last of them was to have been killed with the sword; but he proved one of those sulky, treacherous animals who do not fight fair ; he would not put down his head and charge blindly at anything or everything, but only made a rush now and then, when he thought he had a sure chance. With a bull of this sort there is great danger, while with a furiously savage one there is none at all – so say the bull-fighters ; and after doing all they could, without success, to madden and irritate this sulky animal, he was removed, and another one was brought in, who had already shown a requisite amount of blind fury in his disposition.

A long straight sword was then handed to the *matador*, who, with his flag in his left hand, played with the bull for a little, evading several attacks till he got one to suit him, when, as he stepped aside from before the bull's horns, he plunged the sword into the back of his neck. Without a moan or a struggle the bull fell dead on the instant, coming down all of a heap, in such a way that it was evident that even before he fell he was dead. I have seen cattle butchered in every sort of way, but in none was the transition from life to death so instantaneous.

This was the grand feat of the day, and was thought to have been most beautifully performed. The spectators testified their delight by the most vociferous applause; the Mexican women waved their handkerchiefs, the Mexicans cheered and shouted, and threw their hats in the air, while the *matador* walked proudly round the arena, bowing to the people amid a shower of coin which his particular admirers in their enthusiasm bestowed upon him.

I one day, at some diggings a few miles from Sonora, came across a young fellow hard at work with his pick and shovel, whom I had met several times at Moquelumne Hill and other places. In the course of conversation he told me that he was tired of mining, and intended to practice his profession again; upon which I immediately set him down as either a lawyer or a doctor, there are such lots of them in the mines. I had the curiosity, however, to ask him what profession he belonged to, – "Oh," he said, "I am a magician, a necromancer, a conjuror!" The idea of a magician being reduced to the level of an ordinary mortal, and being obliged to resort to such a matter-of-fact way of making money as digging gold out of the earth, instead of conjuring it ready coined out of other men's pockets, appeared to me so very ridiculous that I could not help laughing at the thought of it. The magician was by no means offended, but joined in the laugh; and for the next hour or more he entertained me with an account of his professional experiences, and the many difficulties he had to encounter in practicing his profession in such a place as the mines, where complete privacy was so hard to be obtained that he was obliged to practice the most secret parts of his mysterious science in all sorts of ragged canvas houses, or else in rooms whose rickety boarded walls were equally ineffectual in excluding the prying gaze of the unwashed. He gave me a great insight into the mysteries of magic, and explained to me how he performed many of his tricks. All the old-fashioned hat-tricks, he said, were quite out of the question in California, where, as no two hats are alike, it would have been impossible to have such an immense assortment ready, from which to select a substitute for any nondescript head-piece which might be given to him to perform upon. I asked him to show me some of his sleight-of-hand tricks, but he said his hands had got so hard with mining that he would have to let them soften for a month or two before he could recover his magical powers.

He was quite a young man, but had been regularly brought up to his profession, having spent several years as confederate to some magician of higher powers in the States – somewhat similar, I presume, to serving an apprenticeship, for when I mentioned the names of several of his professional brethren whose performances I had witnessed, he would say, "Ah, yes, I know him; he was confederate to so-and-so."

As he intended very soon to resume his practice, he was on the look-out for a particularly smart boy to initiate as his confederate; and I imagine he had little difficulty in finding one, for, as a general thing, the rising generation of California are supernaturally smart and precocious.

I met here also an old friend in the person of the Scotch gardener who had been my fellow-passenger from New York to Chagres, and who was also one of our party on the Chagres River. He was now farming, having taken up a "ranch" a few miles from Sonora, near a place called Table Mountain, where he had several acres well fenced and cleared, and bearing a good crop of barley and oats, and was busy clearing and preparing more land for cultivation.

This Table Mountain is a very curious place, being totally different in appearance and formation from any other mountain in the country. It is a long range, several miles in extent, perfectly level, and in width varying from fifty yards to a quarter of a mile, having somewhat the appearance, when seen from a distance, of a colossal railway embankment. In height it is below the average of the surrounding mountains; the sides are very steep, sometimes almost perpendicular, and are formed, as is also the summit, of masses of a burned-looking conglomerate rock, of which the component stones are occasionally as large as a man's head. The summit is smooth, and black with these cinder-like stones;

but at the season of the year at which I was there, it was a most beautiful sight, being thickly grown over with a pale-blue flower, apparently a lupin, which so completely covered this long level tract of ground as to give it in the distance the appearance of a sheet of water. No one at that time had thought of working this place, but it has since been discovered to be immensely rich.

A break in this long narrow Table Mountain was formed by a place called Shaw's Flats, a wide extent of perfectly flat country, four or five miles across, well wooded with oaks, and plentifully sprinkled over with miner's tents and shanties.

The diggings were rich. The gold was very coarse, and frequently found in large lumps; but how it got there was not easy to conjecture, for the flat was on a level with Table Mountain, and hollows intervened between it and any higher ground. Mining here was quite a clean and easy operation. Any old gentleman might have gone in and taken a turn at it for an hour or two before dinner just to give him an appetite, without even wetting the soles of his boots: indeed, he might have fancied he was only digging in his garden, for the gold was found in the very roots of the grass, and in most parts there was only a depth of three or four feet from the surface to the bedrock, which was of singular character, being composed of masses of sandstone full of circular cavities, and presenting all manner of fantastic forms, caused apparently by the long-continued action of water in rapid motion.

CHAPTER XXIV

A CITY BURNED

WHILE I was in Sonora, the entire town, with the greater part of the property it contained, was utterly annihilated by fire. It was about one o'clock in the morning when the fire broke out. I happened to be awake at the time, and at the first alarm I jumped up, and, looking out of my window, I saw a house a short distance up the street on the other side completely enveloped in flames. The street was lighted up as bright as day, and was already alive with people hurriedly removing whatever articles they could from their houses before the fire seized upon them.

I ran downstairs to lend a hand to clear the house, and in the bar-room I found the landlady, *en deshabille,* walking frantically up and down, and putting her hand to her head as though she meant to tear all her hair out by the roots. She had sense enough left, however, not to do so. A waiter was there also, with just as little of his wits about him; he was chattering fiercely, *sacré*ing very freely, and knocking the chairs and tables about in a wild manner, but not making a direct attempt to save anything. It was ridiculous to see them throwing away so much bodily exertion for nothing, when there was so much to be done, so I set the example by opening the door, and carrying out whatever was nearest. The other inmates of the house soon made their appearance, and we succeeded in gutting the bar-room of everything movable, down to the bar furniture, among which was a bottle labelled "Quisqui."

We could save little else, however, for already the fire had reached us. The house was above a hundred yards from where the fire broke out, but from the first alarm till it was in flames scarcely ten minutes elapsed. The fire spread with equal rapidity in the other direction. An attempt was made to save the upper part of the town by tearing down a number of houses some distance in advance of the flames; but it was impossible to remove the combustible materials of which they were composed, and the fire suffered no check in its progress, devouring the demolished houses as voraciously in that state as though they had been left entire.

On the hills, between which lay the town, were crowds of the unfortunate inhabitants, many of whom were but half dressed, and had barely escaped with their lives. One man told me he had been obliged to run for it, and had not even time to take his gold watch from under his pillow.

Those whose houses were so far distant from the origin of the fire as to enable them to do so, had carried out all their movable property, and were sitting among heaps of goods and furniture, confusedly thrown together, watching grimly the destruction of their houses. The whole hillside was lighted up as brightly as a well-lighted room, and the surrounding landscape was distinctly seen by the blaze of the burning town, the hills standing brightly out from the deep black of the horizon, while overhead the glare of the fire was reflected by the smoky atmosphere.

It was a most magnificent sight, and, more than any *fire* I had ever witnessed, it impressed one with the awful power and fury of the destroying element. It was not like a fire in a city where man contends with it for the victory, and where one can mark the varied fortunes of the battle as the flames become gradually more feeble under the efforts of the firemen, or again gain the advantage as they reach some easier prey; but here there were no such fluctuations in the prospects of the doomed city – it lay helplessly waiting its fate, for water there was none, and no resistance could be offered to the raging flames, which burned their way steadily up the street, throwing over the houses which still remained intact the flush of supernatural beauty which precedes dissolution, and leaving the ground already passed over covered with the gradually blackening and falling remains of those whose spirit had already departed.

There was an occasional flash and loud explosion, caused by the quantities of powder in some of the stores, and a continual discharge of firearms was heard above the roaring of the flames, from the numbers of loaded revolvers which had been left to their fate along with more valuable property. The most extraordinary sight was when the fire got firm hold of a Jew's slop-shop; there was then a perfect whirlwind of flame, in which coats, shirts, and blankets were carried up fifty or sixty feet in the air, and became dissolved into a thousand sparkling atoms.

Among the crowds of people on the hillside there was little of the distress and excitement one might have expected to see on such an occasion. The houses and stores had been gutted as far as practicable of the property they contained, and all that it was possible to do to save any part of the town had already been attempted, but the hopelessness of such attempts was perfectly evident.

The greater part of the people, it is true, were individuals whose wealth was safe in their buckskin purses, and to them the pleasure of beholding such a grand pyrotechnic display was unalloyed by any greater individual misfortune than the loss of a few articles of clothing; but even those who were sitting hatless and shoeless among the wreck of their property showed little sign of being at all cast down by their disaster; they had more the air of determined men, waiting for the fire to play out its hand before they again set to work to repair all the destruction it had caused.

The fire commenced about half-past one o'clock in the morning, and by three o'clock it had almost burned itself out. Darkness again prevailed, and when day dawned, the whole city of Sonora had been removed from the face of the earth. The ground on which it had stood, now white with ashes, was covered with still smoldering fragments, and the only objects left standing were three large safes belonging to different banking and express companies, with a small remnant of the walls of an adobe house.

People now began to venture down upon the still smoking site of the city, and, seeing an excitement among them at the lower end of the town, I went down to see what was going on. The atmosphere was smoky and stifling, and the ground was almost too hot to stand on. The crowd was collected on a place which was known to be very rich, as the ground behind the houses had been worked, and a large amount of gold having been there extracted, it was consequently presumed that under the houses equally good diggings would be found. During the fire, miners had flocked in from all quarters, and among them were some unprincipled vagabonds, who were now endeavoring to take up mining claims on the ground where the houses had stood, measuring off the regular number of feet allowed to each man, and driving in stakes to mark out their claims in the usual manner.

The owners of the houses, however, were "on hand," prepared to defend their rights to the utmost. Men who had just seen the greater part of their property destroyed were not likely to relinquish very readily what little still remained to them; and now, armed with pistols, guns, and knives, their eyes bloodshot and their faces scorched and blackened, they were tearing up the stakes as fast as the miners drove them in, while they declared very emphatically, with all sorts of oaths, that any man who dared to put a pick into that ground would not live half a minute. And truly a threat from such men was one not to be disregarded.

By the laws of the mines, the diggings under a man's house are his property, and the law being on their side, the people would have assisted them in defending their rights; and it would not have been absolutely necessary for them to take the trouble of shooting the miscreants, who, as other miners began to assemble on the ground, attracted by the row, found themselves so heartily denounced that they thought it advisable to sneak off as fast as possible.

The only buildings left standing after the fire were a Catholic and a Wesleyan church, which stood on the hill a little off the street, and also a large building which had been erected for a ball-room, or some other public purpose. The proprietor of the principal gambling-saloon, as soon as the fire broke out and he saw that there was no hope for his house, immediately made arrangements for occupying this room, which, from its isolated position, seemed safe enough; and into this place he succeeded in moving the greater part of his furniture, mirrors, chandeliers, and so on. The large sign in front of the house was also removed to the new quarters, and the morning after the fire – but an hour or two after the town had been burned down – the new saloon was in full operation. The same gamblers were sitting at the same tables, dealing monte and faro to crowds of betters; the piano and violin, which had been interrupted by the fire, were now enlivening the people in their distress; and the bar-keeper was as composedly as ever mixing cocktails for the thirsty throats of the million.

No time was lost by the rest of the population. The hot and smoky ground was alive with men clearing away rubbish; others were in the woods cutting down trees and getting out posts and brushwood, or procuring canvas and other supplies from the neighboring camps.

In the afternoon the Phœnix began to rise. Amid the crowds of workers on the long blackened tract of ground which had been the street, posts began here and there to spring up; presently crosspieces connected them; and before one could look around, the framework was filled in with brushwood. As the ground became sufficiently cool, people began to move down their goods and furniture to where their houses had been, where those who were not yet erecting either a canvas or a brush house, built themselves a sort of pen of boxes and casks of merchandise.

The fire originated in a French hotel, and among the ashes of this house were found the remains of a human body. There was merely the head and trunk, the limbs being entirely burned off. It looked like a charred and blackened log of wood, but the contour of the head and figure was preserved; and it would be hard to conceive anything more painfully expressive of intense agony than the few lines which so powerfully indicated what had been the contorted position of the head, neck, and shoulders of the unfortunate man when he ceased to move. The coroner held an inquest as soon as he could raise a jury out of the crowd, and in the afternoon the body was followed to the grave by several hundred Frenchmen.

This was the only death from the fire which was discovered at the time, but among the ruins of an adobe house, which for some reason was not rebuilt for several weeks afterwards, the remains of another body were found, and were never identified.

As for living on that day, one had to do the best one could with raw materials. Every man had to attend to his own commissariat; and when it was time to think about dinner, I went foraging with a friend among the promiscuous heaps of merchandise, and succeeded in getting some boxes of sardines and a bottle of wine. We were also fortunate enough to find some hard bread, so we did not fare very badly; and at night we lay down on the bare hillside, and shared that vast apartment with two or three thousand fellow-lodgers. Happy was the man who had saved his blankets, – mine had gone as a small contribution to the general conflagration; but though the nights were agreeably cool, the want of a covering, even in the open air, was not a very great hardship.

The next day the growth of the town was still more rapid. All sorts of temporary contrivances were erected by the storekeepers and hotel-keepers on the sites of their former houses. Every man was anxious to let the public see that he was "on hand," and carrying on business as before. Sign-painters had been hard at work all night, and now huge signs on yard-wide strips of cotton cloth lined each side of the street, in many cases being merely laid upon the ground, where as yet nothing had been erected whereon to display them. These canvas and brush houses were only temporary. Every one, as soon as lumber could be procured, set to work to build a better house than the one he had lost; and within a month Sonora was in all respects a finer town than it had been before the fire.

CHAPTER XXV

THE DAY WE CELEBRATE

O N the 4th of July I went over to Columbia, four miles distant from Sonora, where there were to be great doings, as the latter place had hardly yet recovered from the effects of the fire, and was still in a state of transition. So Columbia, which was nearly as large a town, was to be the place of celebration for all the surrounding country.

Early in the forenoon an immense concourse of people had assembled to take part in the proceedings, and were employing themselves in the meantime in drinking success to the American eagle, in the numerous saloons and bar-rooms. The town was all stars and stripes; they fluttered over nearly every house, and here and there hung suspended across the street. The day was celebrated in the usual way, with a continual discharge of revolvers, and a vast expenditure of powder and squibs and crackers, together with an unlimited consumption of brandy. But this was only the overflowing of individual enthusiasm; the regular program was a procession, a prayer, and an oration.

The procession was headed by about half-a-dozen ladies and a number of children – the teachers and pupils of a school – who sang hymns at intervals, when the brass band which accompanied them had blown themselves out of breath. They were followed by the freemasons, to the number of a hundred or so, in their aprons and other paraphernalia; and after them came a company of about the same number of horsemen, the most irregular cavalry one could imagine. Whoever could get a four-legged animal to carry him, joined the ranks; and horses, mules, and jackasses were all mixed up together. Next came the hook and ladder company, dragging their hooks and ladders after them in regular firemen fashion; and after them came three or four hundred miners, walking two and two, and dragging, in like manner, by a long rope, a wheelbarrow, in which were placed a pick and shovel, a frying-pan, an old coffee-pot, and a tin cup. They were marshalled by half-a-dozen miners, with long-handled shovels over their shoulders, and all sorts of ribbons tied round their old hats to make a show.

Another mob of miners brought up the rear, drawing after them a long tom on a pair of wheels. In the tom was a lot of "dirt," which one man stirred up with his shovel, as if he were washing, while a number of others alongside were hard at work throwing in imaginary shovelfuls of dirt.

The idea was pretty good; but to understand the meaning of this gorgeous pageant, it was necessary to be familiar with mining life. The pick and shovel in the wheelbarrow were the emblems of the miners' trade, while the old pots and pans were intended to signify the very rough style of his domestic life, particularly of his *cuisine;* and the party of miners at work around the long tom was a representation of the way in which the wealth of the country is wrested from it by all who have stout hearts and willing hands, or stout hands and willing hearts – it amounts to much the same thing.

The procession paraded the streets for two or three hours, and proceeded to the bull-ring, where the ceremonies were to be performed. The bull-ring here was neither so large nor so well got up as the one at Sonora, but still it could accommodate a very large number of people. As the miners entered the arena with their wheelbarrow and long tom, they were immensely cheered by the crowds who had already taken their seats, the band in the meantime playing "Hail Columbia" most lustily.

The Declaration of Independence was read by a gentleman in a white neckcloth, and the oration was then delivered by the "orator of the day," who was a pale-faced, chubby-cheeked young gentleman, with very white and extensive shirt-collars. He indulged in a great deal of buncombe about the Pilgrim Fathers, and Plymouth Rock, the "Blarney-stone of America," as the Americans call it. George the Third and his "red-coated minions" were alluded to in not very flattering terms; and after having exhausted the past, the orator, in his enthusiasm, became prophetic of the future. He fancied he saw a distant vision of a great republic in Ireland, England sunk into insignificance, and all the rest of it.

The speech was full of American and local phraseology, but the richness of the brogue was only the more perceptible from the vain attempt to disguise it. Many of the Americans sitting near me seemed to think that the orator was piling up the agony a little too high, and signified their disapprobation by shouting "Gaas, gaas!" My next neighbor, an old Yankee, informed me that, in his opinion, "them Pilgrim Fathers were no better than their neighbors; they left England because they could not have everything their own way, and in America were more intolerant of other religions than any one had been of theirs in England. I know all about 'em," he said, "for I come from right whar they lived."

In the middle of the arena, during the ceremonies, was a cage containing a grizzly bear, who had fought and killed a bull by torchlight the night before. His cage was boarded up, so that he was deprived of the pleasure of seeing what was going on, but he could hear all that was said, and expressed his opinion from time to time by grunting and growling most savagely.

After the oration, the company dispersed to answer the loud summons of the numerous dinner-bells and gongs, and in the afternoon there was a bull-fight, which went off with great *éclat*.

It was announced in the bills that the celebrated lady bull-fighter, the Señorita Ramona Perez, would despatch a bull with the sword. This celebrated señorita, however, turned out to be only the chief *matador*, who entered the arena very well got up as a woman, with the slight exception of a very fine pair of mustaches, which he had not thought it worth while to sacrifice. He had a fan in his hand, with which he half concealed his face, as if from modesty, as he curtseyed to the audience, who received him with shouts of laughter – mixed with hisses and curses, however, for there were some who had been true believers in the señorita ; but the infidels were the majority, and, thinking it a good joke, enjoyed it accordingly. The señorita played with the bull for some little time with the utmost audacity, and with a great deal of feminine grace, whisking her petticoats in the bull's face with one hand, whilst she smoothed down her hair with the other. At last the sword was handed to her, which she received very gingerly, also a red flag; and after dodging a few passes from the bull, she put the sword most gracefully into the back of his neck, and, hardly condescending to wait to see whether she had killed or not, she dropped both sword and flag, and ran out of the arena, curtsying, and kissing her hand to the spectators, after the manner of a ballet-dancer leaving the stage.

It was a pity the fellow had not shaved off his mustache, as otherwise his acting was so good that one might have deluded oneself with the belief that it was really the celebrated señorita herself who was risking her precious life by such a very ladylike performance.

I had heard from many persons of two natural bridges on a small river called Coyote Creek, some twelve miles off; and as they were represented as being very curious and beautiful objects, I determined to pay them a visit. Accordingly, returning to M'Lean's Ferry on the Stanislaus, at the point where Coyote Creek joins that river, I traveled up the Creek for some miles, clambering over rocks and winding round steep overhanging banks, by a trail so little used that it was hardly discernible. I was amply repaid for my trouble, however, when, after an hour or two of hard climbing in the roasting hot sun, I at last reached the bridges, and found them much more beautiful natural curiosities than I had imagined them to be.

Having never been able to get any very intelligible account of what they really were, I had supposed that some large rocks rolling down the mountain had got jammed over the creek, by the steepness of the rocky banks on each side, which I fancied would be a very easy mode of building a natural bridge. My idea, however, was very far from the reality. In fact, bridges was an inappropriate name; they should rather have been called caves or tunnels. How they were formed is a question for geologists; but their appearance gave the idea that there had been a sort of landslip, which blocked up the bed of the creek for a distance of two or three hundred feet, and to the height of fifty or sixty above the bed of the stream. They were about a quarter of a mile apart, and their surface was, like that of the hills, perfectly smooth, and covered with grass and flowers. The interiors were somewhat the same style of place, but the upper one was the larger and more curious of the two. The faces of the tunnel were perpendicular, presenting an entrance like a church door, about twelve feet high, surrounded by huge stony fungus-like excrescences, of a dark purple-and-green color. The waters of the creek flowed in here, and occupied all the width of the entrance. They were only a few inches in depth, and gave a perfect reflection of the whole of the interior, which was a lofty chamber some hundred feet in length, the straight sides of which met at the top in the form of a Gothic arch. At the further end was a vista of similarly arched small passages, branching off into darkness. The walls were deeply carved into pillars and grotesque forms, in which one could trace all manner of fanciful resemblances; while at the base of some of the columns were most symmetrically formed projections, many of which might be taken for fonts, the top of them being a circular basin containing water. These projections were of stone, and had the appearance of having congealed suddenly while in a boiling state. There was a beautiful regularity in the roughness of their surface, some of the rounded forms being deeply carved with circular lines, similar to the engine-turning on the back of a watch, and others being rippled like a shirt of mail, the rippling getting gradual-ly and regularly finer, till at the top the surface was hardly more rough than that of a file. The walls and roof seemed to have been smothered over with some stuff which had hardened into a sort of cement, presenting a polished surface of a bright cream-color, tinged here and there with pink and pale-green. The entrance was sufficiently large to light up the whole place, which, from its gen-eral outline, gave somewhat the idea of a church; for, besides the pillars, with their flowery ornaments, the Gothic arches and the fonts, there was at one side, near the entrance, one of these stone excrescences much larger than the others, which would have passed for a pulpit, overhung as it was by a projection of a similar nature, spreading out from the wall several feet above it.

The sides of the arches forming the roof did not quite meet at the top, but looked like the crests of two immense foaming waves, between which were seen the extremities of numbers of pendants of a like flowery form.

There was nothing rough or uncertain about the place; every part seemed as if it were elaborately finished, and in strict harmony with the whole; and as the rays of the setting sun fell on the water within the entrance, and reflected a subdued light over the brilliant hues of the interior, it looked like a gorgeous temple, which no art could improve, and such as no human imagination could have designed. At the other end of the tunnel the water emerged from a much smaller cave, which was so low as not to admit of a man crawling in.

The caves, at each end of the other tunnel, were also very small, though the architecture was of the same flowery style. The faces of it, however, were extremely beautiful. To the height of fifty or sixty feet they presented a succession of irregular overhanging projections, bulging out like immense mushrooms, of which the prevailing hue was a delicate pink, with occasional patches of bright green.

In any part of the Old World such a place would be the object of a pil-grimage; and even where it was, it attracted many visitors, numbers of whom had, according to the established custom of snobhood, acknowledged their own insignificance, and had sought a little immortality for their wretched names by scratching them on a large smooth surface by the side of the en-trance to the cave.

While I was there, an old Yankee miner came to see the place. He paid a very hurried visit – he had not even time to scratch his initials; but he was enthusiastic in his admiration of this beautiful object of nature, which, however, he thought was quite thrown away in such an out-of-the-way part of creation. It distressed him to think that such a valuable piece of property could not be turned to any profitable account. "Now," said he, "if I had this here thing jist about ten miles from New York City, I'd show it to the folks at twenty-five cents a head, and make an everlastin' pile of money out of it."

CHAPTER XXVI

FRENCHMEN IN THE MINES

THE only miners on the Creek were Frenchmen, two or three of whom lived in a very neat log cabin, close to the tunnel. Behind it was a small kitchen-garden in a high state of cultivation, and alongside was a very diminutive fac-simile of the cabin itself, which was tenanted by a knowing-looking little terrier-dog.

The whole establishment had a finished and civilized air about it, and was got up with a regard to appearances which was quite unusual.

But of all the men of different nations in the mines, the French were most decidedly those who, judging from their domestic life, appeared to be most at home. Not that they were a bit better than others able to stand the hard work and exposure and privations, but about all their huts and cabins, however roughly constructed they might be, there was something in the minor details which bespoke more permanency than was suggested by the generality of the rude abodes of the miners. It is very certain that, without really expending more time or labor, or even taking more trouble than other men about their domestic arrangements, they did "fix things up" with such a degree of taste, and with so much method about everything, as to give the idea that their life of toil was mitigated by more than a usual share of ease and comfort.

A backwoodsman from the Western States is in some respects a good sort of fellow to be with in the mountains, especially where there are hostile Indians about, for he knows their ways, and can teach them manners with his five-foot-barrel rifle when there is occasion for it; he can also put up a log cabin in no time, and is of course up to all the dodges of border life; but this is his normal condition, and he cannot be expected to appreciate so much as others, or to be so apt at introducing, all the little luxuries of a more civilized existence of which he has no knowledge.

An old sailor is a useful man in the mines, when you can keep brandy out of his reach; and, to do him justice, there is method in his manner of drinking. He lives under the impression that all human existence should be subdivided, as at sea, into watches; for when ashore he only lengthens their duration, and takes his watch below as a regular matter of duty, keeping below as long as the grog lasts; after which he comes on deck again, quite refreshed, and remains as sober as a judge for two or three weeks. His useful qualities, however, consist in the extraordinary delight he takes in patching and mending, and tinkering up whatever stands in need of such service. He is great at sweeping and scrubbing, and keeping things clean generally, and, besides, knows something of tailoring, shoemaking, carpentering; in fact, he can turn his hand to anything, and generally does it artistically, while his resources are endless, for he has a peculiar genius for making one thing serve the purpose of another, and is never at a loss for a substitute.

But whatever the specialties and accomplishments of individuals or of classes, the French, as a nation, were excelled by no other in the practice of the art of making themselves personally comfortable. They generally located themselves in considerable numbers, forming small communities of their own, and always appeared to be jolly, and enjoying themselves. They worked hard enough while they were at it, but in their intervals of leisure they gave themselves up to what seemed at least to be a more unqualified enjoyment of the pleasures of the moment than other miners, who never entirely laid aside the earnest and careworn look of the restless gold-hunter.

This enviable faculty, which the Frenchmen appeared to possess in such a high degree, of bringing somewhat of the comforts of civilized life along with them, was no doubt a great advantage; but whether it operated favorably or otherwise towards their general success as miners, is not so certain. One would naturally suppose that the more thoroughly a man rested from mental or bodily labor, the more able would he be for renewed exertions; but at the same time, a man whose mind is entirely engrossed and preoccupied with one idea, is likely to attain his end before the man who only devotes himself to the pursuit of that object at stated intervals.

However that may be, there is no question that, as miners, the French were far excelled by the Americans and by the English – for they are inseparably mixed up together. There are thoroughgoing Americans who, only a year or two ago, were her Majesty's most faithful subjects, and who still in their hearts cherish the recollection. The Frenchmen, perhaps, possessed industry and energy enough, if they had had a more practical genius to direct it; but in proportion to their numbers, they did not bear a sufficiently conspicuous part, either in mining operations, or in those branches of industry which have for their object the converting of the natural advantages of a country to the service of man. The direction of their energies was more towards the supplying of those wants which presuppose the existence of a sufficiently wealthy and luxurious class of consumers than towards seizing on such resources of the country as offered them the means of enriching themselves in a manner less immediately dependent on their neighbors.

Even as miners, they for the most part congregated round large camps, and were never engaged in the same daring undertakings as the Americans – such as lifting half a mile of a large river from its bed, or trenching for miles the sides of steep mountains, and building lofty viaducts supported on scaffolding which, from its height, looked like a spider's web; while the only pursuits they engaged in, except mining, were the keeping of restaurants, estaminets, cafés chantants, billiard-rooms, and such places, ministering more to the pleasures than to the necessities of man; and not in any way adding to the wealth of the country by rendering its resources more available.

Comparing the men of different nations, the pursuits they were engaged in, and the ends they had accomplished, one could not help being impressed with the idea that if the mines had been peopled entirely by Frenchmen – if all the productive resources of the country had been in their hands – it would yet have been many years before they would have raised California to the rank and position of wealth and importance which she now holds.

And it is quite fair to draw a general conclusion regarding them, based upon such evidences of their capabilities as they afforded in California ; for not only did they form a very considerable proportion of the population, but, as among people of other nations, there were also among them men of all classes.

In many respects they were a most valuable addition to the population of the country, especially in the cities, but as colonizers and subjugators of a new country, their inefficiency was very apparent. They appeared to want that daring and independent spirit of individual self-reliance which impels an American or Englishman to disregard all counsel and companionship, and to enter alone into the wildest enterprise, so long as he himself thinks it feasible; or, disengaging himself for the time being from all communication with his fellow-men, to plunge into the wilderness, and there to labor steadily, uncheered by any passing pleasure, and with nothing to sustain him in his determination but his own confidence in his ability ultimately to attain his object.

One scarcely ever met a Frenchman traveling alone in search of diggings; whereas the Americans and English whom one encountered were nearly always solitary individuals, "on their own hook," going to some distant part where they had heard the diggings were good, but at the same time ready to stop anywhere, or to change their destination according to circumstances.

The Frenchmen were too gregarious; they were either found in large numbers, or not at all. They did not travel about much, and, when they did, were in parties of half-a-dozen. While Americans would travel hundreds of miles to reach a place which they believed to be rich, the great object of the Frenchmen, in their choice of a location, seemed to be, to be near where a number of their countrymen were already settled.

But though they were so fond of each other's company, they did not seem to possess that cohesiveness and mutual confidence necessary for the successful prosecution of a joint undertaking. Many kinds of diggings could only be worked to advantage by companies of fifteen or twenty men, but Frenchmen were never seen attempting such a combination. Occasionally half-a-dozen or so worked together, but even then the chances were that they squabbled among themselves, and broke up before they had got their claim into working order, and so lost their labor from their inability to keep united in one plan of operation.

In this respect the Americans had a very great advantage, for, though strongly imbued with the spirit of individual independence, they are certainly of all people in the world the most prompt to organize and combine to carry out a common object. They are trained to it from their youth in their innumerable, and to a foreigner unintelligible, caucus-meetings, committees, conventions, and so forth, by means of which they bring about the election of every officer in the State, from the President down to the policeman ; while the fact of every man belonging to a fire company, a militia company, or something of that sort, while it increases their idea of individual importance, and impresses upon them the force of combined action, accustoms them also to the duty of choosing their own leaders, and to the necessity of afterwards recognizing them as such by implicit obedience.

Certain it is that, though the companies of American miners were frequently composed of what seemed to be most incongruous materials – rough,
uneducated men, and men of refinement and education – yet they worked together as harmoniously in carrying out difficult mining and engineering operations, under the directions of their "captain," as if they had been a gang
of day-laborers who had no right to interfere as to the way in which the work
should be conducted.

The captain was one of their number, chosen for his supposed ability to
carry out the work; but if they were not satisfied with his performances, it was
a very simple matter to call a meeting, at which the business of deposing, or
accepting the resignation of the incompetent officer, and appointing a succes-
sor, was put through with all the order and formality which accompanies the
election of a president of any public body. Those who would not submit to the
decision of the majority might sell out, but the prosecution of a work undertak-
en was never abandoned or in any way retarded by the discordance of opinion
on the part of the different members of the company.

Individuals could not work alone to any advantage. All mining operations were carried on by parties of men, varying in number according to the
nature of their diggings; and the strange assortment of dissimilar characters
occasionally to be found thus brought into close relationship was but a type
of the general state of society, which was such as completely to realize the
idea of perfect social equality.

There are occasions on which, among small communities, an overwhelming emotion, common to all, may obliterate all feeling of relative superiority;
but the history of the world can show no such picture of human nature upon the
same scale as was to be seen in the mines, where, among a population of hundreds of thousands of men, from all parts of the world, and from every order of
society, no individual or class was accounted superior to another.

The cause of such a state of things was one which would tend to produce
the same results elsewhere. It consisted in this, that each man enjoyed the capability of making as much money as his neighbor; for hard labor, which any man
could accomplish with legs and arms, without much assistance from his head,
was as remunerative as any other occupation – consequently, all men indiscriminately were found so employing themselves, and mining or any other kind
of labor was considered as dignified and as honorable a pursuit as any other.

By J. D. BORTHWICK

In fact, so paramount was this idea, that in some men it created an impression that not to labor was degrading – that those who did not live by actual physical toil were men who did not come up to the scratch – who rather shirked the common lot of all, "man's original inheritance, that he should sweat for his poor pittance." I recollect once arriving in the middle of the night in San Francisco, when it was not by any means the place it now is, and finding all the hotels full, I was compelled to take refuge in an establishment which offered no other accommodation to the public than a lot of beds – half-a-dozen in a room. When I was paying my dollar in the morning for having enjoyed the privilege of sleeping on one of these concerns, an old miner was doing the same. He had no coin, but weighed out an ounce of dust, and while getting his change he seemed to be studying the keeper of the house, as a novel and interesting specimen of human nature. The result showed itself in an expression of supreme contempt on his worn and sunburnt features, as he addressed the object of his contemplation: "Say now, stranger, do you do nothin' else but just sit thar and take a dollar from every man that sleeps on them beds?"

"Yes, that's my business," replied the man.

"Well, then," said the miner after a little further reflection, "it's a d – d mean way of making your living, that's all I can say."

This idea was natural enough to the man who so honestly expressed it, but it was an exaggeration of that which prevailed in the mines, for no occupation gave any man a superiority over his neighbors; there was no social scale in which different classes held different positions, and the only way in which a man could distinguish himself from others was by what he actually had in him, by his own personal qualities, and by the use he could make of them; and any man's intrinsic merit it was not difficult to discover ; for it was not as in countries where the whole population is divided into classes, and where individuals from widely different stations are, when thrown together, prevented, by a degree of restraint and hypocrisy on both sides, from exhibiting themselves exactly as they would to their ordinary associates. Here no such obstacle existed to the most unreserved intercourse; the habitual veil of imposition and humbug, under which men usually disguise themselves from the rest of the world, was thrown aside as a useless inconvenience. They took no trouble to conceal what passed within them, but showed themselves as they were, for better or for worse as the case might be – sometimes, no doubt, very much for the worse;

but in most instances first impressions were not so favorable as those formed upon further acquaintance.

Society – so to call it – certainly wanted that superfine polish which gives only a cold reflection of what is offered to it. There was no pinchbeck or Brummagem ware; every man was a genuine solid article, whether gold, silver, or copper: he was the same sterling metal all the way through which he was on the surface; and the generous frankness and hearty goodwill which, however roughly expressed, were the prevailing characteristics of the miners, were the more grateful to the feelings, as one knew that no secondary or personal motive sneaked beneath them.

It would be hard to say what particular class of men was the most numerous in the mines, because few retained any distinguishing characteristic to denote their former position.

The backwoodsman and the small farmer from the Western States, who formed a very large proportion of the people, could be easily recognized by many peculiarities. The educated man, who had lived and moved among gentlemen, was also to be detected under any disguise; but the great mass of the people were men who, in their appearance and manners, afforded little clue to their antecedents.

From the mode of life and the style of dress, men became very much assimilated in outward appearance, and acquired also a certain individuality of manner, which was more characteristic of what they now were – of the independent gold-hunter – than of any other order of mankind.

It was easy enough, if one had any curiosity on the subject, to learn something of a man's history, for there was little reserve used in alluding to it. What a man had been mattered as little to him as it did to any one else; and it was refreshing to find, as was generally the case, that one's preconceived ideas of a man were so utterly at variance with the truth.

Among such a motley crowd one could select his own associates, but the best-informed the most entertaining, and those in many respects the most desirable, were not always those whose company one could have enjoyed where the inseparable barriers of class are erected; – and it is difficult to believe that any one, after circulating much among the different types of mankind to be found in the mines, should not have a higher respect than before for the various classes which they represented.

CHAPTER XXVII

THE RESOURCEFUL AMERICANS

A FTER a month or two spent on the Tuolumne and Merced rivers, and in the more sparsely populated section of country lying still farther south, I returned to Sonora, on my way to San Francisco.

Here I took the stage for Stockton – a large open wagon, drawn by five horses, three leaders abreast. We were well ballasted with about a dozen passengers, the most amusing of whom was a hard, dried-up man, dressed in a greasy old leathern hunting-shirt, and inexpressibles to match, all covered with tags and fringes, and clasping in his hand a long rifle, which had probably been his bosom-friend all his life. He took an early opportunity of informing us all that he was from Arkansas; that he came to "Calaforny" across the plains, and having been successful in the diggings, he was now on his way home. He was like a schoolboy going home for the holidays, so delighted was he with the prospect before him. It seemed to surprise him very much that all the rest of the party were not also bound for Arkansas, and he evidently looked upon us, in consequence, with a degree of compassionate interest, as much less fortunate mortals, and very much to be pitied.

We started at four o'clock in the morning, so as to accomplish the sixty or seventy miles to Stockton before the departure of the San Francisco steamer. The first ten or twelve miles of our journey were consequently performed in the dark, but that did not affect our speed; the road was good, and it was only in crossing the hollows between the hills that the navigation was difficult; for in such places the diggings had frequently encroached so much on the road as to leave only sufficient space for a wagon to pass between the miners' excavations.

We drove about thirty miles before we were quite out of the mining regions. The country, however, became gradually less mountainous, and more suitable for cultivation, and every half-mile or so we passed a house by the roadside, with ploughed fields around it, whose occupant combined farming with tavern-keeping. This was all very pleasant traveling, but the most wretch-ed part of the journey was when we reached the plains. The earth was scorched and baked, the heat was more oppressive than in the mountains, and for about thirty miles we moved along enveloped in a cloud of dust, which soaked into one's clothes and hair and skin as if it had been a liquid substance. On our arrival in Stockton we were of a uniform color all over – all identity of person was lost as much as in a party of chimney-sweeps; but fortunately the steamer did not start for an hour, so I had time to take a bath, and make myself look somewhat like a white man before going on board.

The Stockton steamboats, though not so large as those which run to Sacra-mento, were not inferior in speed. We steamed down the San Joaquin at about twenty miles an hour, and reached San Francisco at ten o'clock at night.

San Francisco retained now but little resemblance to what it had been in its earlier days. The same extraordinary contrasts and incongruities were not to be seen either in the people or in the appearance of the streets. Men had settled down into their proper places; the various branches of business and trade had worked for themselves their own distinct channels; and the general style of the place was very much the same as that of any flourishing commercial city.

It had increased immensely in extent, and its growth had been in all directions. The barren sandhills which surrounded the city had been graded down to an even slope, and were covered with streets of well-built houses, and skirted by populous suburbs. Four or five wide streets, more than a mile in length, built up with solid and uniform brick warehouses, stretched all along in front of the city, upon ground which had been reclaimed from the bay; and between these and the upper part of the city was the region of fash-ionable shops and hotels, banks and other public offices.

The large fleet of ships which for a long time, while seamen's wages were exorbitantly high, lay idly in the harbor, was now dispersed, and all the shipping actually engaged in discharging cargo found accommodation along-side of the numerous piers which had been built out for nearly a mile into the bay. All manner of trades and manufactures were flourishing as in a place a hundred years old. Omnibuses plied upon the principal thoroughfares, and numbers of small steamboats ran to the watering-places which had sprung up on the opposite shore.

The style of life had improved with the growth of the city, and with the increased facilities of procuring servants and house-room. The ordinary conventionalities of life were observed, and public opinion exercised its wonted control over men's conduct; for the female part of creation was so numerously represented that births and marriages occupied a space in the daily papers larger than they require in many more populous places.

Female influence was particularly observable in the great attention men paid to their outward appearance. There was but little of the independent taste and individuality in dress of other days; all had succumbed to the sway of the goddess of fashion, and the usual style of gentleman's dress was even more elaborate than in New York. All classes had changed, to a certain extent, in this respect. The miner, as he is seen in the mines, was not to be met with in San Francisco; he attired himself in suitable raiment in Sacramento or Stockton before venturing to show himself in the metropolis.

Gambling was decidedly on the wane. Two or three saloons were still extant, but the company to be found in them was not what it used to be. The scum of the population was there ; but respectable men, with a character to lose, were chary of risking it by being seen in a public gambling-room; and, moreover, the greater domestic comfort which men enjoyed, and the usual attractions of social life, removed all excuse for frequenting such places.

Public amusements were of a hign order. Biscaccianti and Catherine Hayes were giving concerts, Madame Anne Bishop was singing in English opera, and the performances at the various theaters were sustained by the most favorite actors from the Atlantic States.

Extravagant expenditure is a marked feature in San Francisco life. The same style of ostentation, however, which is practiced in older countries, is unattainable in California, and in such a country would entirely fail in its effect. Extravagance, accordingly, was indulged more for the purpose of procuring tangible enjoyment than for the sake of show. Men spent their money in surrounding themselves with the best of everything, not so much for display as from due appreciation of its excellence; for there is no city of the same size or age where there is so little provincialism; the inhabitants, generally, are eminently cosmopolitan in their character, and judge of merit by the highest standard.

As yet, the influence of California upon this country [England] is not so much felt by direct communication as through the medium of the States. A very large proportion of the English goods consumed in the country find their way there through the New York market, and in many cases in such a shape, as in articles manufactured in the States from English materials, that the actual value of the trade cannot be accurately estimated. The tide of emigration from this country to California follows very much the same course. The English are there very numerous, but those direct from England bear but an exceedingly small proportion to those from the United States, from New South Wales, and other countries; and the latter, no doubt, possessed a great advantage, for, without undervaluing the merit of English mechanics and workmen in their own particular trade, it must be allowed that the same class of Americans are less confined to one speciality, and have more general knowledge of other trades, which makes them better men to be turned adrift in a new country, where they may have to employ themselves in a hundred different ways before they find an opportunity of following the trade to which they have been brought up. An English mechanic, after a few years' experience of a younger country, without losing any of the superiority he may possess in his own trade, becomes more fitted to compete with the rest of the world when placed in a position where that speciality is unavailable.

California has afforded the Americans their first opportunity of showing their capacity as colonists. The other States which have, of late years, been added to the Union, are not a fair criterion, for they have been created merely by the expansion of the outer circumference of civilization, by the restlessness of the backwoodsman unaided by any other class; but the attractions offered by California were such as to draw to it a complete ready-made population of active and capable men, of every trade and profession.

The majority of men went there with the idea of digging gold, or without any definite idea of how they would employ themselves; but as the wants of a large community began to be felt, the men were already at hand capable of supplying them; and the result was, that in many professions, and in all the various branches of mechanical industry, the same degree of excellence was exhibited as is known in any part of the world.

Certainly no new country ever so rapidly advanced to the same high position as California; but it is equally true that no country ever commenced its career with such an effective population, or with the same elements of wealth to work upon. There are circumstances, however, connected with the early history of the country which may not appear to be so favorable to immediate prosperity and progress. Other new countries have been peopled by gradual accessions to an already formed center, from which the rest of the mass received character and consistency; but in the case of California the process was much more abrupt. Thousands of men, hitherto unknown to each other, and without mutual relationship, were thrown suddenly together, unrestrained by conventional or domestic obligations, and all more intently bent than men usually are upon the one immediate object of acquiring wealth. It is to be wondered that chaos and anarchy were not at first the result of such a state of things; but such was never the case in any part of the country; and it is, no doubt, greatly owing to the large proportion of superior men among the early settlers, and to the capacity for self-government possessed by all classes of Americans, that a system of government was at once organized and maintained, and that the country was so soon entitled to rank as one of the most important States of the Union.

The consequences to the rest of the world of the gold of California it is not easy to determine, and it is not for me to enter upon the great question as to the effect on prices of an addition to the quantity of precious metals in the world of £250,000,000, which in round numbers is the estimated amount of gold and silver produced within the last eight years* It seems, however, more than probable that the present high range of prices may, to a certain extent, be caused by this immense addition to our stock of gold and silver. But the question becomes more complicated when we consider the extraordinary impetus given to commerce and manufactures by this sudden production of gold acting simultaneously with the equally expanding influence of Free Trade. The time cannot be far off when this important investigation must be entered upon with all that talent which can be brought to bear upon it. But this is the domain of philosophers, and of those whose part in life it is to do the deep-thinking for the rest of the world. I have no desire to trespass on such ground, and abstain also from fruitlessly wandering in the endless mazes of the Currency question.

There are other thoughts, however, which cannot but arise on considering the modem discoveries of gold. When we see a new country and a new home provided for our surplus population, at a time when it was most required – when a fresh supply of gold, now a necessary to civilization, is discovered, as we were evidently and notoriously becoming so urgently in want of it, we cannot but recognize the ruling hand of Providence. And when we see the uttermost parts of the earth suddenly attracting such an immense population of enterprising, intelligent, earnest Anglo-Saxon men, forming, with a rapidity which seems miraculous, new communities and new powers such as California and Australia, we must indeed look upon this whole Gold-en Legend as one of the most wondrous episodes in the history of mankind.

Note
* An overestimate: probably about $500,000,000. – Ed.

THE END.